LAUGHING MATTER

The British are a funny lot – and this book sets out to collect the funniest material of the best of our humorists (and before some smart-alec starts on about the American contributors – they've all been temporarily – and painlessly – naturalized!)

Individual thanks are impossible – but to all the marvellously funny and generous contributors, our combined and everlasting thanks. Our readers will find the source of our excerpts clearly indicated when their appetites have been whetted.

So – here's to laughter – one of the few good things in a gloomy world.

Kay Batchelor

Published by TOPAZ RECORDS LTD
67 High Street, Great Missenden, Bucks, 1976

ISBN 0 905553 00 4

Printed in the Republic of Ireland by
Richview Browne & Nolan Ltd. Dublin

Book layout by Keith Maylin
Book cover designed by Frank Watkins
Book illustrations by George Robinson

It's all very well for the poet, Walt Whitman, to say 'I think I could turn and live with animals' because whether *he* knew it or not, an awful lot of us are already doing just that. And when he goes on

'They are so placid and self-contained' it's obvious the man had never had an animal of any sort under his roof. Placid? self-contained? when they are forever jumping up at you, dribbling over you, taking possession of your lap (leaving hairs and fishy breath behind), talking your ear off (till you throw a cloth over the cage) or bitin' the hand that feeds them (you should always remember, deah, to hold your hand *flat* when you offer a horse sugar – else who's fault is it if he takes off a finger or two).

That's something else – the way people side with their pets. It's never the animal's fault if it accidentally takes a chunk out of you – it was only trying to make friends, as its owner explains in a way that leaves you feeling that *you're* the one to blame. Should you have the bad luck to have a stirrup break under you when you least expect it, and you fall off your horse, don't expect any of your horsey companions to give you a glance as you lie there with your back broken (you think) – they all rush to your horse, and they tell him what a splendid fellow he is for not kicking your head in 'isn't he *marvellous*, doesn't he *know*' (know what? that you're an idiot who shouldn't have let yourself be talked into that early morning trot through the village?)

And what about the man I know who's got a goose so much in love with him that the damn bird won't let you through his gate, and you have to go to the cottage across the road and ring him up to say you want to see him?

Walt Whitman, I've got news for you – it's safer in the long run to stick to humans.

The lion was feeling pretty good as he prowled through the jungle. Seeing a tiger, the lion stopped it.

'Who is the King of the jungle?' the lion demanded.

'You, O lion, are the King of the jungle,' replied the tiger.

Satisfied, the lion strolled on, until he came across a large, ferocious-looking leopard.

'Who is the King of the jungle?' asked the lion, and the leopard bowed in awe. 'You, mighty lion, you are the King of the jungle,' it said humbly and walked off.

Feeling on top of the world, the lion proudly marched up to a huge elephant and asked the same question. 'Who is the King of the jungle.'

Without answering, the elephant picked up the lion, swirled him round in the air, smashed him to the ground and jumped on him.

'Look,' said the lion, 'there's no need to get mad just because you didn't know the answer.'

No trace had been found of the escaped circus elephant, until a panic-stricken old lady telephoned the police.

'You must come quickly,' she trilled, 'there's a very strange-looking animal in my garden pulling up cabbages with its tail. What is even worse, is the vicar is on his way round for tea and I don't want him to see what he is doing with them.'

PUPPY FAT

by GRAHAM

"Just a precaution—somebody might step on him."

"I just couldn't stand that pathetic whimpering from downstairs."

"Poor little thing—he's shaking all over."

"You know your astrakhan hat?"

"Apparently tummy upsets aren't uncommon in young puppies."

*"He certainly **sounded** as if he wanted to go out."*

from 'All Other Men Have Mellowed.' Published by Garnstone Press Ltd.

DUD & PETE

At The Zoo

Excerpt from
'The Dagenham Dialogues'
by Peter Cook & Dudley Moore
Published by Methuen & Co.

DUD. Nice and warm in here, isn't it, Pete?

PETE. Nothing like a nice warm reptile house

DUD. Nothing like a nice warm reptile house.

PETE. Have you seen those geckos over there?

DUD. Geckos, what are they?

PETE. A gecko, Dud, is a lizard what has sucking pads on its feet.

DUD. So it can hang on glass.

PETE. It can if it likes. It can hang on anything it fancies. It has a wonderful life, except, of course, it has to eat flies. Did you know that?

DUD. No I didn't.

PETE. Oh yes, it has to eat flies, 'cause, as you know, God created it, like he did everything else in his almighty wisdom, and all the animals have to eat each other to keep the population down. And geckos got lumbered with flies. It's all right when it's born. Its mother gives it some flies, all mashed up, daintily garnished with a daisy on top of it, so it can't tell what it's eating. But as soon as it learns to speak, Dud, and communicate, it says to its mother, 'Excuse me, what's this I'm eating?' and she has to reply 'Flies.'

DUD. 'Darling'.

PETE. Of course. She says, 'Flies, darling, and they're very good for you.' But that's why the gecko doesn't live very long, because he can't bear eating the stuff.

DUD. Eating flies, I couldn't bear that. I wouldn't like to be a gecko. I'd like to be a poisonous snake – get a real feeling of power with all them fangs.

PETE. Well you've got prominent teeth already, haven't you?

DUD. I could sharpen 'em up and put a bit of cyanide in 'em and go round and, you know, sort of put my teeth into people's arms and kill 'em.

PETE. What sort of a poisonous snake would you be? Would you be an asp?'

DUD. No I'd like to be a viper.

PETE. That's the same thing as an asp but an asp's bigger, Dud.

DUD. Is it?

PETE. Asp was a word invented by Shakespeare during the thirteenth century to denote a viper, 'cause, as you know, Shakespeare was a wonderful writer.

DUD. Knockout.

PETE. And he was doing this wonderful verse play about Cleopatra – how she got wrapped up in the carpet. Shakespeare had been writing this couplet to describe the scene when the snake comes rustling up her undies and begins to start biting into her busty substances. And he'd almost finished this magnificence verse couplet, you see, but the only thing is he only had one syllable left to describe the snake, and 'viper' was too long for the snake so he invented the word 'asp', and a very good word it is too.

DUD. Wonderful. I suppose it was a sort of Shakespearian abbreviation for 'A Stinging Personality'.

PETE. A.S.P., yes I suppose that's the reason.

DUD. Here, I don't reckon it was an asp what stung Cleopatra in the chest, I bet it was a bra constrictor.

PETE. What do you mean? It was an asp.

DUD. No, a bra constrictor, Pete – boa constrictor, it's a joke, Pete.

PETE. Oh, it was a joke, was it? Oh. It was very bad taste. You shouldn't make jokes about people who are dead, 'cause they can't fight back, Dud.

DUD. Sorry, Pete.

PETE. I wouldn't be a reptile at all if I had a choice. If I had a choice I'd be something lovely and cuddly and lovable. Something like those lovely humming birds, which hum with their various hues above the flowers. Those long tongues, all coiled up like watch springs. They can poke them out to forty yards long. A humming bird, Dud, can kiss at immense distances.

DUD. That means that you could stand on the Chiswick flyover and kiss someone up the Staines bypass.

PETE. Hovering four foot above the ground and humming, a wonderful opportunity. I tell you a creature I think is a very cuddly little thing, that's the chameleon. Very versatile.

DUD. Versatile creature, Pete. They can take on the shape and colour of anything they like, all the hues. You remember Mr Rigby?

PETE. Yer.

DUD. He nearly went through a wedding ceremony with one.

PETE. He would have been very happy with a chameleon. They make lovely wives.

DUD. You know, I was here last week, Pete, I don't know if I told you.

PETE. Yer.

DUD. I saw this big sign saying 'Topical fish this way'. I thought, that's OK, see a few topical fish, a few up-to-the-minute bits of satire. You know, topical barbs, about the current situation in the world today.

PETE. What did you see?

DUD. Well I go in there and it's just a lot of fish swimming about, more timeless than topical.

PETE. I tell you what you done, you gone into the tropical fish department – that's *tropical* rather than topical, you see. What happens is that during the winter months, all through the blustery weather, sometimes some of the letters become dislodged because of the gales. And obviously the letter 'r' had become dislodged in this way. I was talking to the keeper about it actually, and he said that very often during the winter months, his 'r's blew off. During the winter months, his 'r's blew off.

DUD. I think I've had enough of the reptile house. Let's go on to the wonkey house.

PETE. No, that's an 'M' what's got blown upside down.

Strictly for the BIRDS

"If we're very quiet we might see Peter Scott."

"Steady on Charlie! It's on the Protected List."

from Thelwell's 'Book of Leisure' Published by Eyre Methuen from 'Top Dog' Published by Eyre Methuen

MAN'S BEST FRIEND

by THELWELL

THE SHEEP DOG

THE GUN DOG

THE HUNTING DOG

THE TRACKER DOG

THE GUIDE DOG

THE LAP DOG

THE GUARD DOG

THE DRAUGHT DOG

THE TOY DOG

OUR HOME'S MUST SUFFER

It can make you a bit uneasy, laughing at the people and the services run for the public, which is them as well as us of course – partly because not many of them strike you as being brimful of laughs on the job, and what they say and do and are can make all the difference when it comes to getting that licence, receiving an allowance, having your plans passed, your car taxed, your dog quarantined, your cesspit emptied, your children schooled, your hard skin scraped, your meters read, your telephone mended – and your head examined:

The Workers' Bag is Deepest Red

By
ALAN COREN

'The Scottish council of the Labour Party today approved almost unanimously a policy for the complete nationalisation of the vast privately owned Highland estates and the salmon fisheries if a Labour government is returned to power.'

The Times

I followed the clerk down the eau-de-nil corridor and through a brown door marked FISH DIVISION: ENQUIRIES. Inside, a bald man sat at a steel desk beneath a wall-map of the Highlands pinned with tiny flags and a graph on which a curve plummeted into its lower margin.

'Man here wants to have a go at the salmon,' said the clerk.

The bald man glanced at me over his bifocals.

'Where's your ferret?' he said.

'Ferret?' I said.

'Little bugger with short legs,' said the clerk. 'Can't half run, though.'

'I know what a ferret is, I said. 'But I'm after salmon. Ferrets go down rabbit holes.'

'Funny place to look for salmon,' said the clerk. 'Still, it takes all sorts, that's what I always say.'

'We can lease you a government ferret,' said the bald man. He reached for a file, wet his thumb, began plucking forms out. 'Need a 121/436/18g, a 72A/ff, and two pound deposit against loss or damage.'

I cleared my throat.

'There seems to be some mistake,' I said. 'You don't catch salmon with ferrets.'

'He's got a point,' said the clerk. 'They go down like stones.' He indicated the graph. 'Salmon production's been dropping off sunnink terrible lately.'

'Who told you to use ferrets?' I asked.

The bald man tapped a thick grey-covered book beside his in-tray.

'Come down from Central Division,' he said.

'We're radicalising,' said the clerk. 'And rationalising.'

'Sounds to me as though they've got their lines crossed somewhere,' I said.

They looked at me.

'Troublemaker here,' said the bald man.

'There's channels, you know,' said the clerk.

'How you going to catch salmon, then,' said the bald man, 'without a ferret?'

'Flies,' I said.

'Show him out, Sid,' said the bald man.

'I don't understand,' I said.

'We got work to do,' said the bald man, 'without comedians.'

'I'm serious,' I said.

'Pull this one,' said the clerk. 'It's hard enough training ferrets to jump out of a boat, let alone flies.'

'You'd open your jam jar,' said the bald man, 'and they'd be off. I know flies.'

'Look,' I said, 'you do it with a rod and line. You tie the fly to the hook, you cast the line with the rod, you . . .'

'Ah,' said the bald man. He nodded. 'Cross purposes here, Sidney. I thought he was talking about salmon. It's grouse he's after.'

'You should've said,' said the clerk, irritably tearing up his half-filled forms and reaching for a new batch 'And it's not flies, it's worms you use for grouse.'

'Don't be ridiculous,' I said, 'how can you catch a grouse with a worm?'

'Don't ask me,' said the clerk, 'you're supposed to be the sportsman. We only work here. On attachment.'

'From Swindon,' said the bald man. 'Personally, I prefer trains. You know where you are with trains.'

'We're working on a pilot project,' said the clerk, 'to put grouse on rails. It's up before the Recommendations & Amendments Committee. It could revolutionise the entire industry.'

'You'd know when they was coming, then,' said the bald man. 'None of this hanging about with a worm on the end of a string. You'd just sit there with your timetable, and soon as the 8.40 grouse showed up, bang!'

'With your stick,' said the clerk. 'Any old stick. Think of the saving!'

NO WATER – SO FIREMEN IMPROVISED

Liverpool Daily Post

'And once you had your rails laid,' said the bald man 'there's no end to the spin-offs. You could have a dog-track. There's all these hounds we've got, not doing nothing, just walking about and peeing against the van. Train 'em to run after a grouse, you got an entire leisure industry.'

'It seems somewhat less than sporting,' I said.

The bald man looked at the clerk.

'There's your private enterprise talking, Sidney,' he said. 'See what I mean? No grasp of basic concepts.' He turned back to me. 'You don't seem to realise,' he said, 'what the meat industry entails. Mouths to feed, son, mouths to feed. We got an output target of four million grouse this year. Going over to battery production in August. Biggest aluminium shed complex north of Doncaster.'

I sighed.

'Not much sport there, I'm afraid,' I said.

'Don't see why not,' said the clerk. 'You could help with the plucking.'

'It's a far cry from shooting,' I said.

'I thought we was talking about grouse,' said the bald man. 'Not trout.'

'You *shoot* trout?'

He drew a large buff book from a shelf and threw it on the desk.

'Central Division Beige Paper,' he said. 'All in there. Results of the Research Division work-study. They went into the question of how you catch these bleeders when they're only in the air about 1.8 seconds, on average. Tried holding nets over the streams, but they're too sharp. Time you've seen 'em and got your wrists going, they're back in the water again. Only way is to lie on the bank with shotguns, soon as they leap you're on 'em.'

'And how, exactly,' I said, 'do you bring them in?'

'Retrievers,' said the clerk.

'Oh, come on,' I cried. 'Dogs will never go in after fish!'

'Cats will,' said the bald man.

'Got him there, Harold!' said the clerk. 'He'd never thought of cats.'

'Private enterprise again, Sidney. In blinkers. Hidebound by tradition. Good enough for daddy, it's good enough for me, what? This is 1971, mate!'

'4,' said the clerk.

'1974,' said the bald man.

'And how do you propose,' I said, 'to train cats to swim?'

'Listen,' said the bald man. 'If you can train flies, we can train bloody cats.'

'I think I'll be going,' I said, and stood up. They stared at my waders. 'For trout,' I explained.

'First good idea you've had,' said the clerk. 'The nettles are terrible.'

'Hallo,' said the bald man, glancing suddenly past us, and pushing his spectacles up his nose, 'the stock's arrived.' He rose.

I followed them to the window. Between the administration building, on the fourth floor of which we stood, and the Amalgamated Ghillie Union tower block opposite, ran a bright tarn that had risen in some now invisible mountain. Beside it, a dump truck was unloading a wriggling pile of small silver fish directly into the hurtling water. Upon entering which, they all turned belly-up. I peered, but we were fifty feet above.

'There's something wrong with those trout,' I said.

'Shows how much *you* know,' said the clerk. 'They're pilchards.'

'Calls himself a sportsman,' said the bald man.

'But pilchards are saltwater fish!' I cried.

'And very popular, too,' said the clerk. 'On toast, with a bit of tomato sauce.'

'But they're all dying!'

'So I should hope,' said the bald man. 'Easy to see he's never tried packing six pilchards in a tin, innit, Sidney?'

'If you did it his way,' said the clerk, 'it'd take six weeks to get the lid on. They hop about like nobody's business, pilchards.'

'Prob'ly never seen a tin,' said the bald man, jabbing a thumb at me. 'His lot prob'ly hunt pilchards on horseback.'

The clerk thought about this for a moment or two.

'Doubt it,' he said at last, 'you'd have a hell of a job aiming.'

The bald man nodded, slowly.

'Common sense, really,' he said.

Excerpts from 'The Sanity Inspector' Published by Robson Books.

It's a cardinal rule, of course, that even though you may start with a very simple clearly set out request to some public body or other, you'll find yourself knee-deep in gobbledegook from the moment the first buff envelope in reply to yours of the 1st inst. drops stealthily (and paid for by you) through your letterbox. Remember always that the character (who you'll never know by anything but initials and even *they* change) has a pile of other cogent reasonably written letters just like yours – well, so much like yours that it only takes one false flick into the wrong Pending tray for you to be granted a licence to keep a pig instead of getting an appointment with the chiropodist. *If you think I'm joking take a look at these genuine extracts. . . . .*

I want money as quick as you can send it. I have been in bed with the doctor for a week and he doesn't seem to be doing any good. If things don't improve I shall have to send for another doctor.

Unless I get my husband's money I will be forced to live an immortal life.

Please find out if my husband is dead as the man I am now living with won't do anything until he is sure.

In answer to your letter I have given birth to a boy weighing 10 lbs. Is this satisfactory?

In accordance with your instructions I have given birth to twins in the enclosed envelope.

Sir, I am forwarding my marriage certificate and two children, one of which is a mistake as you will see.

In reply to your letter, I have already co-habited with your officer, so far nothing has happened.

Please send some money as I have fallen into errors with my landlord.

You have changed my boy to a girl. Will this make any difference?

I cannot get sick pay. I have nine children. Can you tell me why this is?

Milk is needed for the baby and Father is unable to supply it.

SPIKE MILLIGAN

The discovery of the telephone came about by accident. In 1873 a young, spotty research chemist, called Dr MacTomjim, had left a plate of virus mould culture on the window-sill to cool before serving and, absent-mindedly, forgot it. Next morning as he was counting the dead children around it, eureka! Whereas the mould had, originally been white, there, looming in the middle was an ominous black shape. At first the Doctor thought it was an illegal Jamaican immigrant with a wondrous new way of entering the U.K. But no, closer inspection showed it to be the first telephone. Unaware of his great discovery, the Doctor placed it up on a shelf and forgot it. How, then, you say, did he discover it by accident? I'll tell you. It fell on his head.

His devoted Bronte-like wife, who up till then was happily vivisecting away removing the eyes from live rabbits, etc., etc., rushed to her beloved's side. Seeing the bruise on his head, she swooned to the floor. There, seeing the telephone, she swooned upright and *instinctively* dialled POLICE – FIRE – AMBULANCE. In a trice the police arrived, set fire to the doctor and drove away in an ambulance. Friends, the telephone had arrived!

The first telephone proved to be useless until the arrival of the second. It rapidly became the status symbol of the Industrial Nouveau Riche. Daguerrotypes show important men posing alongside their new telephones; families grouped lovingly *around* their telephones; generals pointing to their military telephones. Tunesmiths wrote 'Will Willy tinkle Tilly on the Telephone Tonight'. No play was complete without a telephone in the first act. It was a boon to the atrocious plays and playwrights that fouled the English stage from 1926 to '38. Soon millionaires were ordering ornate Victorian-rococo telephones of satin brass and glazed steel. The Czar of all the Russias commanded the famed Romanov court jeweller, Fabergé, to fashion a telephonic masterpiece. Made of pure Irish gold, inlaid with lapis lazuli taken from the tomb of Tutankamen, and blazing with rare Australian fire opals, it caused the fiend Rasputin to say of it, 'This is a great day for Russia!' It turned out he was right, they shot him. (He died defiantly singing 'Anything you can do I kon do better'.)

In British West Pongoland, warring Zulu chiefs were placated with great crates of Victorian telephones. It was common fare to see two chieftains sitting two feet apart talking to each other on the new 'White Magic'; while outside, a snide British Lieutenant was hurriedly running up a Union

Jack, and claiming the flagpole for the Queen, (back home Prince Albert had gone one better, he was claiming the Queen).

Henry Irving boosted the sale of telephones with his play *The Bells:* the morning after the first night the G.P.O. was besieged with applications for second night tickets. One man resented the intrusion of the instrument; William McGonagall, self-appointed Poet Laureate, and idiot, wrote:

> What a sinful thing is the electrified telephone,
> Such a disgrace hitherto before has never been known,
> I would rather see those to whom I speak,
> Otherwise, for all I know I may be speaking to a freak.

The tintinabulation of the Bells, drove Poe insane; he stabbed himself to death with a state-controlled raven. With good reason; the G.P.O. phone bell could be heard three miles away as the crow flies, and is the direct cause of deafness among crows today. This nerve-shattering bell is the same one installed at the bedsides of wax-frail old ladies in private nursing homes. Now, by shorting the circuit in the early hours, mercenary doctors in need of bed space can set off a carillon that reaps a fine crop of Coronary Occulusions.

My first phone was a 'party' line, that is, when your T.V., radio, wife and mistress break down, you can pick up the phone and listen to the neighbours. It soon became a burden. One of my writers would phone me at midnight, and indulge in seeing how far he could walk away from the phone and still be heard; last time he got as far as King's Road, Chelsea, where he was knocked down by a bus.

My friend Mr Sellers had it bad. He installed a phone in his car. Rather than let it lie idle all night, he would drive into the Kentish Weald and phone back to tell his mother he was 'Out'. It was becoming evident to me that the phone was a drug, and vieing with cigarettes for cancer of the inner ear.

Victim: Doctor, I've *got* to have more phone calls.

Dr: But Mrs Leigh, you're up to seventy a day!

Victim: I know. I've tried to cut them down but I can't.

Dr: Very well Mrs Leigh. Do you want them on the G.P.O. or do you want to be phoned privately.

Victim: My husband is rich.

Dr: Very well, I want you to ring this number ten times a day after meals.

I invited a fellow sufferer to dine with me. To music by Debussy, and candlelight, we sat down. As we commenced soup, the phone in the next room rang. My guest stiffened, half rose and dropped his spoon. For a moment he listened. 'Aren't you going to answer it?' he said, his voice strangely castrati. 'We never answer the telephone on Fridays, we are Catholics, and the Jews next door are watching us.' My guest was now quite pale, trembling, and his wig had slipped. 'Would you like me to answer it for you?' he whined from his foetus position on the floor. I pointed a threatening obstetrical finger at him but, half-crazed by the bells, he ran screaming to the phone. Lifting the handset he received the following message, 'Your soup's getting cold you silly B——r.' It had all been prearranged twixt me and a certain Mr Secombe.

Which brings us to the promoters of this malaise, those faceless sons of fun, the G.P.O.! Who from time to time issue little pain-killing brochures telling of fresh G.P.O. triumphs in a world of absolutely no competition. 'VALUE FOR MONEY' says their latest bit of bumph, 'When you pick up your telephone, you have a thousand million pounds worth of equipment at your finger-tips.' That's O.K. with me man, what I complain about are those five-pound-a-week brains that answer them.

Published by Dobson Books Ltd.

At a meeting to discuss the route of a proposed ring road, the highways committee chairman said: "We intend to take the road through the cemetary—provided we can get permission from the various bodies concerned."

West London Observer

PASSENGERS HIT BY CANCELLED TRAINS

Manchester Evening News

The services of a woman chief inspector in uniform can be had for £14 5s 1d daily (£1 15s 7d hourly) sliding down to £9 8s 4d daily for a uniformed policewoman or £3s 6d an hour. But a woman C.I.D. inspector will cost £13 7s 2d daily.

Buckinghamshire Advertiser

DURING NUCLEAR ATTACK THERE WILL BE A SCHOOL HOLIDAY —official

By WILLIAM HARROLD

In the event of a nuclear attack, children will be given a day off school, says the Scottish Home and Health Department.

M4 contract for Monk?

A. Monk is expected to be awarded the contract for a 12.2 mile stretch of the M4 motorway from Liddington to Wickham worth about £7.25m.

Constructors' World

INSURED NO DOUBT

Bedford firemen today received 28 letters thanking them for their efforts which destroyed 3 houses last Wednesday night.

Bedford paper

Probation

At Frome yesterday, Mrs. Jennifer Anne Ayres of 5, Duke Street, Frome was placed on probation for three yrs. for stealing the Gas Board.

Bath Evening Chronicle

BEWARE

TO TOUCH THESE WIRES IS INSTANT DEATH

Anyone found doing so will be prosecuted

Titbits

WEATHER SERVICE

From next Tuesday, the B.B.C. will include weather hints for mars in the early morning Home Service programme "Farming Today."

Daily Mirror

Families with, in all, more than 500,000 children to be better off as from next August through the family income supplement, some by as much as £3 a week;

Oldham Evening News

FIREMAN SYDNEY JACOBS *is expected to get his massive tender out in 30 seconds*

Weekend Telegraph

British Rail said it was hoped that from 8 a.m. today a normal service would run, with trains liable to delays of up to 20 minutes.

Times

PICK OF THE PICS No.1

From 'SMILES' by David McEnery

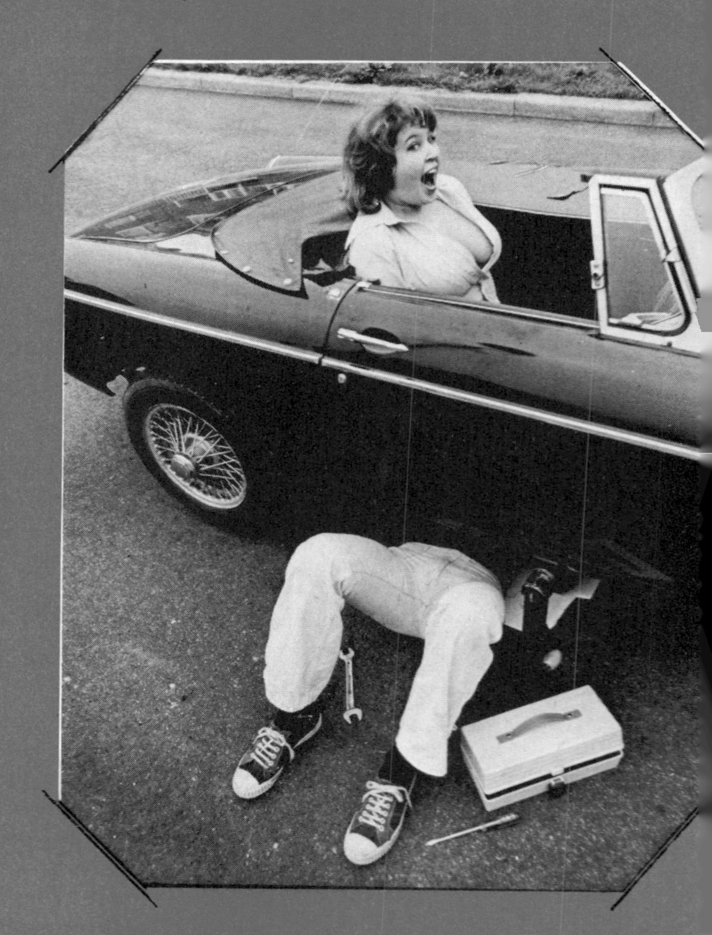

FROM THE BEST OF

MORECAMBE & WISE

by EDDIE BRABEN
Published by Woburn Press

☆☆☆☆☆☆☆☆☆☆☆☆☆☆☆☆☆☆☆☆☆☆☆☆☆☆☆☆☆☆

NAPOLEON & JOSEPHINE

☆☆☆☆☆☆☆☆☆☆☆☆☆☆☆☆☆☆☆☆☆☆☆☆☆☆☆☆☆☆

Ernie My famous play about Napoleon next.
Eric With Vanessa Redcoat?
Ernie Redgrave. She gave us a few problems.
Eric With her being such a tall girl?
Ernie Do you know she wanted paying by the inch.
Eric We'd have been skint. A delightful lady to work with.
Ernie Affable.
Eric Always thought she was British.
Ernie She worked hard at rehearsal.
Eric Did you see her during the breaks? She was stretched out fast asleep in three separate dressing rooms
Ernie Vanessa rather liked me.
Eric Oh?
Ernie Offered me a lift home in her car.
Eric Fool!
Ernie What do you mean?
Eric It was only because she didn't have a dipstick.
Ernie This is the play of mine we did in one of our Christmas Shows with Vanessa Redgrave.
Eric We wanted a big bird for Christmas and we got one.

Cast in order of height
Empress Josephine – Vanilla Redgrave
Duke of Ellington – Eric Morecambe
Napoleon Bonaparte – Lord Ern of Peterborough
Lord Brighton – Brian Clough
Minister without Portfolio – Larry Grayson
Regimental Goat – Richard Attenborough
Horses trained by Mrs Mark Phillips
Cannon balls supplied by Fanny Craddock
The BBC wishes to thank the British Museum for the uniforms and the jokes.

Scene: in the richly furnished tent used by Napoleon on the battlefield of Waterloo Tent is deserted. F/X heavy gun fire and the distant shouting of men in battle. Ernie enters as Napoleon: staggers around the tent before standing still and looking very distressed.
Ernie Sacré Beaujolais! That it should come to this – that I, Napoleon Bonaparte, the tenacious Corsican, should come to this. Defeated by that devil, Wellington. Sacré Beaujolais and bon appétit.
Ernie bows his head and is sobbing . . . as Vanessa Redgrave enters as Josephine, looking seductive, she stops and sees Ernie sobbing.
Vanessa He is crying again. I wish he wouldn't cry. The tears roll down his legs and make them shrink. I do love him. When he kisses me I can feel his heart beating against my knee-caps.
She crosses to Ernie and places an arm on his shoulder.
Vanessa Napoleon, sit down.
Ernie I am sat down.
Vanessa Napoleon, my beloved, tell your Josephine what has happened.
Ernie The flower of the French Army lies crushed upon the battlefield of Waterloo. I have lost some of my finest men.
Vanessa What about the big red-headed drummer lad?
Ernie What?
Vanessa The one with the big cymbals.
Ernie Oh him. Gone. Your Napoleon has been defeated.
Vanessa You must have known in your heart that defeat was inevitable.
Ernie I must be honest, two nights ago I had a slight inkling.
Vanessa Why didn't you tell me? I was awake. I take it that you have lost to the Duke of Wellington.
Ernie He is at this very moment on his way here with the terms of the surrender.
Sound of horses' hooves. Eric enters as Wellington. Hooves continue.

Eric That horse never stops . . . Evenin' all. Sorry I'm late. Some fool kept me talking. Said he wanted to name a rubber boot after me. The Duke of Wellington at your service.

Eric salutes.

Ernie salutes: pulls rabbit out of jacket

Ernie Napoleon Bonaparte.

Eric (*walks past Vanessa, to Ernie*) I don't want to worry you but this tent pole's loose.

Ernie How dare you sir. That tent pole is the Empress Josephine.

Ernie places a small box in front of Vanessa He stands on it and faces her.

Ernie Tell him who you are.

Vanessa I am indeed the Empress Josephine of France.

Eric And what are you doing up at the front? Not that it matters – it suits you.

Vanessa The Emperor wishes to discuss the Battle of Waterloo.

Eric Odd name for a battle There was no water and I couldn't find a . . .

Ernie (*getting off box*) How dare you!

Vanessa Boney, my darling.

Ernie Not tonight, Josephine.

Eric What does he mean?

Ernie It is of little consequence.

Vanessa (*looking at Eric*) I'll second that.

Eric (*to standard*) What do you think of it so far – (*vents*) 'Ruggish'.

Ernie Now let's sit down and discuss these terms properly.

Vanessa I'll take everything down.

Eric That'll get a few laughs.

Vanessa and Eric sit down.

Vanessa Have you got the scrolls?

Eric No, I always walk like this.

Ernie The meeting is now in session.

He bangs table with mallet: hits Eric's finger.

Eric Ow!

Vanessa (*reads paper*) These terms are a bit one-sided.

Ernie I'll say they are. Are you prepared to ratify *my* proposals?

Eric Certainly. Put them on the table and pass me that mallet.

Vanessa You want everything your own way.

Eric Oh, you've heard!

Ernie We are having no part of this document.

Vanessa What happens when Napoleon signs these surrender terms?

Eric He will be dragged out by the dragoons. Not a pretty sight! (*To Vanessa*) I wouldn't look if I were you.

Vanessa I've never heard anything so terrible.

Eric Oh, you must have done! Have you heard Max Bygraves singing 'Deck of Cards' – that takes a bit of beating.

Ernie Perfectly true, Duke.

Eric Anyway, you will be taken to St Helena and incarcerated.

Vanessa *That'll* bring tears to his eyes.

Eric (*to camera*) They're all at it.

Ernie I think I should have a word with you, Josephine. (*Stands*) Over here. (*Points and pulls rabbit out*)

Vanessa and Ernie move to one side. Eric moves behind them and listens.

Ernie We've got to find a way out of this.

Vanessa He's such a stubborn man.

Ernie It's not going to be easy.

Vanessa We could offer him money.

Ernie I've got an idea.

Vanessa What's that?

Eric Seduce him.

Vanessa (*to Ernie*) Do you think I could?

Eric Yes. He'd love it.

Ernie That's a good idea.

Ernie turns to Eric.

Ernie My Lord Duke . . .

Eric Oh, there you are. I didn't understand a word because you were talking in French. Are you talking in French now?

Ernie No, I'm not . . . I need time to study these terms.

Vanessa (*aside to Ernie*) Just give me five minutes alone with him.

Eric That's no good. It takes me 20 minutes to get my wellies off.

Ernie I shall be in the anteroom. (*Exits*)

Vanessa We are alone.

Eric Ready when you are, pally.

Vanessa Poor Napoleon, he's been going through a bad time. Since his retreat from Moscow, he's been very cold towards me.

Eric Well, with that deep snow and those short legs . . . say no more. (*Nudges Vanessa*) Would um . . . (*Moves centre, to bed*) . . . would you like something to warm you up?

Vanessa I would very much.

Eric Good. I think I've got some extra strong mints in my greatcoat.

Vanessa I think not. Wellie . . . ?

Eric Yes.

Vanessa Napoleon has been so engrossed in the battle that he's tended to neglect me.

Eric Oh.

Vanessa I am a woman.

Eric Have you told him?

Vanessa I like you. (*She sprays perfume on to her neck*) Midnight in Paris.

Eric (*picks up bottle and dabs his cheeks with it*) 2.15 in Darlington – just before kick-off.

Vanessa indicates to sofa for Eric to sit.

Vanessa Please?

Eric Do you want to sell it?

Vanessa Sit by me. I only wish we had some music.
Eric That's easily arranged.
Picks up hat: turns into accordion.
Vanessa I am beginning to like you very much. I wish we could have met in Paris. It's a beautiful city. Put the candle out.
Eric Where's the switch?
Vanessa Blow it out and we can make love.
Eric Yes. (*Attempts to blow candle out, but it relights each time*) By the time I blow this thing out I'll be too tired to make love.
Vanessa Never mind the candle. (*She cuddles up to Eric*) The better the light, the better the love.
Eric It's no use, I've just had a power cut.
Vanessa I think that I'm falling in love with you.
Eric I have a wife at home in England.
Vanessa It's common knowledge that your wife has another.
Eric Now there's a novelty.
Vanessa Kiss me.
She throws her arms about Eric. A very long kiss. Eric shudders and bangs his legs.
Eric Good lord. Have you got shares in Mothercare?
Vanessa I don't know what it is you're doing to me, but I can feel a pounding in my bosom.
Eric Have a look, it might be one of his rabbits.
Vanessa (*sits up*) So you think you can resist me.
Eric lunges and misses.
Eric Oh yes.
Vanessa Really?
She raises her skirt and reveals a Luton Town rosette just below her knee.
Eric I've got news for you, we're going up the League.
Eric and Vanessa embrace and lean back. Ernie enters.
Ernie Sacré Beaujolais and bon appétit. What is going on?
Vanessa and Eric both quickly rise.
Vanessa Napoleon!
Eric Don't jump to conclusions. I can explain everything. I was carrying on with your wife behind your back.
Ernie This is too much.
Takes hand from tunic and brings out rabbit.
Eric Have you got Harry Corbett in there passing them up to you?
Ernie First I lose a battle. Now I have lost my wife.
Vanessa That's not true.
Ernie I love you so much, Josephine. You must choose between me or him.
Eric (*pulls his hand out – no rabbit*) Yes, you must choose between me or him. And remember, this is the book of the play and we can't finish with a song.
Vanessa What a shame because I thought I sang so well.
Eric I couldn't hear you. You were too high up.
Ernie Josephine, the time has come for you to choose.
Eric I know we finished the sketch with a song on the telly but this is the book so think of a new tag or we're all in trouble.
Vanessa Very well.
Ernie You have made your choice, Josephine?
Vanessa I have.
Ernie Is it me?
Vanessa No.
Eric Then it is me!
Vanessa No.
Eric If it's not me . . .
Ernie And it's not me . . .
Vanessa It is Christmas and with the money you're paying me I won't have a decent dinner so I'll take the rabbit.
She reaches inside Eric's tunic and takes the rabbit.
Eric Don't go. I've got twelve more rabbits hidden away in there if you'd care to get them out.
Vanessa Gladly.
She puts hand inside Eric's tunic.
Eric Oh yes! Keep going.

It's well-known, of course, that children have no sense of humour – at least not *our* kind. If they laugh, it's mostly at adults in trouble. Apart from that, their approach to life is relentlessly practical and realistic. They have no natural hesitations. In fact, one of the more terrifying things about children is that they know what they want – and go all out for it. Whatever they set their beady little eyes on, they have to have – no matter who they have to threaten. They can even write, bold as brass:

'Dear God, O.K. I kept my half of the deal. Where's the bike. (signed) Bert.'

They also see everything and understand everything:

My mummy and daddy like Peace. They dont often get it.

David aged 7

and they can – at the age of five or six anyway – get it profoundly right:

You must take care of Love – if You Don't it goez bad

James aged 5

They can also get it wrong:

you have to love your baby brother otherwise he geos wind

Alice aged 4

I wouldn't fall in love because girls are all spotty and They Wisper

Norman aged 6

I once saw some one fall in love In a car. It wasn't going though.

Sally aged 7

And occasionally, accidentally, they can hit you right between the eyes;

I don't think there should be Rich churches when there Are poor people

Fiona aged 11

Mostly though the very young look at religion pretty much as they look at everything else –

My sister is always writing to Jesus an he sends her chaolates an once he sent her Two lots of choclates on the same day but she won't tell me where to write.

Ian aged 6

Everybody loves baby Jesus even my uncle and both my bruthers but I don't I love the three wizmen best becus they broat presense.

John aged 5

Excerpts from 'God Bless Love'
by Nanette Newman
Published by Wm. Collins Sons & Co Ltd.

In relation to God, children are at their most basic – short, sharp and to the point

'Dear God, Count me in Your friend Herbie' and who knows, the Almighty may find that a lot more honest and attractive than the dreary old verbiage the rest of us throw at Him. They've also realized that God is the best bet when it comes to their impossible questions – they may not get a recognizable answer but at least their ghastly life-or-death queries are not swept hysterically aside by wild-eyed parents who've given up asking themselves things like:

Dear God,
Do plastic flowers make you mad? I would be if I made the real ones.
Lucy

Dear God
Did you mean for giraffe to look like that or was it an accident
Norma

Dear God,
Are boys better than girls, I know you are one but try to be fair.
Sylvia.

Younger children are particularly skilled at the Question Oblique – that is, a request made apparently to a third party, but with the parent, grandparent, teacher – whatever useful adult happens to be within range – strictly in their sights; thus mother or grandmother is the obvious target for 'Dear God. I would like a duck next Easter I am tired of the same thing every time O.K.? Love. Margaret' – religion being blatantly used here to embarrass the beseiged adult:

Dear God,
Christmas should be earlier because kids can only be good for so long.
Beth

Dear God,
Your book has a lot of zip to it. I like science fiction stories. You had very good ideas and I would like to know where you found them.
Your reader
Jimmy

Dear God
I have to know who Shakespeare is before next Friday.
Melissa

Dear God,
I would like to be a Doctor But not for the Reason you think.
Ferd.

Talking to animals is used very effectively, too, in the everlasting quest for what they want.

Indeed another popular misconception about children is that they like animals. They don't. They *use* them:

"Sandra's pony's broken a leg."

"Hat off in the house."

And when they've worked through all the questions, direct and indirect, tried with all their sweaty little hearts to get what they're after, they sit back and slam a few final unanswerables in the only possible direction left:

Dear God,
If we live after we die why do we have to die then?
Ron

Dear God
Where does everybody come from? I hope you explain it better than my father.
Ward

Dear God,
Do you hear us pray to you? It must drive you crazy.
Charles

Dear God -
If we had fur like The animals we wouldn't have to wear clothes.
Did you ever think of that?
Wally W.

What children *do* learn, of course is how to play the system, particularly for laughs – you can bet the sweet little horrors of this anxious father already knew it all:

> ' "Facts of Life". Father of boy and girl would deeply appreciate a beautifully written essay on this subject. *The Times.*'

– had been gloating secretly indeed for years over each and every intimate, grotty detail. They just wanted to see how snarled up and confused they could get him, trying to explain it to them:

Birds & Bees

By BASIL BOOTHROYD

You must have noticed that often when a lady and gentleman kiss on the pictures or TV it is not the same sort of kiss that you give your Mummy and Daddy, or even the same sort that Mummy and Daddy give each other. This is one of what we call the facts of life, just as girls and boys have different bicycles. They are different in other ways, too, though not as different as they used to be before jeans were invented. And, by the by, do not confuse jeans with genes, because these were invented much, much earlier, though you have only just begun to hear about them on the BBC.

I know you are very interested in birds, and love to see the blue tits hanging upside down from half a coconut, but I am sure you know that it is cruel to take their eggs – because if those eggs are left to ripen they will have other birds in them, and in time they will hang on half coconuts and *they* will have eggs with other birds in them. Yet there is a difference between the bird and the coconut, which does not have eggs but is a native of the Malay Arch-i-pelago, whence it has been carried by human agency to tropical and sub-tropical regions in all parts of the world. Perhaps you can most easily associate the word 'coconut' with the word 'shy', and if so I am very pleased as shyness was the next thing I was going to talk about.

Little boys and girls are often 'shy' with one another, though not, of course, if they are brothers and sisters. When it comes to the facts of life, brothers and sisters are not boys and girls in that sense at all, but often ride each others' bicycles and think nothing of it. I expect you have noticed, too, that a boy throws a ball at a coconut shy quite differently from a girl, except when the girl is what is called a 'tomboy'. I expect that will remind you of a 'tomcat', and it is true that a tomcat is very much more boy than girl, and cannot have kittens, any more than little boys can. Boys often ask their Mummies, 'Can I have a kitten?' and do not understand why they are always told No. It is a fact of life.

One thing that must have puzzled you, since you were about six, was where you were seven years ago? You ask Mummy and Daddy where *they* were seven years ago and they tell you at once, Twickenham, or perhaps even Esher, but when you ask where *you* were they put you off with e-vas-ive answers. You must remember that even your parents do not know the exact answer to everything, and though there are such songs as 'Only a Baby Small, Dropped from the Skies' these are not really giving the facts of life in a true form, as your friends at school may have told you. This does not mean that you should believe all that your friends at school tell you. It is much better to pay attention to a beautifully written essay like this and try to understand what is being said to you.

When a bird . . .

When a cat . . .

I realize that I should have said that coconuts are not the only natives of the Malay archipelago. Many of the natives there are Mummies and Daddies in the same way that your Mummy and Daddy are, exactly. The population was nearly six million in 1947, very unevenly dis-tri-but-ed, leaving large, virtually uninhabited areas of mountain and swamp jungles. When you are older I will lend you some books about the facts of life in that part of the world, by a writer named Somerset Maugham.

Rabbits are . . .

A bee is a fer-ti-lizer, but instead of being spread, like other kinds, it buzzes from flower to flower.

Perhaps the best thing is to think of your Daddy as a great big bee, with only one flower to go at (Mummy!). I expect he has talked to you about the facts of life from time to time, and seemed the biggest bee you ever listened to. If so, remember that that's just what *he* was feeling all the time.

Excerpt from 'Whole Things Laughable'
Published by Geo. Allen & Unwin Ltd.

Once in a while a rare, incredibly tough human being survives to get the better, temporarily, of a school girl or boy:

Noulded into a Shake

By PATRICK CAMPBELL

When I was a tall, sensitive boy at school I once sent up for a booklet about how to be a ventriloquist.

I was always 'sending up' for things – variable focus lamps, propelling pencils with choice of six differently-coloured leads, air-pistols discharging wooden bullets, scale model tanks with genuine caterpillar action, tricks in glass-topped boxes, and so on – anything, I suppose, to vary the monotony of straight games and education.

The booklet arrived at breakfast time one morning in a large square envelope. I told the other boys it was a new stamp album, and got on with my shredded liver poached in water. I wanted the voice-throwing to come as a real surprise.

We had twenty minutes after breakfast in which to get our things ready for first school. I had a quick run through the new book.

It was called *Ventriloquism in Three Weeks*. On the first page it explained that the word ventriloquism came from the Latin *ventriloqus* – 'a speaking from the belly'. There was also a drawing of a schoolboy smiling pleasantly at a railway porter carrying a trunk. From the trunk came hysterical cries of, 'Help! Help! Murder! Police!'

It was just the sort of thing I was aiming at. I slipped the book in with my other ones, and hurried off to first school.

In the next fortnight I put in a good deal of practice, sitting right at the back of the class, watching my lips in a small piece of mirror, and murmuring, 'Dah, dee, day, di, doy, doo.'

It was necessary, however, to be rather careful. Dr. Farvox, the author of the book, suggested that it might be as well to perform the earlier exercises 'in the privacy of one's bedroom or den.' Dr. Farvox was afraid that 'chums or relatives' might laugh, particularly while one was practising the 'muffled voice in the box'.

The best way to get this going, Dr. Farvox said, was to experiment 'with a continuous grunting sound in a high key, straining from the chest as if in pain'.

He was right in thinking that this exercise ought to be performed in the privacy of the bedroom. It was inclined to be noisy – so noisy, indeed, that I was caught twice straining in a high key from the chest during practical chemistry, and had to pretend that I'd been overcome by the fumes of nitric acid.

But, in the end, it was the easy, pleasant smile that terminated my study of what Dr. Farvox described as 'this amusing art'.

It happened one Saturday morning, in the hour before lunch, ordinarily a pleasant enough period devoted to constitutional history. Bill the Bull, who took the class, was usually fairly mellow with the prospect of the weekend before him, and there was not much need to do any work.

As was by now my invariable custom I was seated right at the back of the room with a large pile of books in front of me, and the mirror lying on the desk. I was working on the Whisper Voice, which had been giving me quite a considerable amount of difficulty.

'Lie down, Neddy, lie down,' I whispered, watching my lips closely in the glass.

'It's due to dock at nine o'clock.'

Not bad.

'Take Ted's Kodak down to Roy.'

'There it was again – the old familiar twitch on 'Kodak'.

I sat back, relaxing a little, and smiled. Dr. Farvox was strongly in favour of the Smile. 'What the young student,' he said, 'should aim at from the first is an easy and natural expression. He should Smile.'

I smiled. Smiling, I whispered, 'Take Ted's Kodak down to Roy.'

To my absolute horror I found myself smiling straight into the face of Bill the Bull.

He stopped dead. He was in the middle of something about the growth of common law, but my smile stopped him dead in his tracks.

'Well, well,' said Bill, after a moment. 'How charming. And good morning to you, too.'

I at once buried my face in my books, and tried to shove the mirror and *Ventriloquism in Three Weeks* on one side.

Bill rolled slowly down the passageway between the desks. He was an enormous Welshman with a bullet head, and very greasy, straight black hair. He took a subtle and delicate pleasure in driving the more impressionable amongst us half mad with fear at least five days a week.

'Such pretty teeth,' said Bill. 'How nice of you to smile at me. I have always wanted to win your admiration.'

The other boys sat back. They knew they were on to something good.

I kept my head lowered. I'd actually succeeded in opening my constitutional history somewhere near the middle but the corner of Dr. Farvox was clearly visible under a heap of exercise books.

Bill reached my desk. 'But who knows,' he said, 'perhaps you love me too. Perchance you've been sitting there all morning just dreaming of a little home – just you and I. And later, perhaps, some little ones . . . ?'

A gasp of incredulous delight came from the other boys. This was Bill at his very best.

I looked up. It was no longer possible to pretend I thought he was talking to someone else.

'I'm sorry, sir,' I said. 'I was just smiling.'

Suddenly, Bill pounced. He snatched up Dr. Farvox.

'Cripes,' he said. 'What in the world have we here? Ventriloquism in three weeks?'

He turned a couple of pages.

'Scholars,' he said, 'be so good as to listen to this.'

He read aloud: 'To imitate a Fly. Close the lips tight at one corner. Fill that cheek full of wind and force it to escape through the aperture. Make the sound suddenly loud, and then softer, which will make it appear as though the insect were flying in different parts of the room. The illusion may be helped out by the performer chasing the imaginary fly, and flapping at it with his handkerchief.'

'Strewth,' said Bill. He looked round the class. 'We'd better get ourselves a little bit of this. Here am I taking up your time with the monotonies of constitutional history, while in this very room we have a trained performer who can imitate a fly.'

Suddenly, he caught me by the back of the

neck, 'Come,' he said, 'my little love, and let us hear this astounding impression.'

He dragged me down to the dais.

'Begin,' said Bill. 'Be so kind as to fill your cheek with wind, and at all costs do not omit the flapping of the handkerchief.'

'Sir,' I said, 'that's animal noises. I haven't got that far yet.'

'Sir,' squeaked Bill, in a high falsetto, 'that's animal noises. I 'aven't got that far yet.'

He surveyed the convulsed class calmly.

'Come, come,' he said, 'this art is not as difficult as I had imagined it to be. Did anyone see my lips move?'

They cheered him. They banged the lids of their desks. 'Try it again, sir!' they cried. 'It's splendid!'

Bill raised his hand, 'Gentlemen,' he said, 'I thank you for your kindness. I am, however, but an amateur. Am I not right in thinking that we would like to hear something more from Professor Smallpox?'

They cheered again. Someone shouted, 'Make him sing a song, sir!'

Bill turned to me. 'Can you,' he said, 'Professor Smallpox, sing a song?'

It was the worst thing that had ever happened to me in my life. I tried to extricate myself.

'No, sir,' I said. 'I haven't mastered the labials yet.'

Bill started back. He pressed his hand to his heart.

'No labials?' he said. 'You have reached the age of fifteen without having mastered the labials. But, dear Professor Smallpox, we must look into this. Perhaps you would be so kind as to give us some outline of your difficulties?'

I picked up *Ventriloquism in Three Weeks*. There was no way out.

'There's a sentence here, sir, that goes, "A pat of butter moulded into the shape of a boat".'

Bill inclined his head. 'Is there, indeed? A

most illuminating remark. You propose to put it to music?'

'No, sir,' I said. 'I'm just trying to show you how hard it is. You see, you have to call that, "A cat of gutter noulded into the shake of a goat".'

Bill fell right back into his chair.

'You have to call it *what*?' he said.

'A cat of gutter, sir, noulded into the shake of a goat.'

Bill's eyes bulged.

'Professor,' he said, 'you astound me. You bewilder me. You take my breath away. A cat of gutter–' He repeated it reverently, savouring each individual syllable.

Then he sprang up. 'But we must hear this,' he cried. 'We must have this cat of gutter delivered by someone who knows what he is at. This – this is valuable stuff.'

He caught me by the ear. 'Professor,' he said, 'why does it have to be noulded into the shake of a goat?'

'Well, sir,' I said, 'if you say it like that you don't have to move your lips. You sort of avoid the labials.'

'To be sure you do,' said Bill. 'Why didn't I think of that myself. Well, now, we will have a demonstration.'

He turned to face the class. 'Gentlemen,' he said, 'Professor Smallpox will now say, "A pat of butter moulded into the shape of a boat," *without moving the lips*! I entreat your closest attention. You have almost certainly never in your lives heard anything like this before.'

He picked up his heavy ebony ruler. His little pig-like eyes gleamed.

'And,' he went on, 'to make sure that Professor Smallpox will really give us of his best I shall make it my personal business to give Professor Smallpox a clonk on the conk with this tiny weapon should any of you see even the faintest movement of the facial muscles as he delivers this unforgettable message.'

Bill brought down the ruler with a sharp crack on my skull.

'Professor,' he said, 'it's all yours.'

I don't have to go into the next twenty-five minutes. The other boys yelled practically on every syllable. I got the meaningless words tangled up, and said, 'A cack of rutter roulded into the gake of a shote.'

At times Bill was so helpless with laughter that he missed me with the ruler altogether.

When the bell went for the end of the hour he insisted on being helped out into the passage, wiping his eyes with the blackboard cloth.

After that, I gave up ventriloquism, feeling no recurrence of interest even after reading Bill's observation on my end-of-term report: 'He ought to do well on the stage.'

Excertp from '35 Years on the Job'
Published by Blond & Briggs Ltd.

FORM 2B

FUNNY
Q. WHAT IS AN OCTOPUS?
A. AN EIGHT SIDED CAT
Q. WHAT IS A FJORD
A. A NORWEGIAN MOTOR-CAR
Q. WHAT IS A MYTH
A. A FEMALE MOTH

'Dad,' said young Johnny, 'I have a message for you. There's going to be a small meeting of the Parent-Teachers Association tomorrow morning at school.'
'What do you mean a "small" meeting?' asked his father.
'Just you, me and the headmaster,' said the boy.

The subject for the essay class was A Cricket Match.
One small boy finished long before everybody else. In fact his essay consisted of just three words — 'Rain Stopped Play'.

Two little girls wre discussing their respective families. 'Why does your grandfather read his bible so much?' asked one. Replied the other: 'I think he's cramming for his finals.'

DORA LOVES FRED

The teacher was explaining that surnames often referred to the occupations of their owners in days gone by, and he quoted the usual examples — Taylor, Baker, Smith, Mariner and so on. Turning to a boy called Webb, he said,
'And what do you think your ancestors were?
'Spiders, sir?' said the boy hopefully.

Many schools today contain a high proportion of coloured and negro children and this can give rise to some peculiar misunderstandings. A teacher asked a class one day how far away Nigeria was.
'I don't know, miss,' said a little white boy, 'but it can't be far. My mate here's from Nigeria and he goes home to lunch every day.'

Philip: I hear the headmaster is trying to stop necking during the school hours.
Little Johnny: It's not an easy habit to break.

Over a row of hooks in the school cloakroom was a sign saying: 'THESE HOOKS ARE FOR TEACHERS ONLY', Underneath, some bright spark had added the words: 'THEY MAY ALSO BE USED FOR HATS AND COATS'.

Teacher: What is a cannibal?
Child: Don't know, miss.
Teacher: Well, what would you be if you ate your mother and father?
Child: Please miss — an orphan.

A teacher caught a small boy of 10 smoking in the school playground.
'Aren't you a bit young to be smoking?' he asked.
'Course not,' replied the lad. 'I go out with girls an' all — I'ad one only last night.'
'Good heavens!' said the teacher. 'And how old was she?'
'No idea,' said the youngster. 'I was too drunk to ask!'

'Now this is a very useful text book,' said the teacher.
'If you use it properly, it will do half your work for you.'
'Please miss,' said little Albert, 'could I have two of them?'

In a small school in Dublin, the teacher had offered a 50p piece to whoever could give her the name of the most holy man in history. Only one hand went up, that of the only Jewish boy in the class, Manny O'Cohen.
'Well, Manny,' said the teacher.
'Saint Patrick, miss,' said Manny.
The teacher handed over the 50p piece and then said, 'Now how is it that the only boy who knows the correct answer is Jewish?'
To which Manny replied, 'Well, miss, in my heart of hearts I knew it was Moses — but business is business!'

An Examination by GRAHAM

"He seems to have aged in the last day or two."

"At first glance I'd say I won't be getting that new bicycle."

"Nonsense! Best years of his life!"

"A word of advice . . . Don't ask her how Biology went."

"Hullo! Another case of examination nerves."

Excerpts from 'All Other Men Have Mellowed'
Published by Garnstone Press Ltd.

The Daily Blooper

OUR WOMEN LICK MALE SPORTSMEN
Sportsweek

Bodies in the garden are a plant says wife
Hong Kong Standard

Recent tests conducted by a zoo-ologist prove that grasshoppers hear with their legs. In all cases the insects hopped when a tuning fork was sounded nearby. There was no reaction to this stimulus, however, when the insects' legs had been removed.
Corning Glass Works Magazine

The Vicar, the Rev. C. O. Marston, reported an increased number of communicants during the year. He also stated that the death watch beetle had been confirmed in the church.
Banbury Guardian

Primary School's summer festival was supported by 800 parents and friends last week. The evening began with the drowning of the Summer Queen, Susan F—.
Horley Advertiser

THREE BATTERED IN FISH SHOP
Man gaoled for assault
Evening News

Lost his head

The driver had a narrow escape, as a broken board penetrated his cabin and just missed his head. This had to be removed before he could be released.
Leicester paper

CHEERFUL CHOPPERS

Why is it, I wonder, that butchers always seem cheerful? It's not that their job is a enviable one, for in cold weather meat must be very cold to handle. Maybe they get rid of any bad temper by bashing away with their choppers? *Mrs. J. R. Stevenson, Southampton, Hants.*
Woman's Own

Blood and Thunder

□ In a popularity poll staged by Madame Tussaud's in London, Dracula tied for fifth place in the 'hate and fear' section with Mr. Enoch Powell.
Daily Mirror

She proceeded on her way until 7, or rather later, when a noise was heard as of a heavy body like an anchor or a chain being dragged along the deck from about the funnel aft. It was the mate's watch.
Liverpool paper

Crash courses for private pilots
Daily Telegraph

GLYNDEBOURNE — Young lady mid to late 20s needed to undertake highly interesting secretarial / administrative post. Must be prepared to live locally. Initial months as assistant, then promotion to Head-of-department status with excellent long-term possibilities. Applications in writing to front of Horse Manager, Glyndebourne, Lewes, Sussex.
Times

Women leaps from coffin, is Killed

Moinesti, Rumania, Wednesday. Mourners of the burial of Anna Bochinsky were astonished to see the 'dead' woman jump out of her coffin while it was being carried with the lid open—as is the custom in Rumania—from the cemetary to the grave.

She ran into the road and was run over and killed by a motor-car.
Daily Express

Ghana is to change over to driving on the right. The change will be made gradually.
Ghana paper

Should get some money

The County Council's veterinary inspector yesterday certified that death was due to anthrax, and was cremated by the police.
Yorkshire Post

Will the parents of the boy who gave a little boy an apple in exchange for his tricycle outside the Sale Lido on Friday between 6 & 7, kindly return it at once?
Advert in Manchester Evening News

COPPER BOILER?

Some of the fresh eggs came from hens kept at St. Bartholomew's Hospital for nutritional tests; one or two came from a police-sergeant at Scotland Yard.
The Times

Extracts from "Bumper Book of Boobs" published by Private Ey

QUICK AS A FLASH

There are times when it must be no joke at all being funny; when as a comedian, you find yourself in a tight corner, and you've got to be fast on the draw or you're a dead duck; and nowhere can it be rougher or tougher than in the bawdy boozy atmosphere of the halls and the clubs – where audience participation (even supposing they stop drinking and talking long enough to listen to you) can mean beer cans and boos, cat-calls and heckling. You've got to be quick-witted then – and how – or you're done for. Les Dawson *(like his fictional hero "Joe King")* – **slogged his way through this jungle, was tough enough and fast enough to come out on top, and this is what it was like to come on to do his act in a northern club after watching the preceding acts, comedian and folk singers alike, get murdered by hecklers:**

Les Dawson

'Well . . . I thought, as the compere went on to the stage to announce me, most of the bill had died, so let's make it a communal burial. The "Band" struck up with "There's No Business Like Show Business" . . . I looked at the ocean of faces down in front of me; pale saucers with open mouths, curiosity in some, indifference in the majority. The noise was deafening, so I never said a word, just stood deadpan of feature, and looked back at them . . . I uttered no sound. After what seemed an eternity, the audience began to quieten and gaze from their pots to me. I gave it another few seconds or so, and then began:

"Coming up here takes me back to my childhood . . . You see my father was so lazy, during the hunger march from Jarrow in the Thirties, he was the only one singing". The roof lifted off at that one, and I knew it was going to be all right.

"We were so poor at home we used to go out selling clothes pegs . . . to Gypsies. I waited so long between meals that the doctor warned mother that if she didn't force the odd crust down, my mouth would heal up.

"Mind you I wasn't expected . . . mother was firmly convinced that she was going into hospital to have a boil lanced.

"Dad didn't like me . . . when they took me to be christened, he threw a depth charge in the font.

"My ma had no idea how to look after a baby . . . I was the only kid in the street with nappy rash on his head.

"She was short sighted, and she would persist in putting talcum powder on my face . . . I've often wondered what the hell she did with my dummy".'

Another time – while he was still fighting his way up – 'Joe King' nightly faced a dull silent club audience and saw the previous act fail to reach them at all:

'The audience kept on talking, and remembering my nightly debacle, I couldn't blame them.

"Thank you ladies and gentlemen for your kind applause . . . I'm very grateful, because if success breeds success . . . then it looks as if I'm on the pill".

I'd hardly said that when I was aware that the room was listening to me, indeed the opening had got a laugh . . . without any set routine, I started talking:

"Mind you I don't have to do this for a living; I could always starve to death. To give you some idea of my act, last night a fisherman stood up in the front and fired off a distress signal. My agent said to me never mind Joe, one day your ship will come in . . . after the week I've had at this club it must have been the Titanic. Let's face it, as you well know I'm a flop . . . you should have seen my engagement book, the pages are so blank and white, you get snow-blindness looking through it".'

He made it, he had the audience roaring with laughter, and roaring for more – and success grew with the act:

'Thanks for the applause . . . if clapping is music to an artiste's ears, then the only song I've heard for the last five years has been "Silent Night". Mind you I don't have to do this for a living . . . I only do it for the luxuries in life . . . little things like bread and shoes.

'I've been out of work so often when I sign on the dole now they ask me to MC their staff dances.

'The manager of the club has been very nice to me . . . at rehearsal he said to me, "there's only one thing wrong with your act Joe . . . the seats face the stage".'

'Joe King' went on making it – and as Les Dawson says in his book, this was partly because he'd found his style – and carried it through all the tough spots and the heckling. Something that all successful comedians have to learn to do – as Mike Yarwood says:

Mike Yarwood

" There are stock answers which every stand-up comedian has to have in his repertoire, but I prefer off-the-cuff ripostes if I can get them in. I was once being persistently interrupted by a man, and I finally stopped my act and told him: 'Look, sir, I don't mind working with you, but I would appreciate if we could have rehearsed.' That was pointed enough to get a smile from the rest of the audience, and delicate enough to have them appreciate my difficulties and get them on my side. It is their opposition that finally silences most hecklers. But it depends how much drink has been taken.

Because of my particular act, I get hecklers who are not so much disagreeing with me as with the characters of whom I am giving impressions – particularly the political figures. I was once doing Harold Wilson in a club in Southport, when a woman who had had a few drinks obviously mistook me for Harold Wilson himself. She gave a wild diatribe against me for not having allowed her to make the profits out of rented property that she thought she had a right to. What I did was to answer her back in the voice of Harold Wilson, and actually using one of Harold's lines which, in my studious researches, I had once heard him say to a heckler. I said: 'Madam, if you'll be quiet, I'll give you the facts. I can only give you the facts, I cannot give you the intellectual apparatus to appreciate them.'

I like to go to the big meetings of the political leaders, not only to study them, but to see how they deal with heckling. I heard someone shout at Harold, 'What about housing?' Quick as a flash he replied, 'How many have *you* built?'

I did the autumn season in Coventry. My impersonations then included Macmillan, Heath, Wilson and Muggeridge as well as the comedians. I met Malcolm Muggeridge, and he asked me how I mimicked him. I said, 'I just put a lot of big words together, but I don't really know what I'm talking about.' He looked at me confidentially. 'Neither do I, dear boy,' he said. I didn't mention that one of my Muggeridgisms was, 'Edible tubers fragmented and subsequently immersed in seething emollient fluid, transmogrified into brittle morsels of an amber hue' – a rather roundabout description of chips!"

Billy Connolly

Billy Connolly is another fast-thinking comedian who's taken on the hecklers – and beaten them at their own game:

" The great problem with hecklers is that quite often you just can't hear what they're trying to say to you, especially in the Apollo, Glasgow, because they're all so far away. All you can hear on stage is a sort of 'Giewabeennarrack'. So of course I shout back something rude and then find out afterwards that all they were trying to say was: 'Just keep goin', Big Yin – ye're magic.'

Some ripostes . . .

(To noisy, aggressive hecklers):

'Last time I saw a mouth like yours, pal, Lester Piggott was sitting behind it.'

'The more I hear of you, the more I believe in birth control.'

'Just keep talkin' so's the bouncers can find ye . . . on ye go, Igor – kill!'

'If you're in the next seat, put a net over her, will ye?'

'To an artiste, applause is like a banquet. Thanks for the cheese sandwich.'

'You're a great crowd . . . what's wrang wi' ye? Got yer balaclavas on back tae front?'

(When tuning up):

'Aye . . . just tae think that when Mozart was my age, he'd been deid for seventeen years.'

'I just washed ma hair – cannae dae a thing wi' the sink.'

(To noisy hecklers in Dublin):

'Hey, put the house lights on. I want tae *see* an Irish joke.'

'Does the Mother Superior know ye're out?'

(To photographer taking flash photo):

'Take as many as ye want. It doesnae worry me – I used tae be a welder.'

(Sudden giggle in the audience):

'Unexpected laugh – always check your fly.'

And from the quick riposte and heckler-getter, Billy goes on to repartee:

" George Bernard Shaw, too. I like some of the things he used to say. One particularly because of what I'm doing now – he sent a card to Churchill inviting him to the first night of his play and he put: 'Bring a friend – if you have one.' Churchill writes back and says he can't make the first night, but he'll come to the second night, '– if you have one.'

And it reminds me of the story about Arnold Palmer, the golfer. He was playing in this big golf tournament somewhere and he hits the ball on to the top of the bunker and it sticks there – thunk! So he takes out a club and does this delicate wee chip. The ball goes right up, out of the bunker and lands just beside the hole, a few inches away. One of the spectators comes up to Palmer.

'You were lucky there, Arnold.'

'Yes,' he says. 'And it's an amazing thing: but the more I practise, the luckier I get.'

I wish I'd said that."

Oscar Wilde

And of course it was when someone else once sighed 'I wish I'd said that', that Oscar Wilde flashed back with 'And you will, dear boy, you will.' Wilde's wit is legendary – sometimes it seems like the accumulation of all the wit of the times in which he lived – and it's stood the test of time too, because you can still dine out wonderfully on his tight, taut and sometimes stinging witticisms:

'I hope you have not been leading a double life, pretending to be wicked and being really good all the time. That would be hypocrisy.'

'Women are meant to be loved, not to be understood.'

'I never put off till tomorrow what I can possibly do – the day after.'

'Laughter is not at all a bad beginning for a friendship, and it is far the best ending for one.'

'Gold-tipped cigarettes are awfully expensive. I can only afford them when I am in debt.'

'If one tells the truth, one is sure, sooner or later, to be found out.'

'The history of women is the history of the worst form of tyranny the world has ever known. The tyranny of the weak over the strong. It is the only tyranny that lasts.'

'I can't help detesting my relations. I suppose it comes from the fact that none of us stand other people having the same faults as ourselves.'

'When I was young I used to think that money was the most important thing in life; now that I am old, I know it.'

'I dislike arguments of any kind. They are always vulgar and often convincing.'

'How marriage ruins a man! It's as demoralising as cigarettes, and far more expensive.'

'I like men who have a future and women who have a past.'

'Experience is the name everyone gives to their mistakes.'

'I hate vulgar realism in literature. The man who could call a spade a spade should be compelled to use one. It is the only thing he is fit for.'

'Of course America had often been discovered before Columbus, but it had always been hushed up.'

'I never travel without my diary. One should always have something sensational to read in the train.'

'The only difference between a caprice and a lifelong passion is that the caprice lasts a little longer.'

'Some Southern Americans have a melancholy tendency to date every event of importance by the late war. "How beautiful the moon is tonight," I once remarked to a gentleman standing near me. "Yes," was his reply, "but you should have seen it before the war".'

'It is perfectly monstrous the way people go about nowadays saying things against one behind one's back that are absolutely and entirely true.'

'She who hesitates is won.'

'Moderation is a fatal thing. Nothing succeeds like excess.'

'Ignorance is like a delicate exotic fruit; touch it and the bloom is gone.'

'The one duty we owe to history is to rewrite it.'

'We live in an age when unnecessary things are our only necessities.'

And finally:

'I like hearing myself talk. It is one of my greatest pleasures. I often have long conversations all by myself, and I am so clever that sometimes I don't understand a single word of what I am saying.'

Noel Coward

Noel Coward seems to be the natural descendant of Oscar Wilde; his wit too is crisp and cool, and seemed even more so when delivered in his famous dry clipped syllables.

- 'Wit,' he said once 'is like caviare. It should be served in small elegant portions, and not splashed about like marmalade.'

And here are some of his small elegant portions:

- 'I often used to think that most of my gift horses seemed to have bad teeth.'
- 'The five most unpopular words of any evening are: waiter, bring me the check.'

'Time has convinced me of one thing. Television is for appearing on, not looking at.'

'The TV spectacular I am going to do with Mary Martin will be completely spontaneous. The kind of spontaneity I like best – the kind that comes after five weeks' rehearsal.'

'I love the weight of American Sunday newspapers. Pulling them up off the floor is good for the figure.'

Then there are the little stories about his repartee. Coward was said, for instance, to have a number of quick squelches for brushing off bores and those who tried to scrape up acquaintance with him. When a woman said to him

'You remember me? I met you with Douglas Fairbanks.'

'Madam' Coward replied icily, 'I don't even remember Douglas Fairbanks.'

'What do you know?' said a late arrival at a party Coward was attending, 'so-and-so's just blown his brains out!' The suicide was an acquaintance who was both a bore and a boor, and Coward lifted the slightly uncomfortable silence by saying casually in his clipped tones: 'He must have been an incredibly good shot.' And there was the young sycophant who buttonholed Coward at another party and gushed

'I've just been reading your marvellous "Present Indicative" again.'

'That's right, my boy' replied Coward benevolently, 'always keep abreast with the classics.'

Watching with Coward a re-screening of the Coronation Procession, one of the guests – highly impressed by the smiling personality of Queen Salote, who was descended way back from cannibals – said

'She's wonderful – but who's the little guy sitting up front in her carriage?'

'That' replied Coward 'is her lunch.'

There are also on record a lot of pronouncements which the Master let go on a wide variety of subjects:

On seeing an actress play Queen Victoria in the provinces:

'Her Victoria made me feel that Albert had married beneath his station.'

To a young actor consulting him about the motivation of a scene:

'My dear boy, forget about the motivation. Just say the lines and don't trip over the furniture.'

Writing to Lawrence of Arabia (who was also Aircraftsman T. E. Shaw No. 338171) and knowing the man's shyness, Coward's letter began:

'Dear 338171, May I call you 338?'

On some dining companions:

'The Blaises were both a bit desiccated and lacked vitality to such a degree that one felt oxygen should be served after the fish.'

On mixed morals:

'I'm not a suspicious woman, but I don't think my husband has been entirely faithful to me.

What makes you think that?

My last child didn't resemble him in the least.'

On a tribe encountered en route to South Africa:

'The natives' claim to fame is that they are very tall, have the longest penises in the world and dye their hair with urine; doubtless, cause and effect.'

Excerpts from:-
Les Dawson "A Card for the Clubs"
Published by Sphere Books Ltd.
Mike Yarwood "And This is Me"
Published by Jupiter Books Ltd.
Oscar Wilde "The Wit of Oscar Wilde"
compiled by Sean McCann
Published by Leslie Frewin Publishers Ltd.
Noel Coward "The wit of Noel Coward"
compiled by Dick Richard
Published by Leslie Frewin Publishers Ltd.
Billy Connolly the Authorised Version
compiled and introduced by Duncan Campbell
Published by Pan Books Ltd.

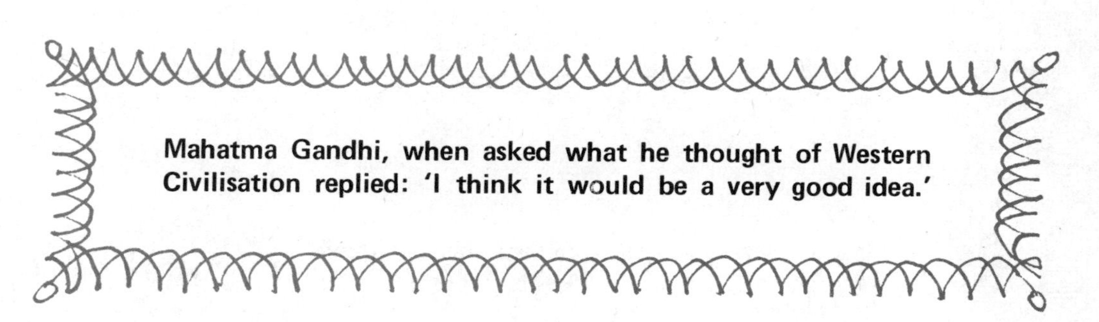

Mahatma Gandhi, when asked what he thought of Western Civilisation replied: 'I think it would be a very good idea.'

TYPO GOOFS

Compiled by Barney Thompson Fawcett Publications USA.

NOTED GEOLOGIST STONED AT ROCK FESTIVAL

—Vienna (Vt.) Vanguara

Police surmised that the *widow* had been pried open with a crowbar and entry made by means of a stepladder found near the scene.

—Castletown (S.D.) Advertiser

However, other Congressmen ribute his *erection* to the fact h of Japanese ancestry.

—Goode (Tenn.) Ne

ANTIQUE SALE

Genuine 1870 Blueridge sewing mac This is a rare small black *gay* model w is screwed on a table and operated b treadle.

—Westport (W.Va.) Messen

Engraved pewter *bowels* were presented to members of the Durley Women's Institute for their efforts in behalf of the cleaner environment movement.

—Durley (Ga.) Democrat

The mayor apologized the remarks attributed to in the newspaper saying had been completely mis oted. He had not said recipients of welfare w lechers and parasites. His tual words had been "leec and parasites."

—Irvington (Md.) Democ

The acoustics of the cathedral have improved tremendously since 1896. In those days, the voluminous skirts of the female parishoners absorbed much of the volume of sound but now with the advent of the miniskirt the old organ really goes to town.

—Granada (Minn.) Star

BARBECUE OF SENIOR CITIZENS BIG SUCCESS WILL BECOME AN ANNUAL EVENT.

—Millstone (Wisc.) Monitor

English drop pounds, shillings a **pants** for faster decimal moneta system.

—Trumbull (Ariz.) Citize

POLICE SHOOT MAN WITH KNIFE

—Arapaho (Ark.) Advertiser

(Well, it's easier than stabbing him with a revolver.)

FOR SALE

Health resort 240 acres in clear Verm air. Two main buildings, 20 cabins plus whirlpool and Sauna baths. Heated swimming pool, hot springs and mineral baths. Organic foods franchise and drug store with complete inventory and registered pharmacist in charge. $250,000. *Must sell due to ill health.*

—Benton Falls (Vt.) Advocate

The *bust* part of his job was the contacts he made with so many attractive women. The salary was secondary.

—La Marr (Colo.) Crusader

PRIVATE INSTRUCTION IN BALLROOM DANCING. PLEASANT, CLEAN ATMOSPHERE. MONDAYS ONLY IN THE *BATHROOM* OF THE MILFORD ACADEMY OF THE DANCE. PHONE FOR APPOINTMENT.

—Red River (Okla.) Citizen

PSYCHIATRIST CLAIMS WOMENS' *LIP* MOVEMENT THE CAUSE OF MALE FRUSTRATION

—Battle Creek (R.I.) Banner

Decrying the growth of hippie communes on the outskirts of town, the alderman asserted, "Johnstown has managed to grow from a small settlement to a thriving town in the last century without the benefit of pot smoking, nudism, and sexual intercourse and there is no reason why any of these things should be necessary now."

—Johnstown (Md.) Journal

Hot Pants

For best results iron pans at least three inches deep should be used to cook the batter. Before baking be sure to line your *pants* with aluminium foil and butter them.

—Beldon (Va.) Times

To the ringing cry of "Hi-yo, Silver the Lone *Banger* rides again.

—T.V. Program Announ

For sale

WEIS *Strumpet*—pro model, used but in goo dition. Hard case $165

—Liondale (Tex.)

Christopher Plummer, who played the *Duck* of Wellington in Waterloo, has signed for another historical role in a film as yet untitled.

(Sir Francis Drake) —Filmplay Review

Now retired, he lives with his wife, a beautiful blonde and a San Francisco girl.

—Ansonia (N.H.) Graphic

BOASTING MAN

Celebrating his 35th wedding anniversary he he had proven his devotion to his wife by t that he had never left his wife alone a single since they had been married.

—Braton (Va.) Tim

The retiring police commissioner has been responsible for all crimes committed in the district for the past twenty years.

Wembley (V.A.) News

DEMAND MAYOR AND COUCIL OPEN *FLIES* TO PUBLIC SCRUTINY

Secret files kept by city officials denounced by group.

—Guernsey (Wisc.) Bulletin

THE LONG ARM OF...

The law is for other people, that's for sure. I mean, who hasn't stood by the roadside while the speed cop takes notes ('I couldn't have been doing more than 65, officer, *honestly*') while the drivers he really *should* be chasing are whizzing by at the speed of light. And how come, incidentally, (taking a long leap forward into court) that the figure of Justice is female – whose bright idea was it to put her above the Old Bailey, blindfold and covered in pigeon droppings. On behalf of my sex, I object m'lud. Ships I'll accept as feminine (long, low, lovely white yachts I mean, not trawlers or tramps) – and even cars, which men tend to pat so affectionately on what they obviously consider is 'her' rump. But Justice ... who needs to be associated with the dry-as-dust implacability of the law? All the rest of the law's trappings are distinctly male, come to think of it, right down to the copper's truncheon.

Sex in one form or another turns up in some pretty way-out forms in the courtroom, as anyone learns who has served on a jury – or read the blue bits in the newspapers. This, appeared recently in a court report under the teasing title

PLASTIC ELEPHANT FOLLOWS MISS GRUNT INTO COURT 11

with a picture of the lovely Miss Grunt armed with what appears to be an outsize toothpick. Now read on:

Courtroom 11 in Glasgow Sheriff's Court, a grim Victorian building heavy with the odour of stale cooking, was the drab setting last week for startling revelations about bribery and sexual high-jinks in the traditionally straitlaced Scottish business community. . . .

The jury heard evidence that might have been scripted by Brian Rix of the night a National Coal Board official is said to have spent with Miss Anna Grunt, a free-lance Polish model; of bribes secreted in cigar-boxes; of businessmen's parties at the Crazy Daisy Discotheque in Sauchiehall Street; and of a girl job applicant who was asked to sit on a plastic elephant with flashing eyes. . . .

When Ross Harper, solicitor for Cochrane, said that a letter signed 'affectionately yours' might be an application to the Liberal Party, the sheriff clamped down hard: 'I do not think we should joke about such things.' . . .

Mr Phillips described one defendant Cochrane as a man of 'unusual habits'. In one of the many colourful exchanges during the trial, Ross Harper, solicitor for Cochrane, asked Mr. Phillips if he remembered an unusual incident when Cochrane called him 'an educated prune' and put ice cubes down his trousers in a London night-club. Mr Phillips said he could not recall that.

However, one former employee, Alexander Drennan, did say that Cochrane used to 'throw projectiles across the room' at him, including an oil lamp and plastic eggs. Asked by Mr Harper if this amused him, Mr Drennan said: 'It was funny because they never hit me.'

Mr Drennan also said he recalled that Cochrane made a young girl, who was applying for a job as a clerk, sit on a small toy elephant, telling her that it was a lie-detector and that its eyes would flash if she told a lie. According to Mr Drennan, there were spotlights on Cochrane's ceiling controlled from switches under his desk which would indeed make the eyes light up. Anyone who didn't know Cochrane, said Mr Drennan, would have thought he was possibly mad.

Donald Green, a former managing director told the court that he was once summoned by Cochrane and found him in bed with his secretary. 'Did both of them have their boots on?' asked Mr Harper. Mr Green said he did not notice.

While they were eating, a glamorous blonde, Anna Grunt, joined them at the table. 'I spent the night with her in bed.' said Mr Sim. She was later paid £35 by Cochrane. She was provided, said Mr Harper, as an 'omelette surprise.' The trial continues.

You bet it does. And to think that anywhere else, you'd have to *pay* to be so entertained.

~~Gentlemen~~ persons of the Jury . . .

Judge: 'What possible reason could you have for acquitting this person, who is on a charge for vagrancy?'
Foreman of the Jury: 'Insanity, your honour.'
Judge: 'What – all of you?'

Judge: What's the charge?
PC: Drunk and disorderly, Your Honour.
Judge to prisoner: What's your name?
Prisoner: Freddie Gunn.
Judge: Well, Gunn, I'll discharge you this time, but don't get loaded again.

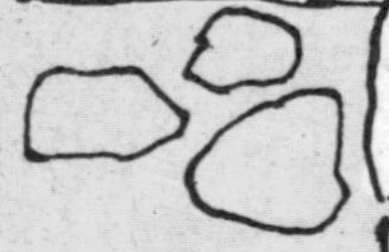

Hear about the tramp that was brought before the Court for stealing a bottle of perfume from a store? He was convicted of fragrancy!

Magistrate: 'Why are you here again?'
Tramp: 'Because of my belief, sir.'
Magistrate: 'And what is your belief?'
Tramp: 'I believed I could get away with it.'

Although my client pleads guilty to murdering his mother and father, m'lud, I would like to make a plea for clemency on the grounds that he is an orphan.

Barrister: 'How can you possibly justify breaking into the same house no less than three times in one week?'
Tramp: 'I put it down to the housing shortage, sir.'

'Before sentencing you,' said the Judge to the poor old tramp, 'I will read a list of your previous convictions.'

'In that case, your honour,' said the ragged old fella, 'I will ask your permission to sit down.'

Judge: I'm afraid I'll have go lock you up for the night.
Defendant: What's the charge?
Judge: There's no charge. It's part of the service.

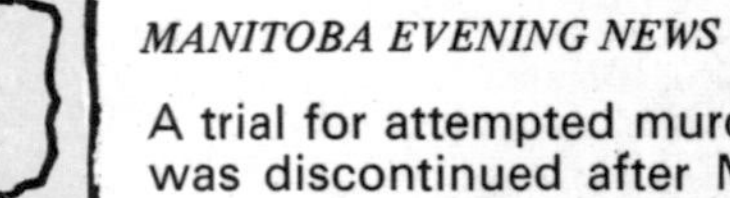

Mr Daniel McNabb, a poet, of Combe by Woodstock, has been fined £10 for his use of abusive and insulting language to Ms Brenda Hathaway, a lady.

'Mr McNabb,' explained his solicitor, Mr Chumpkin, 'spends the greater part of the day in a cloud of inspiration. His solitude, a normal working requirement for one so employed, has been utterly disturbed by visitors to the Cock Inn, a nearby resort.

'Although he has restrained himself for many years past, and has refused to acknowledge cries like "Up Yours" and "Sucks to Shakespear", when he was forced to climb over Ms Hathaway's caravan steps to get to his own garden gate, Mr McNabb finally exploded.

'Although he admits to using such terms as "F . . . Off," and "Get rid of that F . . . ing slum-hutch," Mr McNabb would like to draw attention to the fact that, in fact, he actually felt like killing her, but decided to behave himself in a relatively sensible manner.' *OXFORD MAIL*

MANITOBA EVENING NEWS

A trial for attempted murder being held in Manitoba was discontinued after Mr John Bunn, one of the jury, rose to his feet and asked Mr Justice J. R. Solomon, presiding, to speak up.

An enquiry revealed that Mr Bunn was very deaf and that his fellow juryman, Mr Henry Thorn, was totally deaf.

Further enquiries revealed that three other members of the jury could not understand English.

Mr Thorn admitted that he thought he was hearing a divorce case, while Mr Jaiy Igawar had come to the courthouse in order to apply for a pistol permit.

PORRIDGE

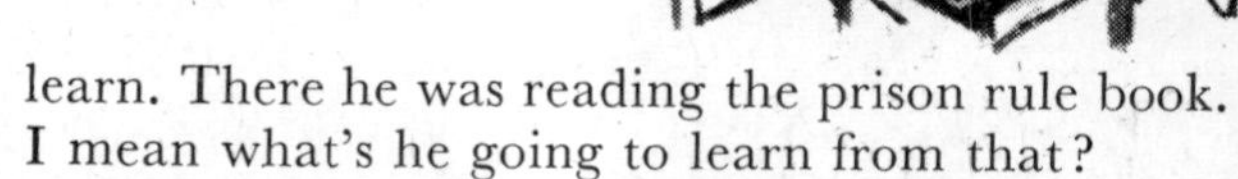

by DICK CLEMENT and IAN LA FRENAIS

The three of us were sitting there in the Reception waiting for the doctor. Three? Well, there was Heslop, Cyril, aged 42. Three years robbery, third time he's been in the nick. Thick as two short planks, about to become Slade's number one nurk. The next was Godber, Leonard Arthur, aged 23. First offender, two years for housebreaking. Seemed somewhat naïve. But a nice looking boy. Then there's me. Fletcher, Norman Stanley, aged 42. Five years for house breaking.

Being the old hand I turned to Godber – said 'Word of advice, son. What you tell 'em today can decide how tolerable your life in this nick is going to be. I mean, if you want to work somewhere cushy and warm, like the kitchens or the library or get the job as teaboy in the main offices, then you've got to invent yourself a new career.'

Barrowclough the interviewing warden called over

'All right, let's have one of you,' he said.

'Me, Mr Barrowclough.' I went to the desk.

'It's Fletcher, of course, isn't it?'

'Yes, that's right, Mr Barrowclough.'

'Christian names?'

'Norman Stanley.'

'Date of birth?'

'2.2.32.'

'Next of kin?'

'My beloved Isobel. The little woman. Well, she ain't so little. I said to her just before I surrendered to my bail, I said to her, Isobel, I said. I'll never get over you, I'll have to get up and go round.'

'Address?'

'107 Alexander Park Crescent, London N5.'

'Occupation?'

'Librarian during the day.'

'During the day?'

'Yeah, at night I was a chef. Library or the kitchen, I don't mind,' I said as I looked at young Godber. Honestly, I don't know what's coming to the younger element, they don't seem prepared to learn. There he was reading the prison rule book. I mean what's he going to learn from that?

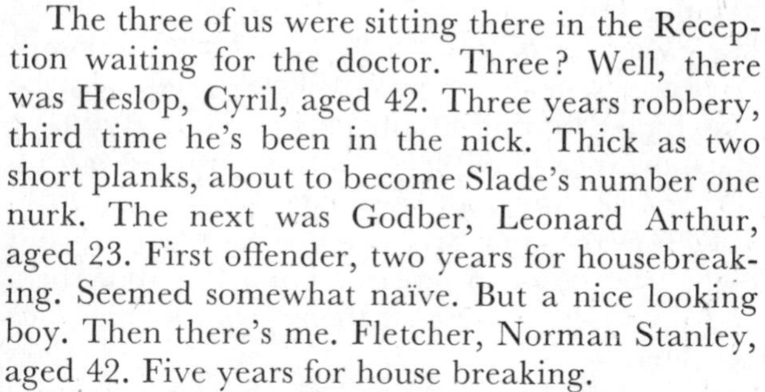

Anyway, we were processed and bathed, them's their terms. And we sat waiting for the medical officer to arrive. I honestly don't know where they dig their medics from. Most of them are alcoholics or skiing fanatics, always going off breaking a leg somewhere. I thought I'd put Godber in the picture a little bit more.

'Look, I meant to tell you, when the doctor comes in, tell him that you've got dodgy plates.'

'What do you mean?' he said.

'Plates of meat, feet. Tell him that they're sweaty or something, then you might get to wear your brothel creepers. Otherwise you'll have to wear the prison issue shoes. Guarantee you bad feet for the rest of your life, they will.'

'Oh, I see,' he said.

That stupid nurk Heslop started to laugh.

'Look, mate, I'm not joking. Perfectly true, you'll see.'

'I don't mean that. I mean your wife. That's funny about your wife. You know, what you said about her being a big woman and you having to get up and go round her.'

'Gawd help us. Take no notice, Godber. Just you remember what I've said about your feet. By the way, what religion are you?'

'C of E, I suppose,' he said.

'That's no good. You get no perks with C of E. What you have to do is think of a nice new one, like Sikh. Now if you was a Sikh you could grow your hair long. Or if you was a Muslim you could have special grub sent in by your loved ones.'

'I don't like Chinese food,' said Godber.

'Muslim ain't Chinese,' I replied.

'Well, what is it?' he asked.

'What? Well, er, it's, it's more erotic than the rubbish they serve up here.'

'Don't you mean exotic? The other means sex.'

'Godber,' I said. 'Godber, that's the trouble with you, you've got sex on the brain. I tell you, you'll have to drink more tea. Now, where was I? Oh yes, it's gotta be better than the filth they eat here otherwise the Muslims wouldn't eat it would they, stands to reason. Or you could say that you were Jewish. Yeah, say that you were Jewish. No, come to think of it you couldn't, could you? Doctor will be here in half a moment and he'd spot the evidence.'

'Evidence?' said Godber. 'What evidence?'

'Well,' I said, 'with Jews it's circumstantial. They been circumstanted.'

The door opened again and in walked this skinny runt with a dirty white coat on. He looked like he worked in the meat market. He was coughing all over the place.

'Tropical fish,' he said.

'Pardon?' I replies.

'Nothing, I'm the medical officer.'

I looked at the others. 'That's reassuring, in'it.'

'Now look,' he said. 'I have to give you men a stringent medical. It's important that we ascertain your medical history and state of health.' He proceeded to cough his guts out. 'Right, Fletcher, you're first.'

I limped forward to where the doctor stood. The conversation after that proceeded at a fast pace.

'Have you ever had crabs?' he said.

'No, I don't eat fish.'

'Lice?'

'No.'

'Suffer from any illness?'

'Bad feet.'

'Paid a recent visit to a doctor?'

'Only for my bad feet.'

'Are you now or have you been at any time a practising homosexual?'

'What, with these feet!'

'Right, you're A1.'

With that he stamps my record with the appropriate stamp.

'A1? Hang on, mate. What about my bad feet? I can hardly walk.'

'Soak them in hot soapy water.'

'What?' I said.

'Look, Fletcher, everyone's trying to pull something in this prison, lying about their feet or their teeth or eyesight. Do you know they even eat light bulbs and razor blades? On top of all the crap I have to take from you I've got a Governor that's got fin rot.'

'Got wot rot?' I says.

'Fish, tropical bloody fish, they've got fin rot.'

'Oh,' I says. 'Interest of the Governor's is it?'

'Yes, Fletcher,' he replies. 'It's an obsession. That and pigs.'

'Pigs?'

'He's started a prison farm to indulge his interest in livestock. Only it's the rest of us who have to look after it. His pigs and his fish and his favourite Jersey cow. I'm a man of medicine not a flaming vet.' He started to pull boxes out of his bag. 'Half the pills in this bag are for his animals. A prisoner came in here yesterday for earache and I gave him pills to dry up his milk. And now the Governor's four-eyed butterfly fish has got fin rot, and he wants me to isolate it.'

By now the poor devil was in a right old two and eight. He took two tablets from a box, put them in his mouth, and rinsed them down with a glass of water.

'You must be rushed off your feet, doc,' I said.

'I can't cope, man.'

'Good job they ain't bad feet like mine.'

'Look, Fletcher, you're A1, I told you so, all right? Now you see that specimen jar over there?' He points to three specimen jars lined up on the table the other side of the room. 'Well, I want you to fill one of them up.'

'What, from here?'

'Behind the screen, man. Now where's Heslop?'

I walked over to the screen. As I did Godber said, 'You didn't pull that one off, did you, Fletch?'

Stupid brummy nurk. 'What did you say?'

'Prison shoes for you, eh?'

'All right, sonny, win a few, lose a few. But my little chat might prove invaluable. Know something about our Governor, don't I? That's another priority for your first day in the nick. Know your Governor.'

'Here, Fletch,' he said, slightly taken aback. 'What's he mean, a practising homosexual?'

'One who hasn't quite got it right yet,' I said as I made my way behind the screen to fill up.

After the other two had been to see the doctor and we'd had our fingerprints taken we were taken to the kitchen to get our midday meal.

As soon as we were seated both Godber and Heslop started to get stuck into the food.

'Will we eat with everyone else tonight?' said Godber.

'Don't,' I said, picking out the tasty bits of food from the rubbish, 'don't be in too much of a hurry to get thrown in with the others. Nothing but a bunch of criminals they are. And don't eat too much of that stuff. Otherwise it'll ruin your palate for tonight's piss-de-resistance.'

'What will it be, Fletch?' said Heslop.

'Lumpy, lukewarm, grey and gritty. Told you to say you were a Muslim.'

'Sheep's eyes,' he said.

Both Godber and I looked at him with amazement.

'What Muslims eat. Figs. Desert. Wadis and things,' he continued.

'Oh, I see. Yeah, we all thank you, Lawrence of Arabia,' I said.

'Why didn't you put down as a Muslim then, Fletch?'

'I don't need to, do I? Going to be working in the kitchens, ain't I?'

'But they haven't allocated us jobs yet,' said Godber.

'Now listen, you see that screw sitting watching telly? Looks like Arthur Askey on stilts. He'll see me all right.'

'How come?'

'Brought me up from Brixton, didn't he. Stands to reason when you're handcuffed to a screw for that long you develop a sort of rapport.'

'Suppose you must do, specially when you go to the lavatory.'

'Oh Godber, I see that you've got a sense of humour. Come in handy during the grim nightmare of your next two years.'

'I'm only here due to unforeseen circumstances,' said Godber.

'Which were?'

'I got caught.'

'Oh yes,' I said. 'I've had a few unfortunate tragedies like that myself.'

'It was my fiancée, Denise. She has this nice flat in a tower block in Smethwick. Well, it's her mum's, like. Very nice. Overlooks the M6. Anyway, I thought I'd get her some nice things for it. But I didn't want to carry the loot too far, so I did the flat next door. I knew he'd be away, like 'cos he's a long-distance lorry driver. He drives a juggernaut from West Bromwich to Brussels. Only thing was, he got a puncture outside Coventry and came back quick like.'

'What did he do? Report you to the police?' I said.

'Not before he kicked my head in.'

'Ramsgate.'

'I beg your pardon, Heslop?'

'Took the wife.'

'Took the wife where, Mr Heslop?'

'To see Lawrence of Arabia. It was raining, see. We couldn't go on the beach, could we? So I took her to the pictures to see Lawrence of Arabia.'

'Yes,' I said. 'Rains a lot in Ramsgate.'

'Rained the next day,' he replied.

'Told you it would,' I said.

'She'd seen the film on at the other cinema, so we come home. Though we did stop for a cup of tea at her sister's in Sidcup.'

'Here, Heslop. Why don't you put that on a postcard and send it to Tony Blackburn's magic moments?'

'Don't like him much, prefer Ronnie Corbett.'

I sat back and surveyed the field. What a right lot they were.

'Tell you what,' I said. 'Tell you what, I shall miss the cut and thrust of your intellectual conversation.'

'Why, Fletch?' said Godber.

'Well, not sharing a cell with you.'

'How come?' he said.

'Well, I'm having a single cell, ain't I? I like my privacy. I prefers to be alone, see. Don't like sharing really. Don't like dominoes, chess, cribbage, ludo or other people's sweaty feet.'

'I prefer a single cell myself. I'd really like to take the opportunity of this enforced confinement to study.'

'Study, Godber?' I said.

'Yes, I've had an education. I've got an O level in geography.'

'On that'll come in handy that will. I can see you now. The escape committee will be calling for your assistance all the time. I mean, they're bound to need you, 'cause you'll help them find the way to Carlisle station.'

'Fletch, you should have tried it, you know. It's very interesting is geography, very educational.'

'Yeah,' I said. 'But it's not the sort of subject you can make a career out of, is it? Now in principle you could learn a trade in here. I mean you could come out with a diploma in, say, house decoration or shoe repairing. Or you might like to be a welder. That's a riveting profession.'

'What?' said Heslop.

'Riveting? No, don't matter, forget it.'

'Do you mean that I won't be able to learn a profession here, Fletch?'

'Course you can, oh yes. There are trades you can learn in here. For starters you could become an expert at how to open a safe, steal a car, forge a banknote. Oh yes, many's the trade you can learn. Bloke I was in Maidstone with, Charlie Mossop, first offender he was, by the time he come out he was a brilliant forger. But brilliant. And he only went in for reckless driving.'

'Do you know, Fletch,' said Godber, 'I really want to finish with this thieving game. I'm fed up with it. There's no profit in it really.'

'How old are you, son?' I was taken back by what he'd just said.

'Twenty-three.'

'Twenty-three and you want to turn it in? What sort of attitude is that? You're at the start of what could be a promising career. Think about it. Where did the train robbers start? Not at the top I can promise you, no, they went in right at the bottom. Then as they progressed, they became more what you might call adventurous. No, old son, you can't throw away the chance of a lifetime. I could teach you so much, how to nick only the best, how not to get caught . . .'

'How come you got caught?'

'Tragic misdirection of the jury by a biased judge.'

'There's something in education though isn't there, Fletch?'

'Right, young Godber. True, very true. Hang about. I'm not saying don't put down for educational classes. Education, that's different. Current affairs, pottery, archaeology. I'll be putting down

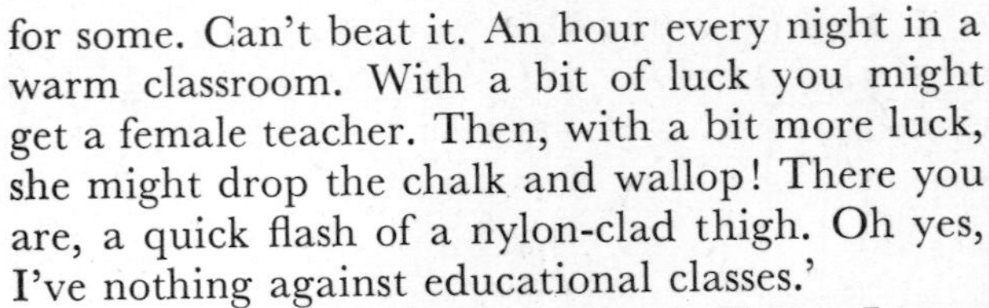

for some. Can't beat it. An hour every night in a warm classroom. With a bit of luck you might get a female teacher. Then, with a bit more luck, she might drop the chalk and wallop! There you are, a quick flash of a nylon-clad thigh. Oh yes, I've nothing against educational classes.'

By now we'd finished our meal. Young Lenny Godber took a packet of cigarettes out of his pocket and offered the packet to me and Heslop. We quickly took one each and put it in our pockets.

'Why'd you do that?' he asked.

'We're not being impolite, Lenny, my son. It's just that Heslop and me have been inside before, an' you see, inside, snout is like gold. You was mad to give us a fag.'

'But you took them.'

'Ah, yes, you gotta learn the hard way, haven't you? Learn not to be lavish, you're not Paul Getty! Should have just lit one and shared it.' And I lean over and takes his fag and has a puff before passing it to Heslop.

'Right, lads,' said Barrowclough, as he turned off the telly and walked over to where we were sitting. 'Drink up, lads.'

'What's next on the agenda, Mr Barrowclough?'

'You should know, Fletcher, all the time you've spent inside.'

'Oh yes,' I said. 'It's the Governor we see now.'

Lenny and Heslop collected up their trays and walked over to the sink to wash them. This gave me the chance I'd been waiting for.

'Did you get what I asked for, Mr Barrowclough?'

'Well, there isn't much in the library in the way of what you want. Just this booklet. *Know your Tropical Fish*.'

'Oh good, it's my hobby you see.'

'Do you know, Fletcher, by an extraordinary coincidence that's the Governor's hobby too.'

'Is it?' I said.

'Oh yes, he likes all animals. He's on the local RSPCA. Between ourselves though, I think he'd be much better off looking after a zoo than a prison.'

'True, but when you think about it, Mr Barrowclough, we're all caged animals, ain't we? Talking of cages, you will get me one on the south side on my own? I'm not a sharer really. I mean, the boy's all right, but his feet smell. And Heslop, well, you can't say that he's on my intellectual level, is he? Don't think he's on anybody's level really. If the Governor did open a zoo, Heslop'd be a big attraction.'

'Fletcher, you must understand that I'm a Prison Officer and you are a prisoner. You must recognise that relationship. I am not here to be coerced or cajoled into doing what you want, when you want it.'

'Mr Barrowclough, please. Would I ever? Here, give this a rinse out while I go and have a slash,' I said as I handed him my tray and mug.

We went into the Governor's office, and the three of us stood in line.

'Stand up straight in front of the Governor,' said MacKay. 'Heslop, Godber and Fletcher, SIR!'

'Thank you, Mr MacKay,' said Mr Venables the Governor. 'Now you men have been sent here for varying offences and varying terms of imprisonment. This is not a maximum security prison, you are in a "C" Class establishment. However, if any of you abuse the less stringent security measures we have here, you will quickly find that we will be on you like a ton of bricks.'

By now I had located the fish tank.

'Are you listening to me, Fletcher?' he said.

'Face the front!' shouted MacKay.

'I'm sorry Mr Venables, sir. I just couldn't help but notice your aquarium. It's an interest of mine, you see. Indoor fish, tropical fish.'

'Is it really?'

'All right, Fletcher, face the front,' butted in MacKay.

'I'm sorry, Mr MacKay. Sorry, Sir. I couldn't help but notice. But something is bothering me.'

'What's that?' said the Governor.

By now I was really into it. I leaned over so that I could see into the fish tank.

'Well, sir. This is only a first impression but . . . I think your four-eyed butterfly fish has got fin rot.'

That ended it. MacKay couldn't believe what was happening. The three of us went back to the wing. They put us all into a three cell until we'd been allocated jobs.

'Crafty old nurk aren't you, Fletch?'

'Hang about, young Godber. I'm finishing off the *Farmer's Weekly*. There's this marvellous article on Artificial Insemination that the Governor said I should read.'

'He fell for it, didn't he? He really believed that you had a deep interest in fish and livestock.'

'It ain't been a bad day all around. I told you this was the day that conditioned how tolerable your life'll become here. No, old son. Porridge is porridge.'

'I think he was impressed by my O level in geography.'

'Oh, I could see that, you'll probably work in the mailbags.'

'Why, Fletch?'

'Well, they'll need someone to understand all them foreign names they have to stencil on the air mailbags.'

The cell door opened and in walked Mr MacKay.

'All right, lads, on your feet. Exam results. It's been a full and exciting day, hasn't it? Right, Godber, you're first, here they are.' With that he hands young Godber a pair of civvy shoes. 'Courtesy of the Medical Officer.'

'How'd you work that?' I said.

'I told him that I had flat feet, didn't I?'

'Which he believed, Fletcher,' said MacKay. 'Young Godber still has a certain amount of credibility, unlike yourself. I'm afraid we're going to have to split this little threesome up. One of you's going to a sing.'

With that I started to pack my kit.

'Oh yes, only right, Mr MacKay,' I said.

'Not so fast, Fletcher.'

'Whot'yer mean?'

'Get your things together, Godber.'

'Godber! Him! A cell on his own?' I said.

'Yes, that's right, the Governor thought it would be more conducive to his studies.'

'Oh, that's lovely. I didn't fancy sharing. No offence, Fletch.'

'You didn't fancy sharing? What about me, you leave me here with the "Brain of Britain"!'

'There'll be three of you. Don't worry, Fletcher, we're moving Evans in here.'

'Evans,' I cried. 'That Welsh lunatic who eats light bulbs.'

'Only when he can't get razor blades,' said MacKay.

'Oh, wonderful. Just bloody wonderful. Can I have permission to grow a beard?'

'Right, now it's jobs. Godber . . . Kitchen.'

Godber grinned. 'Oh that'll be nice. All warm and second helpings.'

'Heslop . . . Library.'

'Library! Him! He's illiterate.'

'I read a book once,' said Heslop indignantly. 'It was green.'

'Look, Mr MacKay. Tell me, what's Godber got the kitchen for? God Almighty, he should be breaking rocks or something. He's gotta pay his dues. This is victimisation. Mr MacKay, sir, look, sir, I'm an old hand. I've been in before, you know me. I should have something befitting my seniority.'

'And you have, Fletcher, you have.'

'I have?'

'Oh yes, oh yes.'

'What?' I asked.

'Special duties.'

'Special duties, Mr MacKay? What special duties?'

'Who's the Governor's blue-eyed boy then?'

'Well,' I said. 'Well we did have a sort of rapport. Cemented by our common interest in all things bright and beautiful, all creatures great and small.'

'The Governor said you're just the man he's been waiting for.'

'What is it, Mr MacKay. Is it fish?'

'Well . . .' said MacKay.

'Fish?'

'Not quite, Fletcher, not quite.'

'What is it then, sir? Come on, tell me.'

'Pigs!' said MacKay with a smarmy smart look on his face.

'Pigs?' I said.

'Yes, pigs,' he answered.

'What about pigs?' I said.

'They're your pigs,' he said.

'My pigs?' I said. 'How are they my pigs?'

'Well, laddie, you showed such a great interest in livestock that the Governor thought you would be the ideal chap to look after the pig farm.'

'But I don't even like the taste of bacon.'

'You'll soon get used to it. Come on, man, time to collect your wellies. You'll need them in the pigsty.'

There I was the next morning up to my neck in . . . Well, there I was. 'Get out of the way, you great big brute.'

'Morning, Fletcher.'

'Morning, sir.'

'It always gives me great pleasure to place a man in a job which gives him real fulfilment.'

'Oh, yes, Mr Venables. Oh yes.'

'Oh, by the way. Have you finished that article in the *Farmer's Weekly* I gave you?'

'I'm afraid I didn't, sir. I would have done, only Evans ate it.'

Published by BBC Publications

"Solitary means solitary, Hannigan."

Two crooks broke into a bank. One went up to the safe, took off his shoes and socks and started to twiddle the combination with his toes. His mate was upset and told him to stop mucking about.

He replied: 'Don't worry. It will take a bit longer, but we'll drive the fingerprint department potty.'

Constable: You've got a nice little lot 'ere, 'aven't yer? Dangerous driving, disregarding my signals, no lights, two flat tyres, no driving licence, no number plates, no windscreen wipers and no indicators.

Driver to accomplice: There – I told you it wasn't worth pinching, didn't I?

he blue light

: to Inspector: I've got a hunch, sir.
spector: Yes, I've noticed it. You must learn to your shoulders back, man!

oliceman stopped a motorist one evening and l him: 'How long have you been driving without r light?'
ne driver jumped out, ran to the rear of his car gave a groan. His distress seemed so obvious that policeman was sympathetic. 'Now, you don't to take it so hard,' he said, 'it isn't all that us.' 'Isn't it?' cried the motorist, 'what's hapd to my caravan?'.

eman: 'Excuse me sir, this is a one-way street.'
r: 'That's right. I'm only going one way.'

M "THE DAILY POST"

d standing beside his lorry with his trousers n, Mr Geoffrey Dent of Mitcham explained that ad been driving along Martin Way when a se dashed across the instrument panel, down the ing column, and up the inside of his left trouser-

n my surprise I carried away two bollards and a -post,' he said.
r Dent sprang from his vehicle and, before the of two astonished lady passers-by, tore off his sers, chased after the mouse that shot from therein, stomped it into oblivion on the pavement.
fear the van was a write-off,' he said.

Man to Welsh PC: Can you tell me where I can find a urinal?
Welsh PC: No, bach. We've got a Huw Jones, a Huw Thomas, but I don't know any Huw Rinal.

Village constable to female camper: Sorry me dear, but ee bain't allowed to swim ure.
Fair one: Why didnt you say so before you saw me undressing?
Constable: Well, there ain't no law 'bout undressing.

"That will do for now, sir. Now just a minute while I take down the Chief Constable's version."

"Tango one to Fox-trot – Sid's arrived – make that three bangers and mash."

A horse had dropped dead in a street named Nebuchadnezzar Street and a policeman was laboriously dragging it round the corner into the next street. 'Whatever are you doing that for?' asked a bystander. Replied the policeman with a knowing look, 'When I make out my report will will be easier to write "King Street" as the place of occurrence.'

A policeman found three girls crying their eyes out at Euston Station, so he took them into the buffet and bought them a large pot of tea and a plate of cakes.
They dried their tears and smiled. Then he plonked the teapot into the centre of the table and asked 'Now, who's going to be mother?'
And they all burst into tears again.

THE FLYING SQUAD

Lest We Forget

By "PAPPAS" first appearing in the Guardian

ARE YOU BEING SERVED

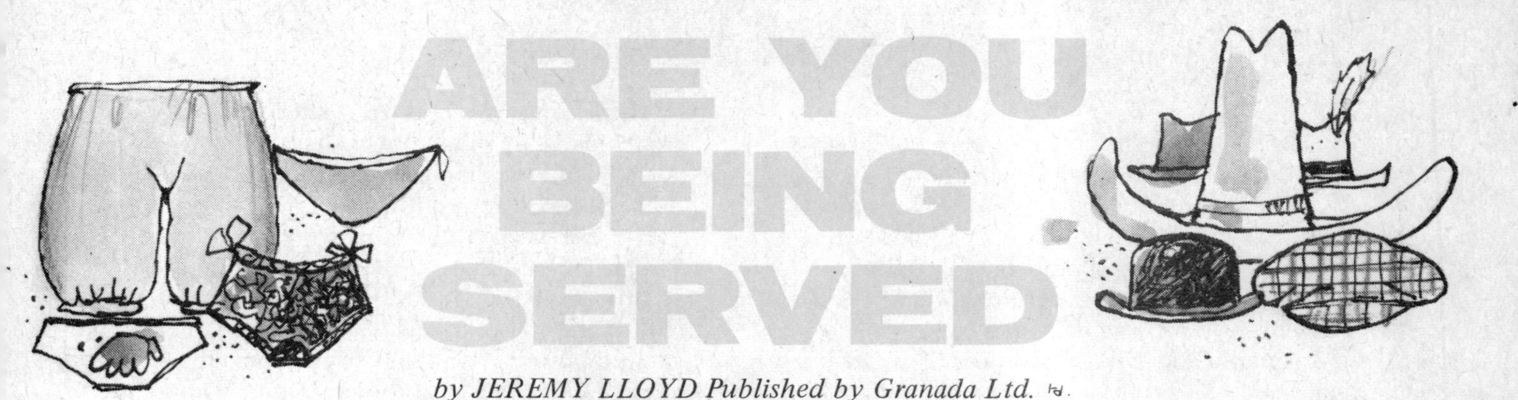

by JEREMY LLOYD Published by Granada Ltd.

The scene is Grace Bros. Dept. Store—Ladies Clothing Section. In charge is Mrs Slocombe.

A clatter of wheels indicated the arrival of the maintenance man Mr. Mash with his trolley.

' 'Ere you are, Mrs. Slocombe, twelve pairs of thirty-denier tights. Unlucky for some. And twelve padded bras for the underprivileged.' Taking them out of the box on the trolley, he plonked them on the counter. Delving into the box again he produced an assortment of ladies' briefs. 'And to continue, 'ere's the *piece de résistance*, twenty-four pairs of novelty briefs, known to such common persons as myself as naughty knickers.'

'I beg your pardon,' said Mrs. Slocombe, placing her glasses firmly on the end of her nose.

' 'Ere, look at this,' said Mr. Mash, holding up a pair. 'See, there's writing on them.'

'So there is,' said Mrs. Slocombe. 'What does it say, Miss Brahms?'

Miss Brahms picked up the knickers and looked at the writing.

'IF YOU CAN READ THIS,' announced Miss Brahms, 'YOU'RE TOO CLOSE.'

Mrs. Slocombe pursed her lips. 'It's disgusting.'

'Yes,' said Miss Brahms, 'but true.'

'What about these then?' said Mr. Mash waving another pair. Then holding them between two hands he stretched them out to show that they had a pair of black hands embroidered on the seat.

'What are they called?' said Miss Brahms. 'An evening out with Johnnie Mathis.'

'That's a good one,' said Mr. Mash delving into his box and pulling out another pair. 'Then there's these. They come in four models: HELLO CHEEKY, I LOVE ELVIS, YOUR FLIES ARE UNDONE and NO PARKING.'

Mrs. Slocombe gazed disdainfully at the offending objects. 'Oh Miss Brahms, did you ever see anything like it?'

Miss Brahms nodded. 'My boyfriend bought me a pair, but I wouldn't wear them.'

'I hardly dare ask,' said Mrs. Slocombe, 'but what did they say?'

'IN CASE OF EMERGENCY PULL DOWN.'

Mr. Mash gave a coarse laugh. 'That'd be worth a five-pound fine.'

Mrs. Slocombe waved her hand in a dismissive gesture. 'That'll be enough, Mr. Mash,' and then, calling out in her best voice, 'Captain Peacock, whether you are free or nor I want you over here.'

Captain Peacock strolled over, hands behind his back, and gazed at the pairs of assorted knickers on the counter. 'Are you having trouble, Mrs. Slocombe?'

'I certainly am, Captain Peacock.'

Captain Peacock glanced at his watch. 'I'm afraid I can only spare you a moment. I have to see Mr. Rumbold in his office.'

Mrs. Slocombe picked up the knickers and dropped them back in the pile on the counter.

'I positively refuse to display these.' Then picking out a pair she held them up for Captain Peacock's inspection and pointed to the 'no parking' sign on them. Captain Peacock raised his eyebrows in surprise.

'You're not being asked to wear them, are you, Mrs. Slocombe?'

'Certainly not,' said Mrs. Slocombe indignantly. 'I wouldn't put them on for a thousand pounds.'

'How much to take them off!' inquired Mr. Mash.

Captain Peacock stretched out his arm and pointed a commanding finger. 'Mr. Mash, get back to your basement.'

Mr. Mash thrust his face under Captain Peacock's nose. 'I see. So the worker's not allowed to have a sense of humour eh? Well, we have our laughs. You should see what's written about you on the walls of our khazi.' And having delivered what he considered a crushing blow, he wheeled his trolley off as noisily as he could.

'Horrid man', said Mrs. Slocombe. 'Now look, Captain Peacock, I refuse to have anything to do with these vulgar garments.'

'They're not all that bad,' said Miss Brahms.

Captain Peacock nodded in agreement. 'Progress must march on, Mrs. Slocombe.'

Mrs. Slocombe waved the offending knickers to emphasize her point. 'Not wearing these it doesn't.'

Captain Peacock adopted a more soothing tone of voice. 'Mrs. Slocombe,' he explained, 'I must remind you that you are all paid by Grace Brothers to sell the goods purchased by the Buying Department.'

'And if I don't,' said Mrs. Slocombe

There was a slight pause while Captain Peacock stared stonily at her. 'No one is irreplaceable.'

Having issued his threat he turned on his heel and disappeared in the direction of Mr. Rumbold's office.

'Oh,' said Miss Brahms. 'You're not going to stand for that, are you?'

Mrs. Slocombe gritted her teeth. 'I very nearly said something very cutting and rude, I can tell you.'

'I'll bet,' said Miss Brahms. 'What are you going to do now?'

Mrs. Slocombe gathered up the assortment of underwear and stuffed it angrily into a drawer. 'I'm seriously thinking of handing my resignation in.'

Miss Brahms took a step back and said in a loud voice: 'Your resignation?'

Mrs. Slocombe held her hand up in alarm.

'Shhh! Not so loud,' she said.

Over in the men's department a short gentleman with a mop of grey hair fought his way gamely into a Fairisle sweater, with the help of Mr. Lucas and Mr. Humphries despite the fact it was quite obviously some sizes too small. Giving it a final tug, Mr. Lucas managed to bring it down till it was only six or seven inches above the customer's waistband.

'There we are, sir,' said Mr. Humphries. 'It's definitely you, sir. Don't you think so, Mr. Lucas?'

'Definitely the customer,' agreed Mr. Lucas.

The customer didn't seem too sure. 'It seems rather tight to me,' he said breathlessly, as he tried to move his arms up and down.

Mr. Humphries nodded. 'They are being worn tight this year, sir.'

'Particularly this one,' said Mr. Lucas.

'I wanted it for golfing, you see.'

'It will keep your arms very stiff,' said Mr. Lucas.

'Just try a swing or two,' said Mr. Humphries, 'to get the feel of it.'

Producing a walking stick from his display stand he handed it to the customer, who gripped it, swung and struck an imaginary ball across the department.

Mr. Humphries clapped his hands admiringly. 'That's a beautiful movement you've got there, sir.'

'Unless I am mistaken,' said Mr. Lucas, 'that was a hole in one.'

'Well,' admitted the customer proudly, 'I do have a very small handicap.'

Mr. Humphries raised his eyebrows. 'Have you?'

'With luck,' said Mr. Lucas, 'we've probably got a tight pair of trousers to go with it.'

The customer handed the stick back to Mr. Humphries and pulled at the sweater under his arm.

'It's gripping me very tightly just here.'

'It would, sir,' nodded Mr. Humphries. 'There's a lot of tension with Shetland wool.'

'It's the nervous sheep,' added Mr. Lucas. 'They live near a shooting range.'

Mr. Humphries handed the customer the walking stick again. 'We know it's all right for driving, sir, but how is it for putting?'

The customer took the stick and bent over an invisible ball, then with a deft movement putted it. He shook his head. 'It's pulling.'

'Maybe it's the way you are holding the club, sir,' suggested Mr. Lucas. 'Try locking the thumbs together and keeping your eye on the ball a bit longer.' The customer tried another imaginary putt. Mr. Lucas and Mr. Humphries both nodded with approval.

'Much better,' said Mr. Lucas. 'If Jack Nicklaus had seen that he'd have gone straight home to bed.'

'There's no doubt,' said Mr. Humphries, 'that that sweater has improved your game enormously, sir.'

'But,' complained the customer, 'the sleeves are only just below my elbows.'

'It's a good sign,' said Mr. Humphries. 'You see, it will definitely stretch after the first wash.'

The customer looked puzzled. 'I thought wool always shrank?'

Mr. Lucas shook his head. 'That's a popular misconception, sir. When you think about it, it can't be true otherwise every time it rained the sheep would get smaller.'

The customer shook his grey head emphatically. 'No, I definitely need the next size.'

Mr. Lucas took Mr. Humphries by the elbow and led him out of earshot.

'We don't have a forty-four,' he hissed. 'We've only got forty-sixes.'

'In that case,' said Mr. Humphries, 'that is the next size.'

With speed that almost deceived the eye, Mr. Lucas bent over the counter and produced an enormous Fairisle sweater and held it out in front of the customer.

'How about that, sir?'

The customer shook his head doubtfully. 'It seems rather long.'

'Ah,' said Mr. Humphries, 'they are being worn long this year, sir.'

'And,' said Mr. Lucas, 'it will be very good for your handicap.'

The customer stared uncertainly at the sweater and shook his head.

Mr. Humphries smiled encouragingly. 'Of course, it will shrink after the first wash.'

'But,' stammered the customer, 'I thought you said wool didn't shrink?'

Mr. Humphries introduced a patient note into his voice. 'That's pure wool, sir, this is half wool and half extruded man-made fibres. The extruded bit shrinks in hot water.'

'And,' added Mr. Lucas, 'the man-made bit shrinks in cold water.'

'In fact,' observed Mr. Humphries, 'there's very little point in your trying it on until you have washed it.'

The customer suddenly looked very tired. 'Very well,' he murmured, I'll take it.'

'Sale, Mr. Lucas!'

As Mr. Lucas rang the till Mr. Humphries produced a carrier bag and placed the sweater in it, but noticed the customer was having trouble taking off the size forty-two.

'Can I help you, sir?'

The customer nodded gratefully.

So Mr. Humphries and Mr. Lucas stood on either side of him and, gripping the bottom of the sweater, began to pull it up, but halfway they ran into difficulties as it stuck over the customer's head.

'Are you all right in there, sir?' inquired Mr. Lucas. There was a note of panic in the mumbled reply.

'If you wouldn't mind bending forward, sir, I'll pull while Mr. Humphries holds your rear. All right, Mr. Humphries?'

'It'll be a pleasure, Mr. Lucas.'

As Mr. Humphries grasped the waistband of the customer's trousers to prevent him going forward, Mr. Lucas tugged at the sweater.

'It's just like pulling a Christmas cracker,' observed Mr. Lucas.

'Yes,' gasped Mr. Humphries, 'I wonder who's going to get the novelty?'

Then with a final effort Mr. Lucas heaved and pulled off the sweater as the customer screamed, his hands flying to his head. He was suddenly bald.

'It's gone!' he cried.

'I beg your pardon?' said Mr. Lucas. 'What's gone?'

'My toupee,' gasped the customer. 'You've lost it.'

'Oh, our Ada!' said Mr. Humphries, his hands flying up with mock horror and falling on his knees to search the floor, while Mr. Lucas shook the sweater.

Seeing what was apparently an unattended customer Mr. Grainger waddled over. 'Are you being looked after, sir?'

The customer pointed. 'They are looking for my very expensive, undetectable hairpiece,' he said grimly.

'And,' added Mr. Lucas shaking the sweater and peering down the armhole, 'we're having a bit of trouble detecting it. Just a minute, I think I can see it.'

Sticking his hand up the arm, he brought out the hairpiece triumphantly.

'Well done,' said Mr. Humphries. 'Shall we comb it now, sir, or when it's back on?'

Angrily the customer snatched the untidy mop of hair and slapped it back on his head.

'Oh, said Mr. Humphries admiringly, 'it takes years off you.'

Fuming, the man paid his bill and turned to go. As he did so Mr. Lucas nudged Mr. Humphries.

'Look, the sweater price tag's stuck on the back of his hair. Shall we tell him?'

Mr. Humphries shook his head. 'He'll see the size, realize it's too big and insist on having his money back. Let's just hope he doesn't notice it before he gets out of the store.'

'What if somebody mentions it,' said Mr. Lucas.

'I hardly think,' observed Mr. Humphries, 'anybody would say, "Excuse me, sir, you've still got the price tag on your wig." Especially when it looks so awful, If they say anything they'll point out that he's wearing it the wrong way round.'

'I'm glad I'm not bald,' observerd Mr. Lucas.

'So am I,' said Mr. Humphries, 'although it won't be long if I get another customer like that.'

In the ladies' department Mrs. Slocombe was looking very pleased with herself as she applied a dab of red nail varnish to stop a run in her tights.

'I think I certainly made my point to Captain Peacock about not displaying those awful knickers.'

But a worried expression crossed Miss Brahms's face as she observed Captain Peacock striding over with Mr. Rumbold.

'Look out, I think he's reported you to Mr. Rumbold.'

Mrs. Slocombe hurriedly put her nail varnish out of sight. 'Oh, he wouldn't sneak, would he, Miss Brahms?'

'Mr. Rumbold's looking very ugly.'

'Look at the start he's got,' observed Mrs. Slocombe as they arrived at the counter.

'Attention a moment if you please,' said Captain Peacock loftily. 'Mr. Rumbold would like to have a word with you.'

Mr. Rumbold cleared his throat, rook off his glasses and mopped his brow with his spotted handkerchief.

'I must tell you,' he said, 'that something very important has come to my ears.'

Mrs. Slocombe gazed at Mr. Rumbold's large ears and decided that it was better not to comment.

'I'm afraid,' said Captain Peacock, 'that I had to tell Mr. Rumbold about your insubordinate attitude.'

Mrs. Slocombe drew herself up to her full height, and adopted her most refined tone of voice.

'There are,' she said, 'some knickers I will display and some I won't. The ones I won't are staying in my drawers.'

Mr. Rumbold nodded. 'I see.'

'And,' added Mrs. Slocombe, 'Miss Brahms backs me up about this, don't you? Miss Brahms . . . where are you?'

'I'm here,' called Miss Brahms peering through the curtains of the ladies' fitting room. And added, 'Mrs. Slocombe feels so strongly about it that she's prepared to resign.'

Mrs. Slocombe appeared to have a sudden choking fit. Mr. Rumbold stared at her sternly through his thick-rimmed spectacles.

'Is that right, Mrs. Slocombe?'

'Er . . .' said Mrs. Slocombe, recovering. 'Well, er . . . that is what I said, I mean what I said was that I will have to give it my very serious consideration.'

'Very well,' snapped Mr. Rumbold who turned on his heel and started to depart.

'Mind you, I haven't had time to consider it yet and I do think a person with my excellent sales record should be allowed some discretion as to what stuff I push.' Mrs. Slocombe hurried after Mr. Rumbold. 'Don't you agree, Mr. Grainger?' she called as she passed the men's counter.

Mr. Grainger gazed at her unsympathetically. 'If you ask my opinion, Mrs. Slocombe, you've been nothing but trouble ever since you put foot on this floor.'

'Oh, said Mrs. Slocombe, 'you two-faced old crab.'

'I take it,' interjected Captain Peacock, 'that you don't support Mrs. Slocombe, Mr. Grainger?'

Mr. Grainger agreed. 'If she wants to resign, let her go. We could do with her floor area to expand my trousers.'

Mr. Humphries nodded vigorously. 'Yes, our trousers have been rather restricted since the ladies arrived, haven't they, Mr. Lucas?'

'Bursting at the seams,' agreed Mr. Lucas.

Mr. Grainger pointed to the centre of the floor which contained the ladies' display dummy.

'That stand,' he announced, 'has been the focal point of my trousers for the last twenty-five years until the ladies arrived. Correct, Mr. Humphries?'

'Correct, Mr. Grainger. In those days it was known as "bargain bags".'

Mr. Lucas stared at Mrs. Slocombe pointedly. 'And now they're here, it still is.'

Mrs. Slocombe looked outraged. 'Captain Peacock, do I have to stand and listen to this?'

It was quite obvious Captain Peacock was enjoying the situation. He nodded. 'One must say in Mr. Grainger's defence that his sales have dropped since the ladies took over half the floor.'

'Perhaps,' said Mrs. Slocombe, bitterly, 'because he's a bit past it.' Mr. Grainger swelled up like a bull frog. 'Past it?' he spluttered. 'Past it?'

Mr. Lucas rushed forward with a chair and called over his shoulder, 'Glass of water for Mr Grainger.'

'Some water coming up,' said Mr. Lucas.

Sitting down heavily Mr. Grainger addressed his next remark to Captain Peacock's left knee.

'Tell that woman I am severing my connections.'

Mr. Lucas stopped in his tracks. 'In that case I'd better cancel the glass of water.'

'I don't know why everybody's getting at me,' said Mrs. Slocombe. 'It wasn't my idea to move into Mr. Grainger's trousers.'

'I think,' observed Mr. Lucas, 'he'd rather have had sports equipment there.'

Captain Peacock indicated Mr. Rumbold who was hovering on the edge of the floor. 'It wasn't Mr. Rumbold's idea to have ladies on the floor.'

Mr. Rumbold frowned as he tried to remember. 'Wasn't it?' he inquired.

'No sir. It was Young Mr. Grace's idea,' Captain Peacock reminded him.

'Aah, yes,' said Mr. Rumbold. 'Well, I hadn't realized Mrs. Slocombe's underwear was causing so much friction.'

'Neither did I,' admitted Mrs. Slocombe. 'But I could very easily get a job somewhere else. Harrods have been making overtures.'

'Where did they want you?' asked Mr. Lucas. 'In the piano department?'

Mrs. Slocombe pretended she hadn't heard.

'I also have very good contacts at Marshall and Snellgrove, and,' she added, 'the Beauty Department of Swan and Edgar's have made a very interesting offer.'

'What was it?' inquired Mr. Lucas. 'A free face lift?'

Mrs. Slocombe's self-control snapped.

'That's it, I'm going!' She turned and marched brusquely towards the steps. Mr. Grainger rose from his chair and hurried after her.

'Mr. Grainger,' called Captain Peacock, 'don't stop her.'

Mr. Grainger turned. 'I won't, I was going to ring for the lift.'

Miss Brahms who had been listening intently from behind the counter picked up Mrs. Slocombe's hat and coat and ran across the department.

'Don't go without these, Mrs. Slocombe.'

Mrs. Slocombe pressed the lift bell and turned.

'I'm not going out,' she snapped. 'I'm going up to see Young Mr. Grace and to put my points before him personally.' As she turned back to face the lift the doors opened and the aged Young Mr. Grace staggered out leaning heavily on his stick.

'Aah, good morning to you, Mrs. Slocombe.'

Mrs. Slocombe's stern expression disappeared and she took a pace back. 'Oh good morning, Mr. Grace.'

Mr. Grace waved his stick vaguely towards the members of the department and a chorus of 'Good morning Mr. Graces' echoed from the assembled sales staff.

Captain Peacock stepped forward. 'May I say, Mr. Grace, how it does our hearts good to see you looking so flamboyant.'

'Thank you,' wavered Mr. Grace. 'You're probably referring to the flower in my buttonhole.'

Captain Peacock's eyes fastened on the anemone that hung limply from the buttonhole in Mr. Grace's tweed jacket. 'A touch of spring, sir.'

'I found it in the lift,' confided Mr. Grace. 'It's a shame to waste it.'

'If you have a moment, sir,' interrupted Mrs. Slocombe, 'I have something I'd like to show you.' And running down the marble steps she headed towards the counter.

'What is it?' called Mr. Grace.

'Her knickers,' retorted Miss Brahms.

'In that case,' said Mr. Grace, 'I'll hang on.'

Mr. Rumbold cast an anxious eye towards Captain Peacock and hurriedly whispered in his ear, 'We don't want a scene here, better keep him talking.'

Captain Peacock nodded and extending his arm helped Mr. Grace down the steps.

'May I suggest, sir, to go with your flower, one of our range of Foulard squares to go in your top pocket.' He snapped his fingers imperiously. Mr. Lucas opened a drawer and produced a silk square and handed it to Mr. Humphries who handed it to Mr. Grainger who handed it to Mr. Rumbold who handed it to Captain Peacock who tucked it into Mr. Grace's top pocket.

'An excellent match I think, sir.'

'It's very kind of you, Peacock, said Mr. Grace. 'There aren't many floorwalkers who would spend that much on a Foulard for their employers. I shall remember that.' Before Captain Peacock could recover, Mr. Lucas pressed the till and called out, 'Sale!'

Mrs. Slocombe reappeared from her counter as Captain Peacock hurriedly removed the silk square from Mr. Grace's top pocket.

'Er, I wasn't actually purchasing it for you, sir, it was just to see if you thought it went with your "ensemble".' A look of disappointment crossed Mr. Grace's face.

'Credit note for Captain Peacock,' called Mr. Lucas and before Captain Peacock could reply, Mrs. Slocombe appeared holding a pair of bright-coloured briefs.

'What do you think about that?' she asked.

'As a matter of fact,' said Mr. Grace peering at them shortsightedly, 'I think I prefer it,' and taking them from her he popped them in his top pocket and nodded approvingly. 'Thank you, Mrs. Slocombe. Now I have an announcement to make.'

'Quiet for Mr. Grace,' boomed Mr. Rumbold.

'It may surprise you all to know that I have been a widower now for forty years,' said Mr. Grace.

'And,' exclaimed Mr. Lucas *sotto voce* for Mr. Humphries's ears alone, 'it don't seem a day too much.'

'Mr. Lucas,' called out Captain Peacock sharply

'I'm no longer a young man,' quavered Mr. Grace.

'I'm sure you have years yet,' said Mr. Rumbold encouragingly.

'Certainly hours,' murmured Mr. Lucas.

'And,' continued Mr. Grace, 'there is a certain someone here in Grace Brothers that I have had my eye on for some time.'

Captain Peacock handed the Foulard square back to Mr. Lucas.

'Any lady,' he announced, 'who has attracted your attention must have great qualities, sir.'

Mr. Rumbold edged forward.

'She will indeed be a lucky lady, sir.'

'She'll have lots of lolly too,' observed Miss Brahms.

Mr. Humphries nodded. 'And not long to wait for it.'

'To sum it up,' whispered Mr. Lucas, 'the maximum of one thing and the minimum of the other.'

Mr. Grainger smiled ingratiatingly, 'May we be permitted to know the lady's name, sir?'

Mr. Grace tapped the side of his nose with his forefinger. 'I'm keeping that secret until I have told her my intentions.'

Mr. Lucas winked. 'That shouldn't take long.'

'But,' added Mr. Grace, 'I shall reveal everything to you all shortly.'

'We will look forward to that, Mr. Grace,' said Mr. Humphries.

Mr. Grace turned to Mrs. Slocombe.

'Give me your arm, I would like a private word with you.' Leaning heavily on Mrs. Slocombe's arm he took a few paces and then stopped 'How long have I known you now, Mrs. Slocombe?'

Mrs. Slocombe visibly simpered. 'Since I was a junior here, Mr. Grace.'

'Yes,' murmured Mr. Grace, 'a very very long time. Well I can't discuss it here, so would you have tea with me in the Board room at, say, four o'clock?' He paused and then added significantly, 'I want to talk to you about a ring.'

Mrs. Slocombe's hand flew to her heart. 'A ring?'

Mr. Grace nodded then waved his walking stick. 'Carry on, everybody, you've all done very well.'

Mrs. Slocombe helped him towards the lift and pressed the bell.

'Ring?' gasped Mr. Rumbold.

'Ring?' mouthed Captain Peacock.

Mr. Lucas addressed Mr. Humphries from the corner of his mouth. 'If he marries Mrs. Slocombe, she'd be in charge of the whole store.'

Mr. Humphries nodded. 'After the contretemps this morning, Mr. Grainger could lose his trousers altogether.'

'Not to mention our jobs,' said Mr. Lucas. 'She'll be the power behind the throne.'

Mr. Humphries looked aghast. 'I never like to think of people having power there,' he observed.

As Mrs. Slocombe marched purposefully down the steps towards the counter, Miss Brahms was hot on her heels.

' 'Ere,' she gasped, 'we all heard that. Does that mean that you and him are going to . . .'

Mrs. Slocombe held up her hand imperiously.

'We don't wish to make any comments at this stage,' she announced. 'Just get me a chair, Miss Brahms.'

Miss Brahms ran into the fitting room and reappeared with the gold wickerwork chair which she placed by the counter.

'Here you are, Mrs. Slocombe.'

Mrs. Slocombe slowly sat down, crossed her

legs and leaned her elbow nonchalantly on the counter. Captain Peacock and Mr. Rumbold walked slowly towards her, followed by the others. Captain Peacock cleared his throat.

'Er . . . Mrs. Slocombe, I'm sorry about our little misunderstanding, but I was only doing my job. As a matter of fact when I mentioned it to Mr. Rumbold I did say my sympathies lay with you.'

Mr. Rumbold shook his head. 'No, no, no, it was you who said we had better put her in her place.'

Captain Peacock gave a short laugh. 'No, what I actually said was, there should be a better place to put her in.'

Mrs. Slocombe gazed at him stonily.

Mr. Grainger extended his hand. 'No hard feelings, Mrs. Slocombe. I have been a little on edge lately because Mr. Humphries kept saying men are so much better on the floor than ladies. Though I disagreed with him of course.'

Mrs. Slocombe ignored the outstretched hand.

Mr. Lucas leant forward. 'On the other hand I was saying how much I enjoyed having ladies on the floor, particularly Mrs. Slocombe, whom we all love and respect.'

'Never in my life,' said Miss Brahms, 'have I seen such crawling since I went to the insect house at the Zoo. What's more . . .'

'That'll do, Miss Brahms,' cut in Mrs. Slocombe.

'I mean,' said Miss Brahms, 'just because you're going to marry the head of the firm, they've gone all smarmy. Let me get you a sweetie, Mrs. Slocombe.'

'You're very kind, Miss Brahms. I think not though, I still have to consider my figure and of course I haven't actually said yes. After all, a girl has to think carefully about all the pros and cons.'

'If you ask me,' said Miss Brahms, 'he's too old and past it.'

Mrs. Slocombe pursed her lips thoughtfully. 'I'm not sure whether that's a pro or a con. Anyway he's not that old, he's only about seventy.'

'He certainly doesn't look seventy,' said Mr. Humphries.

'No,' added Mr. Lucas, 'he looks about eighty-five.'

Mrs. Slocombe produced her handbag from a drawer, opened it, selected a bottle of Eau de Cologne, unscrewed it and shook it down her cleavage.

'Age,' she commented, 'has nothing to do with it.'

A far-away look came in Miss Brahms's eyes. 'I wonder where he will take you for your honeymoon?'

'Well,' said Mrs. Slocombe, 'as he's got a yacht, it could be anywhere. Although I wouldn't say no to Capri.'

'Oh, don't go there,' said Mr. Humphries. 'He might run off with Gracie Fields. She's more his age.'

Mrs. Slocombe stood up and gazed at the racks of dresses behind her. 'Oh dear,' she said anxiously, 'what am I going to wear? I do want to look my best.'

Mr. Grainger leaned across the counter. 'The full facilities of my department, Mrs. Slocombe, are at your disposal.'

'How kind,' said Miss Brahms, 'but she's hardly likely to get proposed to in a three-piece suit.'

'I was referring,' said Mr. Grainger, 'to the superior quality of our fitting rooms and their two-way mirrors.'

Mrs. Slocombe turned in surprise.

'Mr. Grainger means you can see the back and front at the same time,' explained Mr. Lucas.

Mr. Humphries nodded. 'Comes in quite handy sometimes.'

'I'm sure,' suggested Captain Peacock, 'that Mr. Rumbold would welcome your choosing any garment from the stock in the ladies' department.'

With a note of exasperation in his voice, Mr. Rumbold said that he was just about to say that.

'How kind,' said Mrs. Slocombe. 'I shall of course have to choose something appropriate for the occasion.'

Leaning over the counter, Mr. Lucas produced a pair of novelty briefs, and held them out and pointed to the writing on them.

'How about "Opportunity Knocks",' he suggested.

The department clock indicated it was half past three. Captain Peacock walked up and down nervously, hands behind his back, glanced at the clock and then strolled over to Mr. Grainger, shaking his head.

'Half past three, Mrs. Slocombe still not back from lunch.'

Mr. Grainger nodded. 'Such a dear person, I'm very fond of her you know, Stephen.'

'Oh so am I,' said Captain Peacock. 'By the way, Ernest, does Young Mr. Grace have any living relations?'

Mr. Grainger shook his head. 'Only Old Mr. Grace and he doesn't get about much any more.'

'In that case,' sighed Captain Peacock, 'she stands to cop the lot.'

'Yes,' said Mr. Grainger. 'As I said, such a dear person.'

A mechanical ping indicated the arrival of the lift and the doors opened. Mrs. Slocombe stepped out with a hassive halo of curls lacquered into place and strolled forward with her head back as though her balance was in jeopardy.

'How nice your hair looks, Mrs. Slocombe,' called Mr. Grainger.

Captain Peacock nodded in agreement. 'Very *a la mode.*'

'It's lacquered solid,' confided Mrs Slocombe. 'On the way up I bumped into the commissionaire and broke the peak off his hat.'

'Lovely,' said Miss Brahms as Mrs. Slocombe moved regally across the floor. 'It must have cost a fortune.'

'Four pounds fifty,' confided Mrs. Slocombe, 'but an investment.'

Miss Brahms pulled back the curtain of the fitting room. I've got the clothes that you picked out to try on.'

'I'll remember your efficiency,' said Mrs. Slocombe. 'While I change I shall have to leave you in charge.'

With that Mrs. Slocombe disappeared into the fitting room, then came out again with two dresses over her arm.

'Oh yes, that's very nice, I think brown is so dignified.'

'Yes,' said Miss Brahms, 'and it doesn't show the gravy.'

'May I suggest,' said Mr. Grainger, 'that our fitting room, which has fluorescent lighting, would be a far superior place for you to try on your ensemble.'

'Why not?' said Mrs. Slocombe.

'Follow me, madam,' said Mr. Grainger.

Mrs. Slocombe followed Mr. Grainger across the floor.

'Mr. Grainger,' she said, 'your kindness to me will not go unnoticed,' then she paused at the gentlemen's counter. 'Mr. Humphries, your tie is crooked.'

Mr. Grainger with an ingratiating smile pulled back the curtain of the fitting room and bowed as he ushered Mrs. Slocombe in but she recoiled in horror. In the cubicle a customer was in the act of stepping out of his trousers.

Mrs. Slocombe gave a piercing scream and fell back into Mr. Grainger's arms. Mr. Humphries and Captain Peacock rushed to her assistance. Mrs. Slocombe gasped and pointed to the curtain. 'There's a naked man in there, in his underpants.'

Mr. Humphries patted her hand consolingly. 'You've seen nothing yet, Mrs. Slocombe. Just wait until the honeymoon!'

'I think,' said Mrs. Slocombe, gathering up her dress, 'that I shall use my own facilities, thank you.'

'Of course,' added Mr. Humphries, 'to be fair, Young Mr. Grace will have to get used to it too. Tell me, Captain Peacock, you're a man of the world, from your wide experience of these matters, do you think they will make a go of it?'

Captain Peacock pursed his lips. 'Putting it bluntly, Mr. Humphries, neither of them are in a position to be choosey.'

Mr. Humphries shook his head. 'I can't think what has come over the old boy.'

'He wants somebody to be ready to take over, rather like Eva Peron when the Junta collapsed,' suggested Captain Peacock.

'I should be surprised,' said Mr. Humphries, 'if his hasn't collapsed already.'

'Between you and me,' said Captain Peacock, 'I think she could be a bit of a tartar.'

Half an hour later, Mrs. Slocombe reappeared from her fitting room in full bridal regalia, a white veil carefully covering her new hairstyle. The gentlemen's department gasped in surprise.

'Well, Captain Peacock?' said Mrs. Slocombe, posing demurely as she waited for an opinion.

'A little formal for afternoon tea don't you think, Mrs. Slocombe?'

Mrs. Slocombe shook her head. 'I'm not going to wear it this afternoon. I just couldn't resist trying it on, it makes me feel all young and innocent.'

A look of surprise crossed Captain Peacock's face.

'A remarkable garment indeed,' he observed.

'It's a quarter to four,' said Miss Brahms. 'You had better try the afternoon dress on.'

Mrs. Slocombe turned back towards the dressing room and warbled in a wavering voice, 'Oh be still my fluttering heart.'

PECIAL OFFER!

BIKINI'S HALVED

½ PRICE GENTS

Miss Brahms drew the curtains behind her murmuring, 'It was probably the wind from the fairy cake.'

At five minutes to four Mrs. Slocombe reappeared in the brown dress. She poured another generous helping of the Cologne down her bosom, snapped on her best earrings with a businesslike gesture and with cries of 'Good luck' ringing in her ears, entered the lift and disappeared upwards, to her fate.

'Well,' observed Mr. Lucas, 'it looks as if she's made up her mind.'

'Yes,' said Mr. Humphries, 'in two minutes she'll be up in Mr. Grace's office.'

'I wouldn't mind,' said Captain Peacock, 'being a fly on the wall.'

'I'll tell you exactly what you'd see,' said Mr. Lucas, 'tea for two, a silly old muffin and a tired old bit of crumpet.'

In the Board room Mr. Grace sat in his high-backed chair, eyes closed. A loud knock on the door interrupted his reverie.

'Yes, yes,' called Mr. Grace. 'Come in, come in.'

The young bossomy girl holding a tray of engagement rings entered.

'Here are the rings you wanted to have a look at, Mr. Grace.'

'Thank you, Miss Robinson, where's the tea?'

'It's just coming, Mr. Grace.'

A tentative knock at the door indicated the arrival of Mrs. Slocombe.

'Come in,' said Mr. Grace.

'I hope,' said Mrs. Slocombe, 'that I am not late.'

'No,' said Mr. Grace, 'you're early, the tea hasn't come yet. Never mind, come and sit down. I think you know Miss Robinson of jewellery.'

Mrs. Slocombe started to nod then remembered her lacquered hair and stopped just in time. 'Yes, yes, her superior and I are old acquaintances.'

The sound of a foot kicking the door interrupted them.

'That'll be the tea,' said Mr. Grace. 'Come in.'

The grinning face of Mr. Mash appeared holding a large tray on which was a pot of tea, two cups and an assortment of buns on a plate.

'One pot of Rosie Lee,' called Mr. Mash, 'and the usual muffin and crumpet.' With that he banged it down on the table. 'Blimey,' he said, 'those rings are nice,' then aside to Mrs. Slocombe he whispered, 'choose a big one, darling, and pick the honeymoon suite on the ground floor, one flight of those stairs and he won't be able to raise his walking stick until after breakfast.'

'Get out,' hissed Mrs. Slocombe.

'Are you going to be mother?' said Mr. Grace. Mrs. Slocombe almost jumped out of her seat, then recovered.

'We can't be sure,' she murmured with lowered eyes. 'One must wait and see.'

'I mean,' said Mr. Grace, 'are you going to pour out the tea?'

Mrs. Slocombe looked relieved. 'The tea, oh yes, of course.'

'Now I expect,' said Mr. Grace, 'you are wondering why I have asked you up here.'

Mrs. Slocombe gave a secretive smile. 'A girl does have an inkling you know.'

'What?' said Mr. Grace, leaning forward and cupping his hands to his ear.

'An inkling,' shouted Mrs. Slocombe.

'What's that?' said Mr. Grace.

'It's what,' said Mrs. Slocombe, pouring with an unsteady hand, 'a girl has when something special is in the air.'

'Aah,' nodded Mr. Grace, 'you mean like hay fever.'

'Do you take sugar,' inquired Mrs. Slocombe.

'I'm sweet enough,' said Mr. Grace.

Mrs. Slocombe threw back her head and laughed. 'That's a good one,' she said, and to her consternation found that one of her lacquered curls had caught the carved woodwork of her highbacked chair. With a surreptitious effort she managed to release it.

'I expect,' said Mr. Grace, 'that you think I'm a bit of an old fool getting married at my time of life. After all, I am seventy.'

'One or two?' said Mrs. Slocombe, holding up the sugar bowl.

'If I say I am seventy,' snapped Mr. Grace, 'I am seventy.'

'I mean how many sugars,' said Mrs. Slocombe.

'I've already told you,' said Mr. Grace, 'that I don't take sugar.'

'I'm sorry,' said Mrs. Slocombe, 'it's just nerves. In fact I thought you were only in your late sixties. And anyway you are only as old as you feel, and I can see you are very young in spirit. All you need is someone to take you out of yourself. I mean you hardly ever take a holiday, do you?'

'That's true,' agreed Mr. Grace.

Mrs. Slocombe buttered a scone. 'It's very difficult being alone for a man of your position isn't it? I mean supposing you take your yacht to the Caribbino. You'll have those young girls climbing all over you and all because you're rich.'

An interested look crossed Mr. Grace's face. 'Will I?' he inquired.

Mrs. Slocombe nodded. 'And they are all after you for one thing, you know.' She pulled a face

SHOP SOILED GIRLS OUTFITS

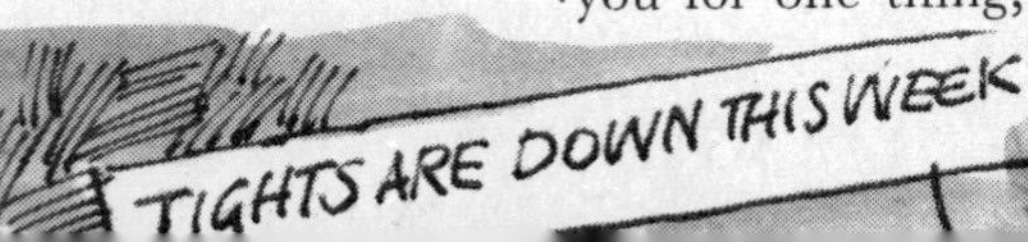

£2

to show how she disapproved of that 'one thing'.

'Are they?' said Mr. Grace, brightening up.

'Yes,' said Mrs. Slocombe, blowing her tea. 'But if you're married to a wife who is devoted to you, she will protect you from all that. You've always got someone at your side sharing your little problems, helping you through life's weary travels.'

The perky look started to disappear from Mr. Grace's face.

'Cherishing,' continued Mrs. Slocombe, 'each other when you are sick, and all that sort of thing.' Taking a large bite of scone she edged her chair a little nearer. Mr. Grace sipped his tea thoughtfully, finally he nodded and put his hand on her knee. She gazed at it anxiously as he continued, 'I'm very grateful to you, Mrs. Slocombe, you have helped me to make up my mind. In fact I brought you up here to choose a ring.'

The scone stuck in Mrs. Slocombe's throat, and she had to take a large gulp of tea to get it down. Stabbing her finger into the box she announced breathlessly 'that big one there' and picking it up forced it on to her engagement finger. She held out her hand and gazed at it admiringly. Mr. Grace appeared not to notice.

'It's for our Miss Robinson of the jewellery department, whom I have had my eye on for some time, almost three weeks,' he added.

Mrs. Slocombe froze. 'Miss Robinson?'

Mr. Grace nodded. 'Yes but now I've spoken to you, you've put me right off the idea of marriage.'

'Oh no,' said Mrs. Slocombe hurriedly, 'that was the last thing I wanted to do.'

With an effort Mr. Grace hauled himself to his feet. 'Anyway thank you very much, Mrs. Slocombe, you must come and help me again.'

Heavy-footed she headed for the door.

'Oh Mrs. Slocombe,' called Mr. Grace after her. Mrs. Slocombe stopped and her face brightened.

She turned eagerly. 'Yes, Mr. Grace?'

'Tell stationery to send me a copy of *Yachting Monthly*. You did say all those girls were in the Caribbean?'

'Yes,' said Mrs. Slocombe, 'I did.'

Mrs. Slocombe stepped from the lift to be greeted by a round of applause.

'Doesn't she look radiant?' said Mr. Humphries.

'Perhaps they've already done it,' said Mr. Lucas. 'He probably had a vicar upstairs in his office.'

'A friend of mine did that,' said Mr. Humphries, 'and he had a small section of the choir hiding behind the curtain, it was a very moving story in court.'

Captain Peacock held up his hands. 'Quiet everybody. Now Mrs. Slocombe, tell us everything that happened.'

Mrs. Slocombe glanced round at the assembled faces. 'Well,' she said, 'before I do, I would like to clear up one or two matters. Mr. Grainger?'

'Yes, Mrs. Slocombe,' Mr. Grainger hurried forward, hands clasped together.

'I take it,' said Mrs. Slocombe, 'that you no longer object to the presence of the ladies' department on this floor?'

'On the contrary,' said Mr. Grainger, 'the ladies' department will always be most welcome.'

'And', continued Mrs. Slocombe, 'I take it, Captain Peacock, that you will not in future insist upon the ladies' department displaying articles they consider to be in bad taste.'

Captain Peacock shook his head. 'The goods on display will be left entirely to whosoever is in charge.'

'Well,' said Mrs. Slocombe, 'I'm glad that's all cleared up.'

'And may one ask,' said Captain Peacock, 'when the happy day will be?'

'Today,' said Mrs. Slocombe.

'Today!' said Captain Peacock.

'Yes,' said Mrs. Slocombe, 'I turned him down.'

THE TWO RONNIES

THE CASE OF MRS MACE:
By Gerald Wiley
(*The scene is a police station* – **Ronnie Barker** *is a plain-clothes North Country detective, sits at a desk.* **Ronnie Corbett** *enters*)

Ronnie Corbett:
Good day, Inspector Jay.
Ronnie Barker:
Morning, Dorning. Any news of the Girder murder?
Ronnie Corbett:
Yessir. He's been shot at Oxshott. Bagshot got him with a slingshot full of buckshot.
Ronnie Barker:
He's a good shot, Bagshot. Well, you must be pleased *that* situation's eased.
Ronnie Corbett:
The relief is beyond belief chief. My mind is once more a blank. And I've only you to thank.
Ronnie Barker:
Alright. Never mind the fawning, Dorning. I'm glad to hear your head's clear: it means there's more space for the Mrs Mace case to take its place.
Ronnie Corbett:
The Mrs Mace case? Have they traced the face? (*Points to photofit blow-up on the wall*)
Ronnie Barker:
No – and the night-dress is still missing.
Ronnie Corbett:
Is she sure it was the right night-dress? She's not mistaken about what was taken?
Ronnie Barker:
How come, little chum?
Ronnie Corbett:
Well, to the voluptuous Mrs Mace, all her night-dresses are equally seductively attractive and attractively seductive. Whatever she wore, she'd still be a bountiful, beautiful nightie-full.
Ronnie Barker:
She's certainly a grand lady to have as a landlady. I've been told, that her teapot's *never* cold.
Ronnie Corbett:
I'd be delighted to be selected to inspect her, inspector. Any prospects of any suspects?
Ronnie Barker:
Yes – two. Two of them are actors who lodge with Grace – Mrs Mace, at her place in the Chase. Leo Mighty, the leading man, known for his portrayals of charmers, farmers, and men in pyjamas. And the other one is Roger Mainger, the stage manager, who once played a mad stranger in a film starring Stewart Granger called 'Deadly Danger'.
Ronnie Corbett:
May I add another to your list? If I'm not being too bumptious or presumptious?
Ronnie Barker:
Who?
Ronnie Corbett:
Sergeant Bodger!
Ronnie Barker:
What? That replacement constable from Dunstable? You must be crazy.
Ronnie Corbett:
It's just a theory, dearie. May I sit down?
Ronnie Barker:
Please – make yourself comfry, Humphrey.
Ronnie Corbett: (*sitting down*)
It's just that Bodger has got a face like a fit: which fits the face on the Photofit in the first place, and he's often to be found at her place, in the Chase, filling his face with fish.
Ronnie Barker:
Fish?
Ronnie Corbett:
Fried by Grace – Mrs Mace. Mostly Dace – or Plaice.
Ronnie Barker:
But what about Leo Mighty? He's there nightly – isn't it slightly more likely? She obviously looks very flighty in her nighty – he's the sort of toff that might try to pull it off.
Ronnie Corbett:
Possibly – but here's something you don't know.
Ronnie Barker:
I don't.
Ronnie Corbett:
No. I've spoken with Roger.
Ronnie Barker:
Roger?
Ronnie Corbett:
The lodger.
Ronnie Barker:
Oh – Roger Mainger, who played the stranger with Granger.
Ronnie Corbett:
He says he saw Leo take the night-gown. He was staring through the keyhole in Mrs Mace's bedroom door.
Ronnie Barker:
He dared to stare through there? Would he swear he saw Leo Mighty take the nightie?

Ronnie Corbett:
He'll do plenty of swearing. No wonder he was staring – it was the one she was wearing!
Ronnie Barker:
What? Surely not!
Ronnie Corbett:
He stood on the bed, and pulled it over her head. She went red, and he fled. He locked himself in the shed, and wished he were dead. She was going to phone her cousin Ted, but felt dizzy in the head, so she lay on the bed instead, and went red.
Ronnie Barker:
So you said. Roger is a liar!
Ronnie Corbett:
Have you any proof, you old poof?
Ronnie Barker:
I've seen where Mrs Mace sleeps. It's an attic! So the story about pulling the garment over her head is false. He would have to pull the nightgown right down! There's no headroom in her bedroom!
Ronnie Corbett:
So Roger's lying! Then he must be the culprit! Game set and match, chief! And so ends the disgraceful Grace Mace case.
Ronnie Barker: (*picks up the phone*)
I'll just tell the Chief Constable – what a relief, constable. (*Into phone*) Hello sir – we've solved the Mace Case. I'm happy to tell you that Leo is innocent, and so is Sergeant Bodger. Yes sir: in other words – t'was not Leo Mighty who lifted the nighty, t'was Roger the Lodger, the soft-footed dodger, and not Sergeant Bodger, thank God!

Published by Hodder Stoughton

DOCTOR SPOONER REVISITED
(By Gerald Wiley)

Ronnie Barker *is seen as the Presenter*
Ronnie Barker:
Some time ago, we visited the abode of Dr William Spooner, the Oxford Don who, a hundred years ago, was confusing all and sundry with his unique habit of transposing the first letters of two adjacent words – hereafter to be known as 'Spoonerisms'. It was he who had proposed a toast to the queer old dean instead of the dear old queen. It was also he who shocked the wife of the new bursar to the college. What he meant to say was that, coming into contact with so many high-spirited young geniuses, she would soon be mad as a hatter, of course. Instead of which, he said she would soon be had as a matter of course.

And so, in a special reconstruction, we return once again to the peaceful confines of Dr Spooner's house in Oxford . . .
(*The scene moves to a Victorian Vicarage – the garden-room, or morning-room; with French doors to the garden. Mrs Spooner sits in a wicker chair, sewing. Enter* **Ronnie Barker** *as Spooner, with a basket, with flowers in it*)
Mrs S:
Good morning, William.
Dr S:
Ah, good ray, Dosey. I mean, good day Rosie.
Mrs S:
You were up early, dear. Where have you been?
Dr S:
I've been rolling the strose-bushes – strolling in the rose-bushes. They love so smelly this morning.
Mrs S:
You do adore your garden, don't you?
Dr S:
Indoo I deed – I mean indood I dee. Nothing makes me gappier than a spot of hardening. But I fear I have neglected it of late – and there is so much to do at this time of year. It's the rutting season for tea-cosies, you know.
Mrs S:
The rutting season? For tea-cosies?
Dr S:
No, no my dear – the cutting season for tea-roses. I declare, you're getting as mad as be!
Mrs S:
Is that what you intend to do today, my love?
Dr S:
No, the roses must wait. The first thing I have to do is to spray my flies against greenbeans. And while I'm at it, I think I'll black my dooberries as well.
Mrs S:
Oh, that reminds me, I need some vegetables for dinner. Would you mind me a farrow?
Dr S:
Mia Farrow? What has she to do with it?
Mrs S:
I'm sorry dear, I mean could you find me a marrow.
Dr S:
Oh I see – a mere tip of the slung. Alas, my dear, I cannot. The garden gate must have been left unlocked. Someone has nip-toed in and tipped my barrow in the mud.
Mrs S:
You mean tip-toed in and nipped your marrow in the bud?
Dr S:
I couldn't have bet it putter myself; I'll wager it was that villainous landlord of the Wig and Pistle.

Mrs S:
What, little Billy Humphris?
Dr S:
Exactly. Little Hilly Bumphris. He's jealous of my prowess in the Shower Flow.
Mrs S:
My name is Rose, dear.
Dr S:
No, the shower flow. The Annual shower flow.
Mrs S:
Oh, I see.
Dr S:
Don't you remember, last year he sabotaged my peas. He covered them with creosote, and left the sore little pods to die.
Mrs S:
The sore little pods? Oh, the poor little –
Dr S:
Exactly.
Mrs S:
William – are you sure it's him? Perhaps it was the bees.
Dr S:
Bees can't open a garden-gate.
Mrs S:
But how do you know the gate was open?
Dr S:
I saw next door's dog loo-ing things on the dawn.
Mrs S:
Their pet poodle?
Dr S:
Yes, their pood pettle.
Mrs S:
Pretty polly?
Dr S:
Yes, prilly potty. That villain! He'll pay for this. I've a good mind to creep over there and put Dertilizer on his failures.
Mrs S:
William dearest, don't get so upset. I will help you with the garden, when I get time. At the moment we both have other duties – our students, remember?
Dr S:
Good heavens. Took at the lime! I mean like at the tomb! I've hissed a mystery lecture.
Mrs S:
And I have a Divinity class waiting. Let us hurry, dear William, and not keep them waiting any longer. (*She takes his arm*) Dearest! You are my William – the sweetest sweet William that ever grew.
Dr S:
And you are my Rose – the ricest nose I ever picked.
Mrs S:
But you know – you're much too Gashionate to be a pardener.
Dr S:
And you're much too titty to be a preacher!
(*They Exit*)

Animal Crackers

The harpsichordist had a theory that music soothed the wildest of animals. So he trekked to the middle of the African jungle, taking his harpsichord with him. All round were the roars and screams of ferocious animals.

When he started to play, the roars died down and a strange hush fell on the jungle. One by one the animals came out to listen, sitting quietly in a circle . . . an elephant, a buffalo, a gorilla, a crocodile, a gigantic snake. Suddenly, with an ear-splitting roar, a lion leapt from the jungle and bit off the harpsichordist's head. The other animals were aghast.

'Why the heck did you do that?' trumpeted the elephant. 'For the first time in our lives we've heard beautiful music. Now you've gone and ruined everything. Why did you do it?'

'Eh'? said the lion, cupping a paw to his ear, 'what did you say?'

The simpleton made a bad mistake and brought a bitch along to the fox hunt. Ten minutes after the chase started, the Master of Foxhounds turned to his companion and asked:

'Which way are they headed?'

'South.'

'Where's the fox?'

'At the moment, running fifth, but he's gaining ground rapidly.'

The animal trainer had a great new animal act – a singing dog and a cat which played the piano. The impresario had seen the act, but was not impressed.

'I think there's a trick somewhere. I don't believe you could train animals to do things like that,' he said emphatically.

Finally the animal trainer broke down and confessed.

'You're right,' he said. 'It *is* a trick. The cat is a ventriloquist.'

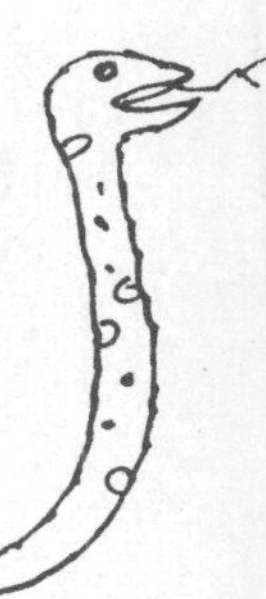

THE BONA BOOK of JULIAN & SANDY
by Barry Took and Marty Feldman Published by Robson Books Ltd.

BONA PETS

Sandy: Hello, Mr. Horne—what brings you trolling in?
Horne: Well, actually I'm looking for a pet.
Sandy: Well, of course, dogs are nice, don't you think, Jule?
Julian: Oh yes, we've got a plethora of dogs here. How do you fancy a little chihuahua?
Horne: No thanks. I don't smoke.
Sandy: Oh, bold! No, he means a Mexican Hairless. I should have thought that was very suitable for *you*. Or you have your poodle. That's a noble beast, isn't it, Jule?
Julian: Yes. And you can have 'em in any colour you like. You can have your blue rinse, your grey rinse—you can have any colour to match your barnet.
Sandy: Now we're back on the Mexican Hairless again.
Julian: No, I tell you what, we got one poodle—very unusual shade, he's streaked with lavender and crimson. We didn't intend it that way, but he rolled in the paint while we was doing the bathroom. He's a very eye-catching little fellow, though.
Sandy: No, he's not the poodle type, Jule. A poodle's not really *him*.
Horne: Well, what sort of dog would you recommend?
Julian: Well, we've got some new strains we've bred ourselves. There's Cyril—he's half-and-half, you know. Half King Charles spaniel, half fox terrier. We call him a fox-cocker.
Sandy: Or you can have your Doberman wolfhound, your wire-haired dalmatian—or then, there's Queenie. She's a cross between a German sausage dog and a greyhound.
Horne: A sort of grey sausage doghound?
Julian: Yes. She stands four foot high with her belly dragging on the ground. She may not look much but she don't half go.
Horne: It's not exactly what I had in mind—I was looking for something a little more exotic.
Sandy: Would you like a Peke?
Horne: I don't really think so—but what about this little chap on the counter? He seems very quiet and well behaved. Yorkshire terrier, isn't he?
Sandy: Not exactly. It's a floor mop.
Horne: Yes, I thought he had rather a long tail.
Sandy: Are you absolutely set on a dog?
Horne: No, not really. I just wanted something out of the ordinary.
Julian: Well, how about our twin set? Hamster and tortoise? Marvellous for dealing with burglars.
Horne: What? A hamster and a tortoise? How?
Julian: Well—the burglar creeps in through the window—sees the hamster sitting there wrinkling his nose and looking all cute—so he gives a squeal of delight, and while he's bending down going 'Kootchy kootchy koo', you creep up behind him and hit him with the tortoise.

BONA LAW

Horne: Can you help me? I've erred.
Sandy: Well, we've all erred, ducky. I mean, it's common knowledge, ennit, Jule?
Horne: Will you take my case?
Julian: Well, it depends on what it is. We've got a criminal practice that takes up most of our time.
Horne: Yes, but apart from that—I need legal advice.
Sandy: Ooh—isn't he bold? Time has not withered nor custom staled *his* infinite variety.
Julian: What is it you've done?
Horne: (*shyly*) I don't like to say.
Julian: Oh, you can tell us. Sand and me have handled the most bizarre briefs—nothing could shock us.
Horne: Well—look, it's here on this charge sheet.
Sandy: Let's have a vada. Oh Jule, look at this!
Julian: Ooh! He didn't!
Sandy: He did. Look, it's written down.
Julian: But I mean—in broad daylight—outside the Corner House—aren't you ashamed?
Horne: Yes—but it is only a parking offence.
Sandy: *Only!* They're very hot on that. What do you think, Jule?
Julian: Hmm—let me look up me tort.
Sandy: Shh—he's looking up his tort. Sometimes it takes him hours to find what he's looking for. Ah, he's found it. Well?
Julian: I recommend we try *Per verulium ad camphorum actus injuria linctus est.*
Sandy: That's your actual Latin.
Horne: What does it mean?
Julian: I dunno—I got it off a bottle of horse rub, but it sounds good, doesn't it? How shall we tackle it, Sand?
Sandy: I think we should plead insanity.
Julian: Yes, but what about Mr. Horne?
Sandy: Oh, him. I'll defend him. I'll do me speech for the defence. Would you like to hear it?
Julian: Go on, do your plea, Sand. Oh, he's an eloquent pleader.
Sandy: Omes and palones of the jury, vada well the eek of the poor ome who stands before you, his lallies trembling. He has his share of guilt, but who is without it? We all have a bit—every one of us. We have our share. His only crime was that he loved not wisely but not too well. This kid never had a chance—born on the wrong side of the tracks, forced to take in washing—society drove him to a life of vice. It is not this ome who is on trial—it is all of us. We made him what he is—without hope, without love, without hair. Give him a chance to become a useful citizen again—a housewife and a mother, so that he can look the world in the face and say, 'I name this ship HMS Ark Royal. God bless all who sail in her!'
Julian: Bravo, Sand! You could have been a Queen's Counsel. Well, Mr. Horne—what do you say?
Horne: Have you got Quintin Hogg's phone number?

Advertising has gone a long way since the days of 'Wanted: bath for baby with copper bottom'.

Some might say it had gone too far – all these girls and fellas floating across the TV hills, their hair streaming out behind them ever so slowly, and only one foot touching the ground every ten minutes – and those commercials with the intimate voice making us all so smell conscious that you're afraid to bat an eyelid in case it lets loose some hideous new personal odour on an ungrateful world. To my mind (if it is my mind they're trying to reach) the best ads. are those that take the micky out of advertising. There was a series on American TV knocking the 'Brand X' idea; every time the luckless demonstrator asked a housewife to choose between a stack of clothes washed in *his* washing powder and those washed by the obviously inferior Brand X powder, she always chose the Brand X pile; or the ones with the enterprising Japanese candy salesman who was always thwarted by some terrible accident to people about to endorse his chocolate – they either fell out of a window as they started speaking, or fell forward over the desk with an unexplained knife in the back. In the end, he pulls out a huge sword, and commits hari-kari himself.

Aside from the commercials, trying to sell you something, there's food for a lot of thought in the 'Sits. Vac.' columns, as Basil Boothroyd has found out:

Take a Joke Miss Wilson

by BASIL BOOTHROYD

'Girl with sense of humour urgently required to replace me as secretary to Temple solicitor. Hard work but entertaining. Box N. 1984.'—The Times.

DEAR BOX: As a kindred spirit I don't need to tell you the relief, seeing a sense of h. advertised for, when everyone else is crying out for women graduates with engineering degrees or A Level in British Constitution. Actually, I couldn't take on some of these jobs for laughing, so it makes no odds really: I mean, I see where they're advertising in Edinburgh for someone to look after what they call a programmeable 16-in. twin reflector. Who wants to reflect twins? is what I'd be sure to come out with at the interview. Same as my father, very highly developed s. of h., I expect that's where I get it from, when Bradfield's Correspondence College wanted him to run their new course in accounting for women and he said there wasn't any accounting for women, just couldn't resist it, and that was the last he heard. Laugh and the world laughs with you, they say, but it hasn't worked out that way in my family. Mum did six months as a hospital almoner and would have been there now except she dressed up as a Maternity Unit sister and dished out the new babies one night; little black celluloid dolls. Dad and I shrieked when she told us, but the next thing was the sack. People like to think they can see a joke, but they're dead serious when you come right down to it. I've had to be filling in as a baker's roundswoman this last few weeks, but got the push last Friday, leaving a loaf at the vicarage with a toy mouse in it.

However, in re your ad. By the way, I hope it is not a leg-pull, don't mind my asking. But my friend says if you are all that humorous you could have inserted same just to get a giggle out of the answers, and her fiancé, who is a big reader (6 foot 1 in his socks, ha-ha, joke) says even the box no. looks fishy but will not divulge why, so I am chancing my arm herewith.

In case I am not suited, what class of humour does your boss like? Would you say verbal, i.e. snappy comments during dictation, or more of the practical, such as he opens a deed box and a pigeon flies out? Personally I am surprised at anyone in the legal line boasting a leaning to mirth, always being under the impression they were a sobersidish lot, otherwise how do they look at each other in those little wigs and not burst out screaming? And incidentally that could be a bad snag with me, being easily tickled, and what if I'm in court being Della Street to your P. Mason and the judge puts on the black doo-dah and I have to laugh? You might think the serious occasion would put a damper, but it goes by opposites with me. Last year's harvest festival our curate had a marrow on the pulpit edgeways on and it struck me it looked so much like Molotov I had to bite on my prayer-book all through the sermon, and anyone who doesn't believe me can see the teeth-marks right up to the Churching of Women.

Still, hold your horses, I haven't got the job yet. Possibly a note of past exploits would assist. I have had five posts since summer 1961, as below, and each one a riot in its way. I expect references could be got as to my sense of fun but there has been no call for them so far.

Ribson, Kyle, Cleaver and Son, Estate Agents. Humour mostly literary, such as inserting light remarks in the Orders to View, e.g. '3 bed., 3 recep., kit., bathroom, polo ground, easy flying distance shops,' but very disappointing how many customers never queried. Left after a practical exercise, couple came enquiring after an architect-built double-fronted detached as advertised and I showed them over an old waterworks. I let myself down by laughing in the end, my old trouble, but soon stopped when they said they'd have it and wanted to write cheque for deposit. It wasn't for sale, needless to relate.

Madame Binns, Coiffeur (Acton). When they were under the drier I used to rap its outside with the scissors, and they used to say, What's that banging noise? and I'd say I couldn't hear anything. You could keep it up for hours with a perm, but of course I had to get the other girls in cahoots. All sacked when Monsieur Binns squinted through the curtains to look at our legs and caught us at it, but had a good run.

Millinery Dept., Anvil & Cooper's Stores. Employed as wages clerk but got to know workroom girls, a rollicking lot, and they let me trim two special order hats with real fruit. Talk about candid camera, it had nothing on Anvil & C.'s three days' later when they brought the hats back. One lady with plum juice running into her eye while complaining. Had my laugh, then left voluntarily.

Invoice Clerk, Swinnerton and Lippett. They were soft toy wholesalers or something, but I never really discovered as I was on a punched-card machine, and used to punch one card at random every day just for the fun of it. Took a long time to enjoy the end-product of this, but after a month it caught up, and a gay old time with shops on the phone saying they'd ordered six dozen Sooties and been delivered three gross of rear-window tigers with lighting-up eyes. My biggest laugh to date, not even barring three days as a cold bar assistant in a roadhouse on the A.23, watching how many customers would eat my speciality sandwich filling, i.e. shredded foam rubber (about 3 out of 5, late on towards closing, but were their facial expressions a treat).

And fifthly the baker's roundswoman, as mentioned.

Of course, I realize I am a fool, setting out specimens of my fun at such length, when you no doubt will be sending me an application pro forma with appropriate questions such as jokes played, repartee engaged in, rhymes composed and laughs raised generally, but doubtless a bit of extra background does no harm.

Trusting to hear from you, therefore, and would just state a proviso, i.e. that I prefer to stay away from my employment on April 1st each year, lest I be tempted to exceed the bounds. And talking of that, I would appreciate hearing just why you are packing up the job.

Yours in good humour,

Heloise Bayonet-Sharpe

(And if you *knew* the trouble I have convincing people it's my real name! H.B-S.)

Excerpt from 'The Whole Things Laughable'
Published by George Allen & Unwin Ltd.

SALES PITCH

"I'm in advertising . . ."

"But Madam, they're not shoes"

"I'm the Advertising Manager of London Buses, and this is my wife."

Let's face it, our coffee machine is the only one required to display a Government health warning notice.

"No thanks, I'm trying to give them up!"

Reproduced from "Private Eye"

It's Yellow! It's Glittering! It's New.

by ALAN COREN

Every copywriter in every advertising agency has, as you know, a half-finished novel tucked away in his lower left-hand drawer. Unable to resist, I picked a lock, and discovered . . .

. . . first met Emma Bovary at a quiet little soirée thrown by the Strive-Glitterings on the croquet lawn beside the moat of Strive-Glittering Castle. It was an unpretentious affair, just sixty eight close friends sitting at a long rosewood table, nibbling thin mint chocolates and laughing, while, in the hazy half-distance, golden-haired chauffeurs in tight grey uniforms strolled arrogantly among the moonlit radiators, practising their leers.

Emma was a ravishing woman, married, as I had found out, to a man earning twenty thousand a year, living in Godalming in a house with gas-fired central heating, two cars, a golden retriever, and a four-berth ketch.

It was when she leaned suddenly in front of me, reaching towards the two tiny silver pots and selecting the butter with an accuracy and an assurance that took one's breath away, that I caught a tantalising whiff of her expensive French perfume.

'I just caught,' I said, 'a tantalising whiff of your expensive French perfume.'

She laughed, tinklingly, and the starlight winked on her stain-free teeth.

'I don't use expensive French perfume,' she murmured, 'in the way you think. But every bar of fabulous pink Camay contains scents made to a special formula by top French parfumiers, exclusively for You. Or, rather, Me. It also contains a cleansing ingredient, a moisture cream, and a thing for keeping gnats off.'

'Your skin is like a baby's bum,' I said.

She lowered demure eyelids, and fluttered lashes that couldn't have gone out at less than £1.49 the pair.

'You're too gallant,' murmured Emma Bovary. 'You've noticed I have no unsightly facial hair?'

I nodded.

'Yes,' I said, 'nor boils, warts, blackheads, acne, barber's rash or moles with bristles on them. Do you use Valderma?'

'Doesn't every girl?' she said, and my blood raced! Inadvertently our warm thighs touched, hesitated, and pressed together.

'I shouldn't be doing this,' I whispered.

'It's quite all right,' she said, 'skirts in the new man-made fibre Finklon will not warp, crease, wither, or ride up. You can even,' and her soft voice dropped an octave, quivering, 'lie flat in them with complete assurance.'

'But your husband?'

'He's on top of a mountain in Spain,' she said, 'drinking Dubonnet.'

'Way up there?'

'Quite.'

Our hands touched, briefly, beneath the cloth.

'Convincing tests have shown,' I said, 'that four out of every five women would rather go home with me than sit around waiting for their husbands to come in and distinguish between different types of instant mashed potato.'

'Incredible!'

'Not incredible,' I said, '*biological*.'

We eased our chairs back, and stood up; but before we could leave, our hostess, the Hon. Fenella Strive-Glittering, shimmered across the dewy grass with a young Apollo on either arm.

'Emma!' she cried. 'Leave Nigel here! I'm prepared to offer not just one, but *two* young men in exchange for the one you've got there!'

Emma shook her lovely wig.

'No, thanks very much, I'll stick to my Nigel.'

Fenella smiled, and shrugged.

'We find most women do,' she said. 'And to think that only last year you had bad breath and forty square feet of clear water every time you got into a swimming-pool!'

'It's amazing what a ring of confidence will do for a girl,' said Emma, 'especially if her haemorrhoids have been shrunk without painful surgery.'

We all smiled, and shook hands, and Emma and I strolled off through the shrubbery. She had removed her shoes, and swung them in her left hand, clasping mine with her right, and leaning her head against the shoulder of my dinner-jacket. My heart pumped madly! Nothing acts faster than adrenalin.

'Is this your car?' she said admiringly, lifting her skirt as she got in and allowing her firm bare leg to set off the mock-lizard, near-leatherette upholstery that comes as standard, together with two-speed wipers, cool-air ventilation, fully reclining seats, walnuteen dashboard, and many other built-in features only obtainable as extras on cars costing hundreds of pounds more.

'Yes,' I said, as she ran her hand up the gear-shift and bit into a Cadbury's Flake, 'I find it outperforms many a sports car while offering limousine-style comfort for five six-feet adults. Heads turn when I drive by.'

'How fortunate, then, that ugly dandruff is not interfering with *your* chance of happiness!' cried Emma.

We got away. In my headlights, cats leapt, and owls watched us, and the dashboard glow picked up Emma's matchless bosom, thrusting deliciously forward, thanks to cross-your-heart straps, designed to lift and separate, that were doing a job which even I could not have improved upon. Happily I reflected that for me, at five-feet-ten and twenty-nine, a worthwhile career awaited in today's Metropolitan Police, should I ever need it. It was then that I noticed the two headlamps in my driving-mirror.

'I think we're being followed,' I said.

She twisted round.

'You're right!' she cried. 'It's a white car, identical to this. Is it merely Paddy Hopkirk testing some new silicone wax polish . . . ?'

'Or your husband, back from his mountain-top, thanks to the unparalleled efficiency and friendly but unobtrusive service which travellers have come to expect from BEA?'

'It cannot be! Tomorrow he is expected off Corfu, drinking tonic water aboard an ocean-going yacht.'

I pressed my Corfam slipper to the floor, and we snaked through the wooded lanes at breakneck speed, thankful alike for Pirelli Cinturatos, Milk of Magnesia, Britax Seat Belts, and Mum Aerosol Deodorant, with the white car barely a furlong behind, and gaining. I had all but resigned myself to discovery and disaster, when the delicious Emma glanced over her shoulder, and cried:

'The white car is stopping!'

I looked in my mirror.

'Thank God for the mileage ingredient!' I shouted.

'You mean?'

'Yes! Our red car will continue for another seven-point-two miles, while the poor sod behind is about to end up as just another case of lupine indigestion, if the rising tide doesn't get him first!'

We did not need to drive even that far: mere minutes later, following Emma's directions, we turned down a narrow track and ended up in front of a splendid neo-Georgian house.

'Is this where you live?' I asked.

'Yes,' she said. 'Fully detached, on two floors only, and with matchless views over the Green Belt, facing south, and a stone's throw from schools, shops, and choice of two stations into London, less than twenty-five miles away. It is, of course, double-glazed, with a mature yet easily managed garden, and the gazebo lights up at night. It was designed for an elderly lady of title, who built it very slowly and only used it at weekends. Shall we go in?.

'What about your children?' I whispered.

'These cold mornings,' said Emma, 'I make sure they don't go out without a good hot breakfast of Weetabix inside them. Its nourishing goodness lasts the whole day through, and keeps rickets away.'

'I meant,' I said, as she slid the key into the lock, 'won't they hear us?'

'No. They're away at their Auntie Eth's. On an egg holiday.'

I followed her into the dark hall, the atmosphere heavy with the intoxicating musk of Air-Wick, and was about to sink my teeth into the fleshy luminescence of her gorgeous neck when something large and black sprang through a shaft of

moonlight and hurled itself upon me with a fearful noise. As I fell backwards, I caught the unmistakable whiff of marrow-bone jelly.

'Good heavens, Bovary!' I cried, never a man to lose my cool, thanks to my training with the Runcorn Correspondence School of Pelmanism, which made me a mental wizard in only three short weeks. 'There's no need to lose your temper, I only dropped in to read the meter and inquire whether you wished to earn money with your pen this winter! I am a Pakistani immigrant, sir, working my way through college, and these magazines—'

'Oh do shut up, Nigel!' exclaimed Emma. 'It's only Prince Osric of Hernia III, Champion of Champions. You wouldn't happen to have a tin of Pal about your person?'

'No!' I snapped, as the dog walked away to practise posing.

'Top breeders use it,' said Emma reproachfully.

I got to my feet, thankful for the creaseproof qualities of Crimplene, and took her delectable elbow in my palm.

'A top breeder I may be,' I said smoothly, 'but I do not engage upon the activity on the lower floors. Where is your staircase?'

I felt her tremble.

'Would you not rather ride with me in the moonlight, Nigel? We have two white horses, you know. We could smoke mentholated cigarettes and let the wind blow through our hair.

'Afterwards,' I breathed, wedging the Polo against an upper bicuspid with a practised tongue and limbering my freshly salved lips.

'But would you not like to watch our Timmy select Kattomeat from not less than five bowls of assorted horse-offal? Will you not come and drop blood-stained garments in the Hoovermatic? Don't you want to see my budgies bounce with health?'

It was this last wild, provocative question that sent my temples into a mad throb of uncontrollable passion! Popping an Iron Jelloid in my mouth, I snatched the luscious Emma into my arms and took the stairs (thank you, Phyllosan!) three at a time, on the run. But—dear Lord, do words exist to limn the agony of what followed!—it was in that dark, desired boudoir that the revelation occurred so harrowing in its extent, so traumatic in its implications, so . . .

Shrieking her small, impassioned shrieks, Emma Bovary began to fumble out of her clothes. First, the sweet Sheerline tights, Designed To Make Your Legs Even Longer, Even Shapelier—these cast aside, her legs suddenly became even shorter, even lumpier; then the Platex girdle, whose Fingertip Panels Hold You In Like Firm Young Muscles To Make You Look Five Pounds Thinner, fell to the floor, making her look five pounds fatter and free from all muscletone, like an ill-knit haggis; and when the bra joined the pile, its cross-your-heart straps gone and leaving a bosom lowered and joined, the decomposing Venus stood before me in the pallid moonlight, rapidly balding with the removal of her assorted hair-pieces, her excitement breaking the porcelain maquillage and sending it running down her face in multi-colour rivulets.

As her dentures fell, hissing, into the Steradent, Emma Bovary advanced upon me, snapping at my outstretched hands with her hungry gums, and, before I could . . .

Excerpt from 'The Sanity Inspector'
Published by Robson Books Ltd.

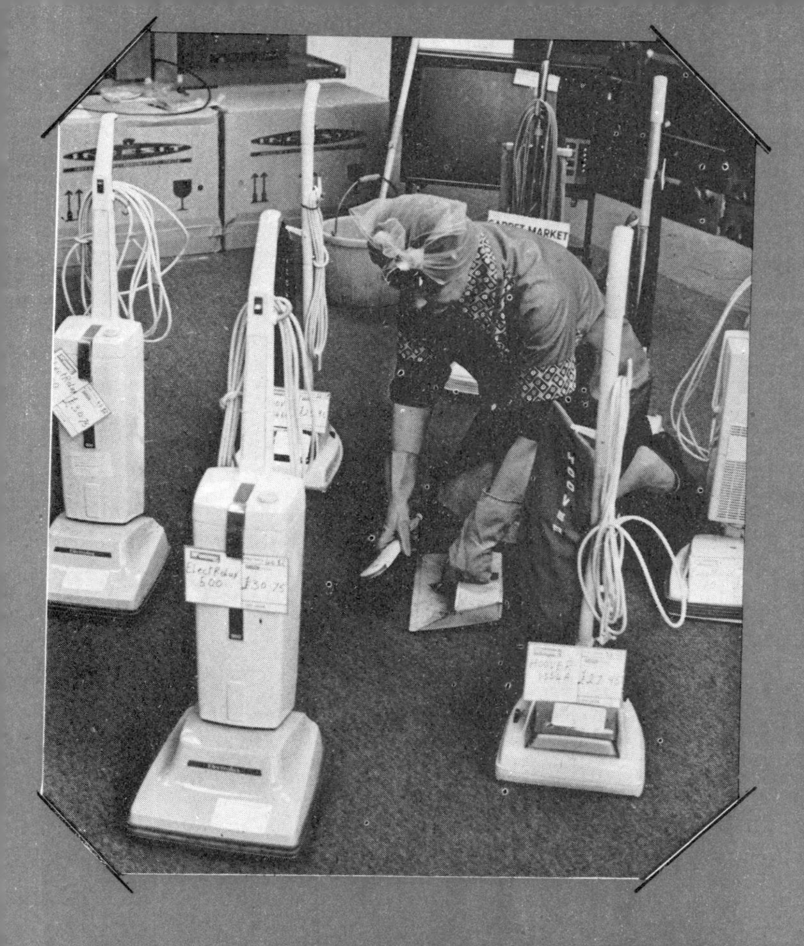

PICK OF THE PICS No. 2

From 'SMILES' by David McEnery

LEEDS: A new German play including scenes of full frontal nudity and love-making opens at Leeds Playhouse tonight. A spokesman for the theatre said: "It was not until the dress rehearsal that we realised there were nude scenes in the play."

Cambridge Evening News

A DESIRABLE HOBBY!

What little time he can spare from his succesful medical practice is spent collecting stamps and rare old *loins.*

—Bradbury (S.C.) Shoppers Guide
(A real crotchety type!)

Renewal notices for thr books from Lincoln City li rary have come from the Sauc Arabian desert, where Mr. Ro nald Paing, a local schooltea- cher, inadvertantly took them on a nine months' stay in Mubbaraz. The books were tre- atises on central heating.

The Guardian

Michael Miles (46) quizmaster of ITV's "Take your Pick," who col- lapsed during rehearsals at Wembley TV studios, Middlesex, on Wednes- day night, was stated yesterday to be resting.

He lives in a corrugated iron shack with his wife, three children, a blind mother, and three brothers. He can't read and can write very little. Yet he's one of the world's top golfers.

The story of his background and an illustrated description of his swing are in tonight's "Evening Telegraph."

Dundee Courier and Advertiser

Flight of Fancy

Forty-year-old Mr. Searl, father of six, says his group could produce a full-size saucer wh- ich could reach the Moon in two seconds. All they need is £12,000,000 and a bit of offi- cial encouragement.

Sunday Mirror

Goldfish is saved from drowning

An R.S.P.C.A. inspector tonight commended Mr. Peter Humphrey, aged 55, for saving a goldfish from drowning, and a full repor of the rescue is to be sent t R.S.P.C.A. headquarters for co sideration by the awards com ittee.

The Daily Blooper

At the instance of the veterinary service of the Dordogne all the wild rabbits are to be vaccinated against myxamotosis. If they do not report at the office of the Department Federation of Hunters the local authoraties are requested to capture them at their war- rens by using ferrets.

Eclaireur du Gâtinais

CENTRAL CHANCERY OF THE ORDERS OF KNIGHTHOOD

St James's Palace, London S.W.1.

The Queen has been graciously pleased to award the **Royal Victorian Medal** (Silver) to the undermentioned: Yeoman Bed Goer Arthur Adams, Her Majesty's Bodyguard of the Yeomen of the Guard.

Better than sex

Sir,—I am not a Welsh tea- cher, but love my country and my language very dearly.

Learning Welsh at school did me no harm, as I received eq- ual marks in both languages. Welsh and English (Full mar- ks).

I think that Welsh is far more pleasant and useful than sex, of which people seem to get so much of these days.

J. Jon

Caergybi,
Sir Fon.

Liverpool Daily P

7.25 The Saint

Girls! Have you ever wondered what *Roger Moore's* legs look like? Now is your chance, for in this episode he wears the kilt! And that is not the only thing to watch for.

T.V. Times

Pair of Pidgins

Recently it was announced that an English cou had adopted Chinese twins aged nine months. M husband says that when the children start talking they will speak Chinese. I say they will speak English. Do you agree?

Letter in Daily Mirror

Tipp Off

The thief also made off with two packets of 20 Peter Styvesant cigarettes. These cigarettes are very long, with double filters, and anyone who notices them being smoked, or saw anything suspicious in Green Lane, is asked to contact Henley CID.

Henley Standard

FUNNY CONFUSING

Nineteen-year-old Texan Roger Martinez set a world record by swallowing 225 live goldfish in 42 minutes in a San Antonio contest. His prize: a free fish dinner.

Sun

Extracts from "Funny Ha Ha & Funny Peculiar" compiled By Denys Parsons, Published by Pan Books.

The best things in life may be free, but it takes money to enjoy them in comfort (an old saying I just made up) – and of what is it truer than of romance. It's a pity that such a lot of tosh and mush gets said, sung, painted, written about what is so stark and simple that it's breathtaking, and so ruthlessly pursued that it's frightening. However, women, being far more basic, seem able to get on with the preliminaries with a lot less fuss than men – and write more pungently about it.

First – before, like the Mounties, you get your man – it's wise to know him *and* his taking little ways.

JILLY COOPER HAS DONE A SURVEY. . . .

DOCTORS

Very easy to get at. Anyone can pretend to have a migraine or pains in the chest. But the Hippocratic oath stops doctors doing anything about it, unless you meet them at a cocktail party or down in the shopping centre. I think most women imagine that because doctors know so much about the female body, they'll be better at making love to it. I should hate to have it off with a doctor in case he found some bump or cavity he shouldn't.

ACTORS

Actors, unlike farmers, get up very late, and go to bed after midnight, unless they are getting up at the crack of dawn to play in some film. As a race, they're inclined to be surprisingly insecure, self-obsessed, only interested in talking shop, and finding out whether Quentin was perfectly frightful at Bristol.

Actors like to make love in front of a looking glass so they can admire their own performance, or with the television on, so they can see how 'perfectly frightfully' all their friends are acting. If they keep their socks on, they're either a blue movie star or terrified of getting foot rot.

On the credit side, they are marvellous at playing out one's fantasies, whether you want them to dress up as a sadistic schoolmaster, a vicar, or a gentleman farmer.

THE SERVICES

'I'm bi-sexual—I like Sailors and Soldiers.'

Soldiers have yelping laughs and very short hair, tend to have very shiny buttons on their blazers, and never talk about women in the mess. They have broad shoulders and narrow outlooks. They are straightforward and uncomplicated. Occasionally they pounce on the wives of junior officers, but the passes they are most interested in are forty-eight hour ones. They wear mental battle dress in bed, and fatigues afterwards.

Soldiers tend to be overridden by their wives. Behind most famous soldiers you will find a very powerful dragon who has rammed her husband up the army list as a gunner might force the charge into the breech.

MUSICIANS

Musicians dress very badly, sometimes suffer from Halle Orchestra and enjoy playing the eternal triangle. Singers however have the most marvellous breath control and can kiss for at least ten mintues without stopping. Trumpeters and any player of woodwind instruments are also very good at kissing, having such mobile lips. Violinists have very versatile left hands—I really dig that double stopping.

Conductors have superb timing: anyone who conducts a whole orchestra shouldn't have much trouble conducting an affaire.

If a man keeps boasting: 'Look no hands,' while making love to you, he's probably a concert pianist or a brain surgeon and frightened of losing his no-claim bonus.

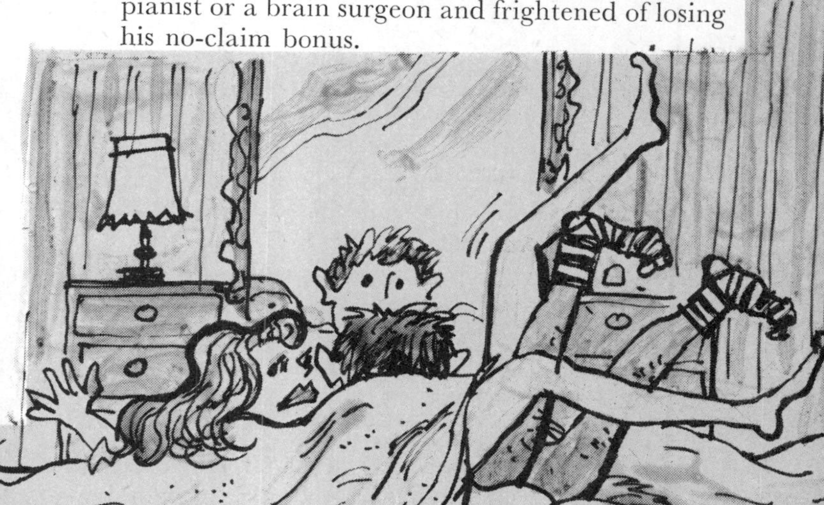

THE LEGAL PROFESSION

Most women, being irrational, will be driven up the wall by the pedantic exactitude of the legal mind. Occasionally a lawyer sends you a legal document covered in kisses, and you really think you're getting somewhere until he tells you he only wants you to sign your name, in three places. And his indecent proposal will be couched in such convoluted jargon, you won't have a hope of defending your honour against him. He will overrule all your objections.

On the whole, barristers are more interested in their briefs than yours. They tend to be pompous and divide you mentally into twelve good men and true when they talk to you. They also put their upper lips in rollers every night, so they can sneer better at their opponents.

ADVERTISING MEN

Most of their time is spent making presentations or discussing whether they should insert their eight-inch single column more than three times a week. They dress very well, if somewhat uniformly – navy blue suit, pink shirt – and are generally doused in free sample scent. When you meet them at parties, they say: 'Actually I'm in advertising,' in a very apologetic way, because *au fond* they feel they ought to get out and do something worthwhile like writing unprofitably, or painting unsellably. Nearly all of them have unsold novels in their bottom drawers and most of them live in Fulham. They have hearts with natural breaks in them.

They wear scarves, berets, long macintoshes, galoshes and often work for the White Fish Authority. They always wash apples before they eat them and suffer from hypochondria. When they say they have relations all the time, they don't mean sexual ones, only that they live at home with their mother and sisters.

They have hot milk with skin on it before they go to bed, and read the Lesson on Sunday. People often say they need the love of a good woman, but what they need is the love of a really bad woman to get them off the hook.

They wear camel-hair dressing gowns and grey striped pyjamas. Penalty for pulling the cord is disillusionment.

BACHELORS

Bachelors begin at thirty-six. Up till this age they are regarded as single men. Most of them are very tidy, smell of mothballs, and have an obsessional old maid's fix about one of their ashtrays being moved an inch to the right. Because they are not married, or living with a woman, they don't feel the need to bath very often. Occasionally they have a shower after cricket and pinch their married friends' towels. They can be recognised by their white underpants. (Married men have pale blue or pink-streaked underpants, because one of their wife's scarves has run in the washing machine.)

Bachelors spend a great deal of time sponging off their married friends, turning up for lunch on Sunday and not leaving until the Epilogue, and knocking their disgusting pipes out on the carpet so that they get a chance to look up the wife's skirt when she bends over to sweep up the mess.

They also get wildly irritated by their friends' children, cast venomous glances at a two-year-old, and say: 'Isn't it time he went to prep school?'

A married man often rings up his bachelor friend and after a lot of humming and hawing asks if he can borrow the flat to 'change in' that afternoon. When the bachelor gets home in the evening, he often finds various bits of female underclothing, and his bed has been far more tidily made than he left it that morning.

More home thoughts from a broad:

It must be difficult being a man. If you pounce too soon everyone calls you a wolf, if you hold off too long everyone calls you a queer. If you make a pass of Khyber-like proportions at a girl who fancies you, she'll say you're wonderfully passionate, if you do exactly the same to a girl who doesn't, she'll complain you're mauling her.

I have also been reading *The Sensuous Man*, which encourages men who want to meet women to hunt them out in the supermarket. Instead of pinching a pretty woman's bottom, a man pinches her trolley 'by mistake' and whisks it down to the check counter. When she rushes shrieking after him, he offers to pay for her groceries, and this way strikes up a friendship. So next time you're in the supermarket, and you see a man lurking, throw a few jars of caviare and peaches in brandy into your wire basket.

Another method the book recommends is for the man to bump into a girl in the High Street and send her parcels flying. He then picks them up, gets into conversation, and offers to buy her a drink to make up for any bruises or breakages he may have inflicted (This ploy can, presumably, only be used in licensing hours.) It strikes me as being rather extreme—one has visions of the pavements of Oxford Street getting as bad as the M1 in a fog. Perhaps they'll install a Pederasts Crossing for men who don't want to get caught up in the rough and tumble.

GOLFERS

If you go out with a man who plays golf, your biggest problem will be not to laugh the first time you see him in action. Once they get on the course, the most sober, steadfast and demure individuals suddenly blossom out like court jesters, in the most brilliant colours and fashions – lemon-yellow caps, pale-blue anoraks, cherry-pink trousers. And when they wiggle their feet to get their stance right they look exactly like cats preparing to pee.

Their language is even more colourful. My uncle had a house near the fourth tee in Yorkshire, and all his children had to wear ear plugs.

In the club house afterwards they will suddenly start kissing your hand, downing gins and tons, asking you what's your poison and saying haw, haw, haw all the time.

Golfers never have one night stands – they hole in one.

RUGGER MEN

Here comes Thunderthighs.

Rugger can be the most romantic game in the world—who could resist Gareth Edwards? It can also be the most boring, if you're watching on the touchline in the icy cold and it's Harlequins 42, H.A.C. nil.

After the game, having covered themselves with mud and glory, rugger players spend hours and hours in the bath, and then expect you to talk to other rugger wives while they down pint after pint of beer. Occasionally in the back of a car, they will make a forward pass at you.

If you marry a rugger player, you won't get sex on Friday night in case you put his eye out, all the towels will disappear, and by the end of the season his suitcase of kit no longer needs carrying, it walks by itself.

Rugger players love orgies, because they remind them of the scrum.

Excerpts from 'Super Men, Super Women
Published by Methuen & Co.

'Sex isn't the best thing in the world, or the worst thing in the world, but there's nothing else quite like it.'
W. C. FIELDS

"The best oral contraceptive is' later, dear!"

The next move is the first date – which can be as sticky as its name suggests – but which has to be got through before the next stage is reached: According to our authority (Jilly Cooper, again) on the first date, most men take you to a restaurant – or a pub:

Superman gives you plenty to drink, doesn't translate the menu from French for you, or spend so much time chatting up the *patron* and asking the waiters about their mothers that he's got no time for you.

'*Darling, I'm so hungry I could eat you.*'

He also arranges for you to sit side by side on a bench seat at a decent distance from other people so that he can brush your hand with his occasionally, or even put a hand on your thigh when he's making a telling point.

'I definitely think Arsenal' (playful pummel) 'are going to win the cup.'

On a bench seat too, it's much easier to make eyes at other people if you get bored.

If you sit at a table opposite a man, you miss half his sweet nothings, you've got nowhere to look if there's a lapse in the conversation, and you're quite likely to waste the whole meal playing footy footy with a table leg.

Another point to remember is that if your dinner-date chooses what he's going to eat with infinite care, then eats all three courses, he's not really keen on you. It's those untouched plates of food that indicate a grand passion.

Meanness of course is a great turn-off. Those men who say: 'I thoroughly recommend the grape-fruit, they sugar it awfully well here, and why not have a pasta for a main course?' afterwards expect you to pay for your dinner horizontally. The same type always fails to conceal that he's keeping the bill afterwards, and if he takes you to a party first, encourages you to fill up on the canapes so you'll only need a very plain omelette later.

24. 'L'Absinthe,' 1876. Paris, Louvre (Jeu de Paume)

Sexual Norm usually takes girls to his pub on the first date, because it's cheap, because his friends will be impressed if they see him with a girl, because there's someone else to talk to if he runs out of conversation. And he knows where the Gents is.

Invariably too your date drinks pints of beer, when you have a gin and tonic, and as you finish long before he does, if you're polite you hide your glass, or if you're like me, you rattle your ice or ostentatiously eat your lemon peel to encourage him to buy you another.

Pubs however are infinitely sexier than Indian restaurants: nothing could be less turning on than flocked wallpaper, bright lights, glasses of warm light ale, a meat vindaloo-flavoured kiss afterwards, and onions, which recur through the night.

Men and their machines:

SAILING is absolutely terrifying. You arrive for the weekend all dressed up in brand-new old clothes with your hair just done, and as soon as you set sail a dirty great wave rolls up and absolutely drenches you. Next moment, the sail is lying on the water, and the darling amiable man who asked you on the boat has turned into Captain Bligh and is yelling blue murder at you. Something about going aft. The nicest men become absolute monsters once they get a bit of string between their hands. Most of your weekend will be spent in the hold, cooking meals which everyone throws up.

The amazing thing about sailing is that although by day the men bellow at you and can't tell the girls from the buoys, at night everything changes. The boat is moored, the whisky comes out and they're all ready to seek out your Jolly Erogenous zones and play deck coitus. If there is another couple aboard, you are bound to have changed partners before the weekend is out, for there is something about lack of space, appallingly uncomfortable beds, and seasickness, that makes people incredibly randy.

CARS are a complete sex substitute. Why else do men refer to the beastly things as 'she'? Let a carman into you life, and you will be woken every morning by the squeak of chamois leather, or be stood up on a date because he's 'moving cars' this weekend. Carmen howl round the shopping centre effing and blinding at every traffic light, wear awful gloves with holes in the back, rush up to anything with a strap round its bonnet and pat it as though it had just won the Grand National, and are so used to lying underneath cars that they always take the underneath position when making love to you, and then complain your big end's gone. Beforehand they wind you up with a starting handle.

On the coldest day in winter, they put woolly hats with pom-poms on, and drive you for hours with the hood down to blow the cobwebs and your wig and everything else away.

BEFORE—

Superman books a room at the Ritz and launches the girl into a sea of vice with a bottle of champagne, ordering smoked salmon in the interval. He believes in mixing pleasure with pleasure.

I've often wondered why smoked salmon is so erotic. Perhaps because it reminds one of rather warm bare flesh.

Some women with marvellous figures like to be undressed before they leap into bed. And for this reason boys ought to take a course in undoing bras

at prep-school. But with most people it's a race to get undressed and into bed before the other person has time to see their stretch marks or spindly calves.

Bachelors sometimes take their clothes off and fold them up in polythene bags. Older hippies get undressed in another room, so they can remove their corsets in private and return with a swish of terry towelling.

Adulterers look in the cupboard or under the bed. Superman takes the telephone off the hook. He also has a fire extinguisher on the wall in case the girl bursts into flames.

Once in bed both parties breathe deeply and say 'A-a-a-ah' several times. This is usually construed as ecstasy, but is in reality because of the coldness of the sheets and other people's hands.

People always try harder with new people. Sexual Norm will spend the next ten minutes worrying whether he's giving the girl enough sexual foreplay or fiveplay, and then grimly thinking about cricket or football to keep his mind off sex. He occasionally says '*Howzat*'.

The girl, remembering what the sex books told her about not lying back and being passive, will be frenziedly stroking Norm's neck, tickling his toes, kissing his navel, and putting on such a display of acrobatics that he has to try and think even harder about cricket or football.

—AND AFTER

Afterwards lovers are supposed to have baths together, which I've always thought was an overrated pastime, particularly if you sit at the wrong end and have the taps digging into your back, with one side scalded and the other one frozen.

Excerpts from 'Super Men, Super Women
Published by Methuen & Co.

NO HONESTLY

by CHARLOTTE BINGHAM

Clever Drawers thought it would be lovely to have a baby, and so did I. We both imagined this gorgeous gurgling creature chuckling in a high chair just like on the advertisements. Well that was all right – until I started being sick.

The trouble was that no one had told us people didn't feel well when they were having babies. As far as we knew they came home with mystical looks on their faces and started knitting things, and then when Cary Grant or Spencer Tracy came through the door they stopped them in their tracks with 'darling, I've got something to tell you . . .'

After that I would spend nine months looking serene and knitting in a rocking chair – not being sick and getting spots – which is actually what happened.

Clever Drawers was just as confused as me about the whole thing, and he's been to University so he's no slouch, if you know what I mean. Although at the time I was dreaming through double Latin he was cutting out pictures of Cyd Charisse's legs – nevertheless even he thought people said 'darling I've got something to tell you . . .'

Of course we were pretty banjaxed by the whole business – particularly the spots. The thing is all my life, through fat and thin, short and squat – I've been able to say 'well at least I've never had spots', and now here I was getting fatter by the minute and covered in spots. No serene and shining skin glowing with the knowledge that I was fulfilling my Greatest Role. No evidence that I had become part of the miracle of life, only hours spent with my head bent over the basin, and skin like a currant bun.

I never realized that having a baby meant you had to go to hospital. I thought you just knitted and knitted, and on the day the doctor told you – it arrived – not exactly by stork – but nearly.

I'd never been inside a hospital before. My knees knocked like there was no tomorrow, and just telling the nurse my name and address seemed like joining the Foreign Legion. Just for a few minutes I thought I didn't want to have a baby after all – it suddenly didn't seem as easy as buying a dog. Then I realized that that was the worst thing about having a baby – you can't change your mind. I mean it's not like a holiday to the Costa Brava – you can't just cancel it and pay a booking charge. I said this to the nurse, but she kept on saying 'where's your specimen?' as if anyone who is anyone always walks about with specimens in their handbags. Nurses can be pretty funny like that.

Still after a bit I stopped being sick, and got quite cheery. I was bursting out of everything so Clever Drawers took me off on a tour of the Maternity Shops. He was extraordinary really. He insisted on coming into the

changing room with me – although it was a dreadful squash – and then kept on charging in and out talking about 'room for growth', as if he'd given birth to nineteen children, and brought them all up by hand himself.

It wasn't enough for him to stick to the dress section either. In the space of about one minute he became an expert on maternity girdles, elastic stockings, and nursing bras. He kept leaping in and out of the cubicle with his hands full, and the assistant kept on saying how nice it was to find a young man who took such an Interest. To which old Clever Drawers would reply 'I think men Should' as he narrowed his eyes and muttered 'room for growth' for the hundredth time.

In the end he kitted me out with enough dresses, and bras and girdles to see me through three pregnancies. It was no use telling him the elastic stockings were for varicose veins – he just muttered 'well you never know' and looked hopefully at my legs.

All the way home on the underground he kept shouting 'look' as someone got in with a baby. But that was nothing compared to the way his eyes would fill with tears when the Heinz baby started gurgling on television, and he would pace up and down the room shouting 'I can't believe it', in between scrutinizing Dr Spock as if it was the Good Food Guide.

I kept on bursting into tears too. I would sit in the kitchen for hours on end with tea towels on my head sobbing about how awful everything was, and then I'd rush out and buy a doughnut and eat it before Clever Drawers came home, because he was very strict about diet – and rubbing yourself with oil – and going to Class.

The first thing you notice when you go into a room full of pregnant women is everyone looking around at everyone else thinking 'How Did *She* Get Pregnant' and 'How Awful To Be *That* Shape.'

Actually you don't quite understand what nature can do to you until you're in a whole room full of pregnancies. I mean some people carry babies round about their knees, some under their chins, and others look as if someone's pinned some washing on their fronts, and they don't have anything to do with what's attached to them.

So anyway, for the first class everyone arrived with tights and jumpers – except me – because I'd left my jumper on the bus. I don't know why, I have this knack of starting off on the wrong foot. My very first school I was the only one without a velvet beret, and everyone called me 'poshy'. Another thing – there's something about my face that makes people want to make a demonstration out of me.

I went redder and redder as the teacher said for the fifteenth time 'don't you know where your knees are? I said bend your knees – not flap your hands' and all the others laughed into their knitting wool. And then the teacher looked round the room and said in that dead tired voice – 'is there anyone who knows where their knees are?' And I had to go and sit down against the wall knowing that everyone else knew that I didn't even know where my *knees* were for heaven's sake. You can hear them thinking 'if she doesn't know where her knees are – how on earth's she going to Cope?' Question mark, question mark.

The next thing we had to do was lie about she floor and relax. The principal of this being that when the time comes to give birth you will be all happy and lovely and not yelling your head-off and biting your teeth on a strap like you've always understood from the movies. Anyway what happens is that you stiffen your arm or your leg and that is a pretend pain, and then you make the rest of you relaxed and you puff and blow to a smaller or a greater degree according to how much pain you're meant to be having, if you know what I mean.

It's not as easy as it sounds, particularly if you're the sort of person who doesn't know where their knees are, and tends to stiffen their breath and relax their arm. The teacher kept on coming round to me and saying 'I can see I'll have to do a lot of work on you', which makes you feel far from better.

Things didn't improve when she got out the Birth Atlas, and I kept looking away, and she kept saying 'I suppose you know all about the placenta? I mean I suppose we have nothing to teach you?' Which are the sort of questions that make 'yes' and 'no' the wrong answer – so you say 'blurp' instead, and everyone else stares at the wrinkles on their tights, or looks keenly at the picture of the placenta to prove how different they are from you.

If you don't like thinking about parts of the body, you are not ideal material for having babies. You can't explain that to teachers and people, because they think everything to do with the body is wonderful. And if you said 'I think the placenta looks revolting' they'd immediately go into the 'do you realize how lucky you are to have one?' line of thinking.

Anyway all the way home on the bus I kept practising stiffening my arm and straightening my leg and doing my breathing, which succeeded in emptying the top deck quicker than anything you've ever seen, so much so that whenever Clever Drawers wanted a seat on the underground afterwards he'd just say 'quick do your breathing' and in a second we'd have a carriage to ourselves. I don't know why, but there's something about a pregnant woman stiffening her arm which puts people off.

Actually the best way to keep cheerful when you're having a baby is never to look at yourself sideways. This is the crux of the matter. If you can get through nine months without ever looking sideways you will keep smiling. It's much easier to say than to do – especially when you're trotting along the road and there's a breeze blowing and you catch sight of yourself in a shop window, you can suddenly feel very distressed. Just for a moment it doesn't seem possible for anyone to be that shape and Human.

And it's no good people telling you that in Italy you would be treated like a sacred cow, that doesn't help one bit, because in England you are treated like the noun – without the adjective. I mean to be openly pregnant in public is an offence. It's as if no one else has been born that way, or that you are some sort of freak. People in shops make remarks, and stare at your hand to see if you've got a nice gold band on. Old ladies are the worst. They can't wait to slam swing doors on your stomach and bash you with their handbags, because to them you are a blatant example of someone who's had sex and Doesn't Mind Who Knows It. Exclamation mark, exclamation mark.

There is nothing worse when you are about to give birth than going to see someone who just has. By the time they've finished removing the nappies from your cup of tea you feel like running out and throwing yourself under a tree.

They always look at you with their heads on one side as if they've been midwives for twenty years, instead of just having given birth to one measly infant, and say things like 'have they X-rayed for twins?' Or 'have you *always* been that shape?' And then with relish they tell you all about how the worst bit is the Injection, or 'I do hope you don't have to be induced' and they talk about 'the drip' as if it was the rack. Then to prove how awful being a mother is they let bits of Marmite fingers drop out of their mouths while they're talking, and undo their bandages to show you their varicose veins.

Clever Drawers used to sit up all night with me as we promised ourselves that we would never become like Them. We wouldn't ever let nappies spill out of the bucket, or leave potties to perfume the hall, or kiss babies' bottoms, or breast feed during dinner parties. The thought of being reduced to talking about Dr Spock and gripe water haunted us, and we spent hours hovering outside Woolworths peering into prams in an effort to harden ourselves to just how ugly babies could be.

Sometimes Clever Drawers would pretend that he wasn't really afraid of Becoming Like Them. 'I know hundreds of people who've had babies who are still all right,' he'd say grandly, but that's as far as he ever got because he could never ever remember who they were, and would end up saying hopelessly 'well, we don't *have* to get like other people.'

Mind you there wasn't much risk of that in some ways. Particularly not with my memory. I know it doesn't sound like it, but not having a memory can be a grave handicap, particularly when you're Expecting. If it's not this it's that, and no sooner have you finished rubbing oil over you than you have to go to class, and as soon as you've finished class you have to go to hospital. One day I forgot my specimen jar so I took it along in an old Miss Dior bottle, and the nurse nearly fainted because when she stuck the piece of paper in it turned green.

Then we both went and forgot what day it was meant to be born. I don't know what it was, I think we were both hoping the other person would remember, but when we woke up one morning – it was suddenly due tomorrow.

And then tomorrow was today, and Clever Drawers was marching up and down and saying 'well?' every five minutes, and if I let out a breath in order to get an intake of oxygen he'd shout 'relax, relax, remember what you've been taught,' and then when nothing happened he kept making helpful suggestions like 'how about a nice cold beer and a hot bath?' Or 'I told you if you packed your suitcase it wouldn't arrive' – as if babies were out to spite you from the start.

Even when I went to the hospital they did nothing to cheer me up. 'What – you still here?' they kept saying as if I was holding up the National Health on purpose. I've never felt such a failure in my life, not even when I failed Grade One Music three times.

When I got home I put a tea towel on my head, until Clever Drawers came up with one of his Ideas. Since, he said, I had been so Foolish as to pack my suitcase and obviously Baby had taken note of this, we would now outwit Baby by giving a non-stop party so that Baby would be fooled into thinking we didn't expect it – because Babies were probably like casting directors – they only wanted you if you were too busy to care.

That sounded a good wheeze, and since Clever Drawers had a craze on playing racing cars – we gave a racing car party. Racing car parties mean that everyone lies on the floor and swears at each other. This was a little more difficult for me than it was for everyone else, so I was shoved into a chair and told to chart the laps. Being a lap counter means that instead of just your own team, everyone in the room swears at you.

Not too many races had gone when I realized this was It. This was what it was all about. This was what all the classes had been for, about, to, or from, so I started to puff and blow just like I'd been taught – the only trouble was that no one had taught me how to puff and blow, and count the laps, so I kept on miscounting between puffs, and everyone kept shouting and Clever Drawers kept saying 'do stop panting and COUNT'.

Once or twice I said to anyone I thought was listening 'I'm in labour you know' – but no one noticed that my bump had slipped down to where my knees used to me. Only when we retired to the pub in the evening and all the little Irish girls behind the bar started to cross themselves and murmur 'there's going to be a miracle in Finch's' did anyone believe me, and then they all kept shouting 'you shouldn't be here' and snatching my drink away, which was a lot of use.

In the end they all came with us to the hospital, principally because it was closing time. Then they all went home again leaving me to watch television with the nurse who kept saying '*which* one was the father did you say?'

After a few hours I was being pushed down the corridor to the labour ward, and Clever Drawers and company were following on in their white coats and masks, and Sister was saying 'I really must insist that only *you* come in, Mr Danby – this isn't a pyjama party you know', and the ward doors closed to shouts of 'five to two it's a girl'.

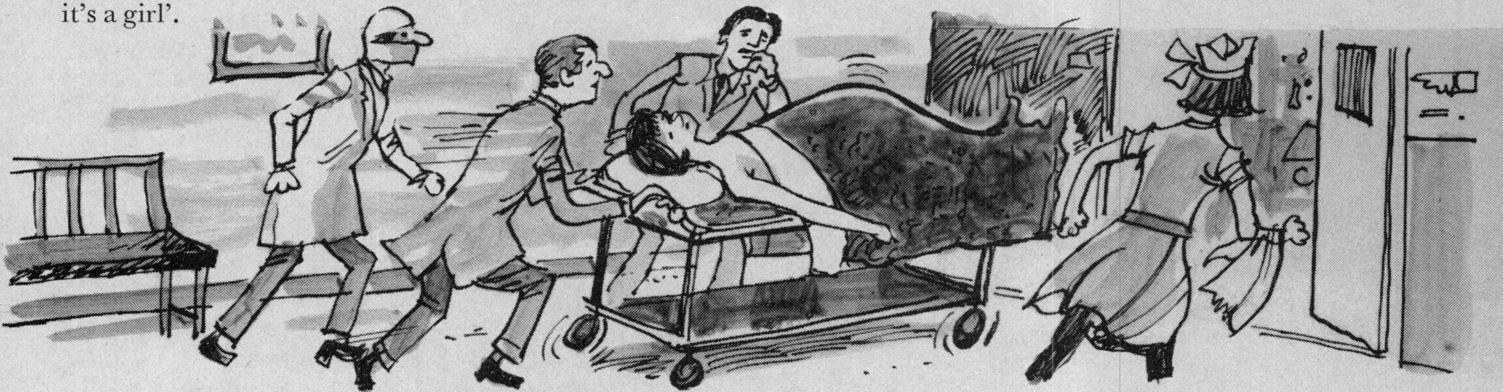

Clever Drawers said to the anaesthetist 'I'll give you three to one because I like your eyes'.

Then the next bit was a little boring. Just me puffing and blowing, and Clever Drawers muttering to the nurse 'do you come here often?' in his best Groucho Marx, and Sister saying 'if you want to *see* anything you'd better put your glasses *inside* your mask', and then suddenly Clever Drawers had hold of my hand and said 'come on pet I've got a lot of money on you', and Sister said 'there we are' and there was a cry like a shout in Spring, and everyone burst into tears because there's something about a pink and crumply face which gets you in the end. No Honestly.

Excerpt from 'Coronet among the Grass'
Published by William Heinemann Ltd.

"He's not too bright—but then I like that in a husband."

BATS IN THE BELFRY

Religion is a dicey subject at the best of times (we all know the old one about never getting into arguments over religion or politics) and its even more dicey when laughter is brought into it. It's an odd thing, really, how humour doesn't seem to have been allowed for in any religion – smiling beatifically – yes; dancing – yes; shaking – yes; singing – you bet; playing tambourine, organ, pipe – but of course; painting, sculpting, writing – yes, yes, yes. So what's so wrong with laughter? So long as its not really cruel or vicious, laughing is one of the great muscle-stretching, soul-lifting experiences in the world. And I wouldn't mind betting we've been laughing just as long as we've been worshipping – and at much the same ludicrous likeable *human* things into the bargain. So let's take a respectfully light-hearted look at various religions as seen by the already immortal Pete and Dud:

PETE & DUD on RELIGION

Excerpts from 'The Dagenham Dialogues'
by Peter Cook & Dudley Moore
Published by Methuen & Co.

PETE. I was reading the Bible the other day, you know.

DUD. It's good, isn't it?

PETE. It's a very good book, Dud, it's beautifully done, it's beautifully bound, it's beautifully put together. I was reading that chapter about Ishmail begat Remus and Remus begat Isobar and Isobar begat this other bloke.

DUD. They were certainly begetting.

PETE. Yer. Every one begat each other.

DUD. Sort of, sort of historical document thing.

PETE. Like, you know, who gave birth to who and that.

DUD. Like at Somerset House, isn't it?

PETE. George Meacham begat Daphne Meacham. Daphne Meacham begat Fred Taylor, and so on.

DUD. Course you can trace it all back to Adam and Eve.

PETE. The first two.

DUD. Yer, they were the first two. But what I don't understand, Pete, is how two people produced so many millions of different colour, kith, race and creed.

PETE. You mean how did Adam and Eve have all these children of myriad hues?

DUD. Yer.

PETE. Well, the point of that, Dud, is that Genesis isn't true in the literal sense, it's an allergy. Genesis is an allergy of *la condition humaine*, it's about the whole lot of the human race. Adam and Eve aren't just Adam and Eve, they're the whole human race personified. Do you believe in God, actually?

DUD. I tell you Pete, when I'm in a tight spot I say to myself, 'God please help me out, if You're there. If You do help me out, I'll believe in You and thank You very much. I'll know You're there for future reference.'

PETE. Yer, I have a similar attitude. Whenever I feel ill, you know, I get a dose of the flu or something, I say a little prayer. I say, 'Dear God in heaven, if You're there, heed my prayer. If You're not there, don't take any notice. But if You are, make me better by Tuesday at twelve o'clock and I'll know You've done it, and I promise to be good for ever more and believe in You.' Of course the trouble is, when you get better you don't know whether it's because God's done it or whether you would have got better in any case. There's no real way of telling what He's up to or even where He is.

DUD. No, you can't tell, can you really.

PETE. I often wish He'd manifest himself a bit more, you know, in the sky.

DUD. Yer, it'd be nice if every now and again He parted the clouds and in a golden burst of sunshine gave you a wave. 'Hello down there, you can believe in me.'

PETE. I asked the Reverend Stephens about this, and he said, 'Much as God would like to keep manifesting Himself, He daren't, you see, because it debases the currency.' He can't go round all the football matches and fetes and everything, so He limits himself to once in a million years if we're lucky.

DUD. Well, you've got to be careful about over-exposure. Course you know, actually, Pete, I wish I'd never been told about God at all 'cause it means we can't get away with nothing, doesn't it? I mean you've been told about Him, you know He's there or you think He's there, and you can't really mess about then, can you?

PETE. You can't.

DUD. No, and what about the people who haven't been told about God?

PETE. Well, I asked the Reverend Stephens this, and he said that if you haven't been told about God, Dud, you're laughing. If you don't know good from evil then you're away. You can do anything you bloody well like. There's these people in New Guinea for example. They wander about with nothing on and they commit adultery, steal, and covet their neighbour's wife, which everyone wants to do. As there are no vicars about, to tell them everything, they can't be got at, so they go up to heaven whatever they do. This means all these nig-nogs are getting up to heaven, and perfectly decent blokes like you and me, who have never even committed adultery, we can't get up there. We're being kept out by these Guineans.

DUD. You see in that case, Pete, it'd be a crime to tell people about God.

PETE. I've never told anyone about God.

DUD. I haven't told anyone, I haven't mentioned it to a soul, Pete.

PETE. St Paul's got a lot to answer for.

DUD. He started it didn't he – all those letters he wrote.

PETE. To the Ephiscans.

DUD. You know, 'Dear Ephiscans, Stop enjoying yourself, God's about the place. Signed Paul.'

PETE. You can just imagine it, can't you. There's a nice Ephiscan family settling down to a good breakfast of fried mussels and hot coffee and just sitting there. It's a lovely day outside and they're thinking of taking the children out for picnic by the sea and everything's happy and the sun's coming through the trees, birds are chirping away.

DUD. The distant cry of happy children, and clouds scudding across the sky.

PETE. In fact an idyllic scene is what you'd call it, an idyllic scene. When suddenly into the midst of it all – tap, tap, on the bloody door. You know who it is?

DUD. No.

PETE. It's a messenger bearing a letter from Paul.

DUD. Dad runs to the door to open it, thinking it may be good news.

PETE. Perhaps Grandfather's died and left them the vineyards.

DUD. They open it up and what do they discover?

PETE. 'Dear George and Dierdre and Family, Stop having a good time, resign yourself to not having a picnic, cover yourself with ashes and start flaying yourselves, until further notice, Signed Paul.'

DUD. A dreadful sort of letter to get, isn't it?

PETE. Terrible.

DUD. Course, you know, actually I'm fascinated by those religions which say you come back in a different form.

PETE. Reincarnation.

DUD. Reincarnation.

PETE. Yer. Buddhists believe in that, coming back as a different creature of some kind or other.

DUD. What would *you* come back as?

PETE. Well, I think if I had a choice, I'd probably come back as a royal corgi and go sniffing about the Palace, you know.

DUD. That's very good, actually, improve your station.

PETE. Course you could come back as something terrible, couldn't you.

DUD. Well, suppose you came back as a humble mayfly.

PETE. Well, of course you'd only live for six hours wouldn't you. They have a very futile life, them mayflies, they only live six hours. As soon as they're born, they're worried about old age. By the time they're three hours old they're really middle aged, they can't run for buses like they used to. They got grey hairs all over their legs, and in another three hours they're gaga and they die.

DUD. Terrible business.

PETE. You know Mr Thomas.

DUD. Yer.

PETE. Next door.

DUD. Yer.

PETE. He's a Buddhist.

DUD. He's not.

PETE. Yer, he's a Buddhist.

DUD. Is he really?

PETE. Yer, he's a Buddhist. He's got this bluebottle in the bathroom. He thinks it's Keats. He thinks it's the poet Keats reincarnated, so he keeps going into the bathroom, takes it in marshmallows and marmalade. The bluebottle's getting very fat, terrible great thing. He puts out bits of paper, hoping he'll complete some poems. He's just got a lot of bluebottle droppings so far. He still frames them, though.

DUD. They'd probably mean something to another bluebottle.

PETE. Well, true bluebottles would understand it wouldn't they.

DUD. Course actually I'd like to come back as a

sparrow so I could see down ladies' blouses.

PETE. There wouldn't be much point in that, Dud. If you came back as a sparrow, you wouldn't want to look down ladies' blouses.

DUD. No, you'd just want to look down sparrows' blouses.

PETE. You'd be interested in them – as a sparrow. If I had my choice I'd like to come back as Grace Kelly.

DUD. Why's that?

PETE. I've always wanted to know what she looks like in the bath. I've always been fascinated by her glacial beauty.

DUD. Course, actually, you know, Pete, in the end, it's a bit of a toss-up as to which religion is right, isn't it? You can't actually know which religion is right.

PETE. No, you can't tell. There are millions of religions. It might be Buddhism, it might be Christianity.

DUD. You don't know what to go for, do you, actually?

PETE. No, you might be a perfectly good Buddhist all your life, get up to heaven and there will be the Reverend Stephens saying, 'Get out, ha, ha, ha, Buddhism is wrong. We're right! Buddha off!'

DUD. Alternatively you might be a very good Christian, Church of England, behave yourself very nicely, get up there and there's Buddha –

PETE. Laughing all over his face and sends you back as a worm.

DUD. I think the best thing is to remain a prognostic.

PETE. An agnostic.

DUD. Do you think God's been listening while we've been talking?

PETE. Well, if He exists, He's been listening because He's omnipresent. He's heard every word we've said.

DUD. Oh, we'd better look religious, then.

PETE. It's no good just looking religious Dud, He can see through that. You have to *be* religious. What do you *really* believe in?

DUD. I believe in having a good time. Food and kip and Joan Whittaker and that.

PETE. That's not religion, Dud. That's Hedonism. You're a Heddist.

DUD. No, I'm a Duddist. That's what I call it.

'Quick. Follow that star!'

EVERY TUESDAY 8 PM.
LET THE PEOPLE SIN
YOUR FAVOURITE HYMNS
BRIGHT & EVANGELICAL
MASSED CHOIRS
GJ.

'About time we got out some fresh posters, Captain.'

'Of course, you know, I wasn't always a celibate!'

'And which of you girls has been wearing stiletto heels?'

'And precisely which doctor ordered Brother Anthony on to this special diet during Lent?'

'. . . And stop saying "Nothing like Lent for the jolly old waistline!" '

Cartoons taken from "More Barnabus" Published by Wolfe Publishing Ltd.

PLAYING WITH WORDS

What's in a word? more than meets the eye apparently, and a lot that wasn't there to start with, too. Take puns – hundreds of years old they are – goodness knows *how* long ago the first man to get locked in somewhere yelled 'O pun the door!' – and I wouldn't mind betting the ancient Greeks did it (made puns, I mean) only it's rather difficult to tell from the peculiar way they wrote their stuff. Punning is like an infectious disease, terribly catching and liable to leave you limp and speechless. Right now there's something like an epidemic going on – with verbal games and contests happening all over the place. Take the **'ANNOUNCED AT THE BALL' WORD GAME,** which can be played straight, like this:

Mr & Mrs Out and their ailing father Peter Out.
Mr & Mrs Star and their singing father, Pop Star.
Mr & Mrs Loaf and their fresh daughter Wanda Loaf.
Mr & Mrs Dar and their cousin the scientist Ray Dar.
Mr & Mrs Coddle and their pampered daughter Molly Coddle.
Mr & Mrs Bite and their son, the leading authority on insects, Nat Bite.
Mr & Mrs Mobile and their German chauffeur Otto Mobile.
Mr and Mrs Pears and their well-preserved aunt, Tina Pears.
Mr & Mrs Russell and their son, the well-known dog trainer, Jack Russell.
Mr & Mrs Koholic and their prostrate son Al Koholic.
Mr & Mrs House and their extremely boring son T. D. House.
Mr & Mrs Bodies and their sexually liberated daughter N. E. Bodies.
Mr & Mrs Rack and their casually dressed daughter Anna Rack.
Mr & Mrs Net and their attractive daughter Mag Net.

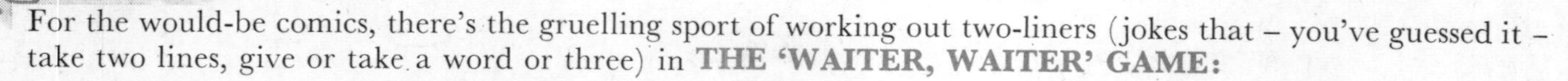

For the would-be comics, there's the gruelling sport of working out two-liners (jokes that – you've guessed it – take two lines, give or take a word or three) in **THE 'WAITER, WAITER' GAME:**

'Waiter, this coffee tastes like tea.' 'Forgive me, sir. I must have given you the hot chocolate by mistake.'

'How did you find the meat, sir?' 'I just lifted up a potato chip, and there it was.'

'Waiter, what's this fly doing in my ice cream?' 'I guess it's learning to ski.'

'Waiter, why is this fly in my soup?' 'Look, I just work here, am I supposed to know everything?'

'Waiter, your thumb's in my soup.' 'That's okay, sir, it's really not very hot.'

'Waiter, there's a fly in my soup.' 'They don't care what they eat do they, sir?'

'Waiter, there's a fly in my apple sauce.' 'Of course, sir, it's a fruit fly.'

'Waiter, there's a dead fly in my soup.' 'I know sir. It's the heat that kills them.'

The 'Worst Book Title' Game is a variation on this sort of verbal gymnastics, like so:

After the Match by Titus A. Newt

Ten Years in the Saddle by Major Bumsore

The Use of Natural Fertilizers by G. G. Dunnit

Fall from the Cliff by Eileen Dover

A Day in the Country by Bab Lyn Brook

British Productivity by General Strike

Learning Golf by T. Off

The Way to Quick Riches by Robin Banks

Playing Cricket by L. B. W. Decision

Holidays in England by A. Pauline Weather

Contagious Diseases by Willie Catchit

or maybe you prefer **THE 'TOM SWIFTLY' GAME,** where the adverb is all:

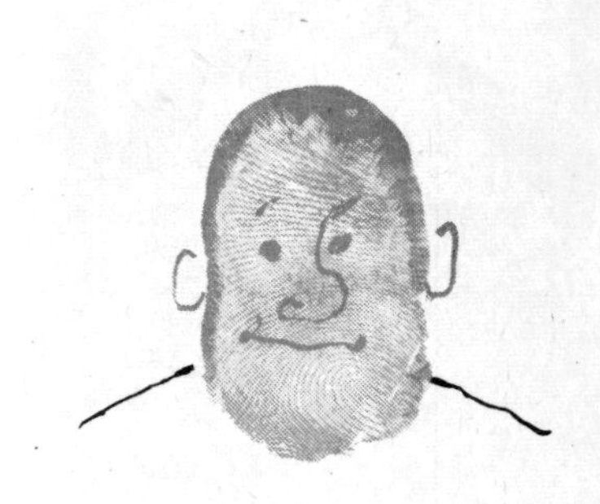

'Keep away, I've got measles,' she said rashly.

'You don't look well,' said the undertaker gravely.

'I think I've just twisted my ankle,' said the girl lamely.

'I've lost my shoes,' said the cobbler defeetedly.

'I've hidden the light bulbs,' said the electrician darkly.

'My sore throat is painful,' said the jockey hoarsely.

'I'm lost for words,' said the author speechlessly.

While for those who like epigrams, especially ones with a sting in the tail, there's **THE 'NEW STYLE PROVERB' GAME:**

He who laughs last doesn't get the joke.

Let us remember that ours is a nation of lawyers and order.

If you can't say something nice about a person, say something nasty.

Two is company, three is an orgy.

Two can live as cheaply as one, for half as long.

Money is the root of all evil and a man needs roots.

Confucius say too much!

A friend in need is a pest indeed.

He who always finds fault in his friends has faulty friends.

I disagree with what you say but will defend to the death your right to tell such lies.

Never put off 'til tomorrow what you can avoid altogether.

If, on the other hand, you're stronger on pictures than words, then DOODLES is the game for you. A Doodle is an odd looking sort of drawing that doesn't make any sense until you know the correct title. For instance, here are some classic Doodles that illustrate this point:

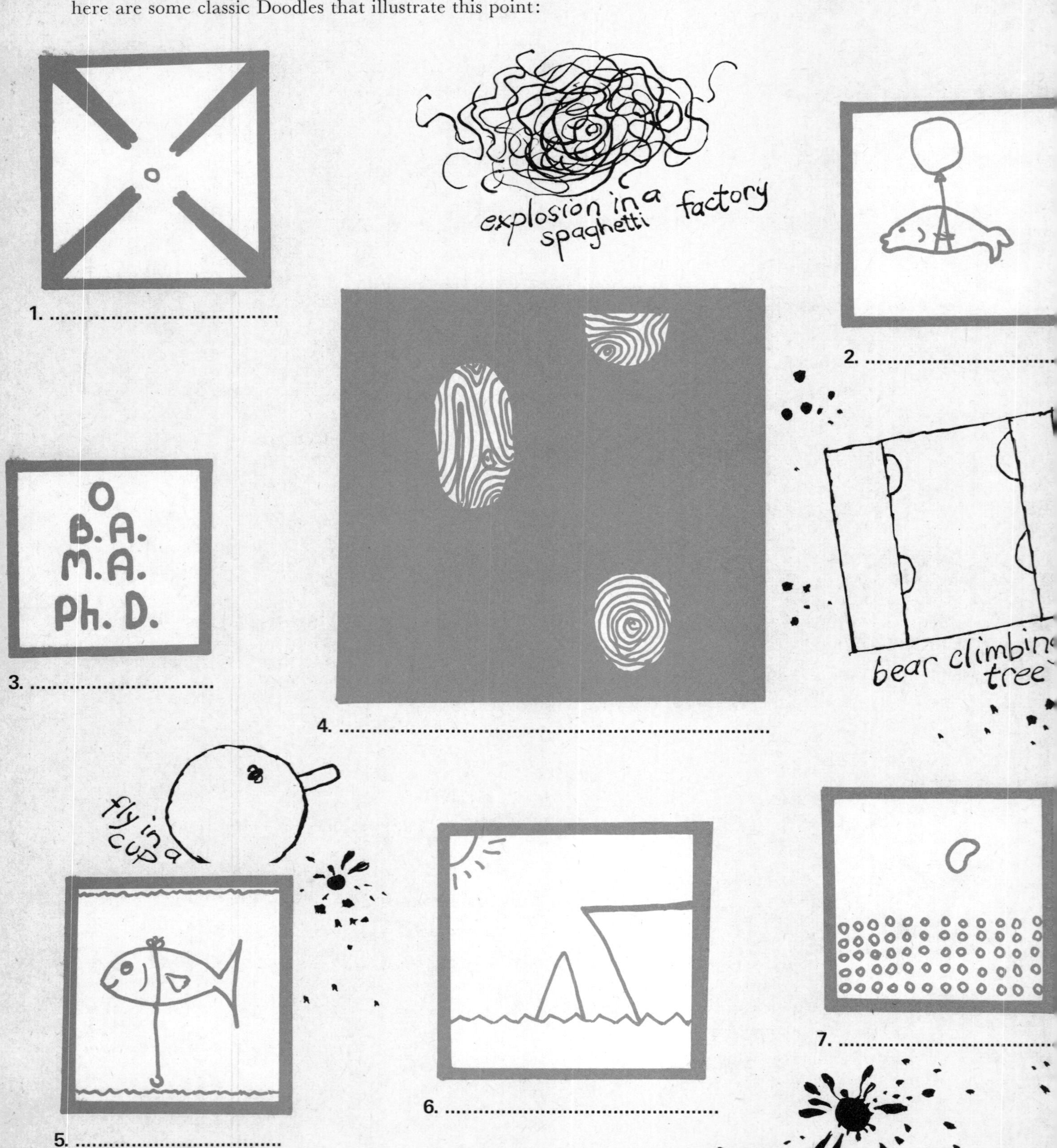

8. ....

9. ....

10. ....

woman looking
for soap in bath

11. ....

12. ....

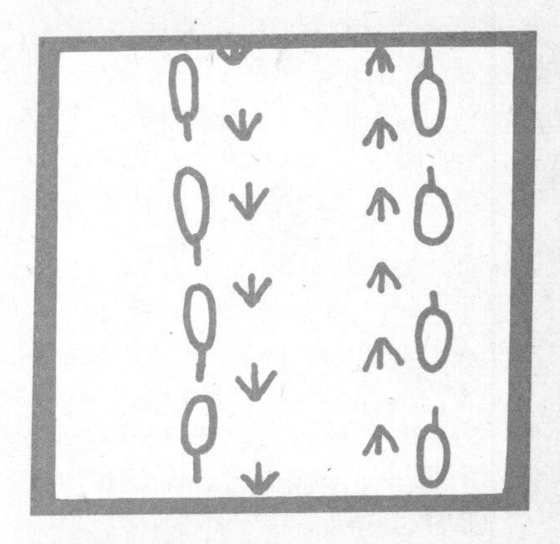

13. ....

ANSWERS

1) Four elephants examining a grapefruit.
2) A fish commiting suicide.
3) Three degrees below zero.
4) A flute player seen from the inside of the flu
5) A fish fishing.
6) A witch drowing after she's fallen overboard.
7) A bean trying to join the peas corps (U.S. Jo
8) Rats deserting ship.
9) Spider doing a handstand.
10) Sign on the dotted line.
11) Elephant stroking an ant.
12) Man getting bow tie caught in a lift.
13) Chicken with only one snow shoe.

Last, and quite definitely most, are the reigning kings of pun and fun – Frank Muir and Dennis Norden – and by them the extended pun has been elevated into an art form, exemplified in these two stories from '*Upon My Word*' the famous BBC radio game (in which, in case anyone hasn't ever heard it, these two panellists are given a well-known phrase and have to spin a story, using the phrase (or something remotely resembling it) as a punch line. Here, for instance, is a phrase Frank was handed:
'What's the good of a home if you are never in it?' (from George & Weedon Grossmith's 'The Diary of a Nobody')

Upon My Word

The other morning at breakfast time I was sitting over a cup of hot coffee when I had a terrific idea. I wasn't even trying to think at the time; I was crouched over the cup trying to steam an egg stain out of the seat of my jeans. If I had a thought in my head at the time it was never again to put a tray with a soft-boiled egg on my chair, move forwards to switch on the television, then back gently and sit down on the egg. If I had been in a thinking mood I might have reflected further on the extraordinary amount of egg there is in an egg; enough in one small oval shell to besmear a cheek and a half of jeans.

But my mind was blank, and into it floated this idea. If pressed for a comparison in the world of nature I would say that it was not at all unlike a mushroom spoor alighting on a damp flannel.

Now every writer dreams about inventing a new character to write novels about. Think how excited Ian Fleming must have been when he dreamed up James Bond, or Galsworthy when he thought of Forsyte Saga. Once a writer has his hero, his Bond or his Saga, the rest is easy; best-sellers, major motion-pictures, television serials.

My idea was a totally original character – a criminal pixie. Or, to put it another way, a bent elf.

For the next three days I put everything else aside and worked like a madman on the plot of the book; I refused all offers of food – except at meal-times, of course – and went without sleep all day, but at the end of it I had a synopsis roughed out.

There are four of them in the gang. Our hero, Norm the Gnome, is the leader. He is a criminal but we make it clear that he is not all that nasty. Nasty-ish but not revolting. He learned his bad habits when he did his National Service – two years in the National Elf Service – and has never since come to terms with society.

Norm's girl-friend is Mustard-Seed, hot stuff, still a bit green, although well past her salad-days. She earns her living as a dancer in the clubs, where she works under her professional name of 'Caustic-Soda'. She is a stripper.

The heavy is Alf the Elf, a huge muscle-bound giant – a giant, that is, up against the elves – who gets all the dirty work to do. He is well known to the police because he unthinkingly allowed himself to be photographed in the nude, rippling his muscles, for the cover of the magazine *Elf and Strength*.

The last member of the group is Puck (real name Robin Badfellow), a layabout who spends most of his time filing his nails and passing remarks. His job with the gang is to act as contact-man and drive the getaway car when they can afford to buy one.

The gang always met on Tuesday evenings because it was a bad night on the telly and one Tuesday Norm strode in very purposefully with a Master Plan.

'Right,' he said. 'From tonight this gang stops being cat burglars. We've had a good year burgling cats but the market for hot cat-collars even with a bell attached, is satiated. We're going into the big time.'

Consternation, as you might well imagine, reigned. The pros and cons were discussed with some heat, but Norm was adamant.

'I'm going to be Mr Big,' he said. 'Caesar of the Undergrowth. Drive round in an Elfa-Romeo. Take Mustard-Seed to the South of France, first-class on the Cross-Channel Fairy. So here's what we're gonna do. Next Saturday evening, after the Western on telly, we're going to rob a bank!'

'I know a bank whereon the wild thyme blows,' said Puck, combing his hair with a thistle.

'That's the one we're going to do!' said Norm.

'I can't manage Saturday,' said Puck. 'I'll be in the middle of an ice hockey match.'

'Then Mustard-Seed can be look-out,' said Norm. 'We're going to nick all the thyme from that bank and then take it to a fence.'

'Which fence?'

'The one at the bottom of my garden. We'll pin it out on the fence to dry, then put it into packets marked "Dried Herbs" and flog it to Health Food addicts up the Goblin Market. There's a fortune in it.'

'Hey boss,' said Alf the Elf, to everybody's surprise as he didn't go in much for talking. 'We'll get caught. That bank's floodlit!'

Norm silenced him with a look 'We are going to tunnel!' he announced. 'I have recruited Mo the Mole and Harry Hedgehog for the job. We are going to go in underneath the plants and pull them up – *downwards*!'

Everything seemed to be going according to plan on the night. Mo the Mole burrowed a rough tunnel, then Harry the Hedgehog went in and scraped the tunnel smooth with his quills. The roots of the thyme dangled down. Norm dragged the thyme down by its roots and passed it to Alf, who staggered down the tunnel and deposited it in piles outside. And then something went wrong. Alf had disappeared with the last load when Norm had a gnomish feeling that all was not well. He ran down the tunnel to the entrance – and it was blocked. He was trapped by a large clod of turf, which had been rolled over the entrance.

'Somebody has grassed on me!' he groaned. and sat down to wait for the police.

The story ends with Norm the Gnome staring through his prison bars, while Mustard-Seed dances cheek to cheek with Puck in some thieves' hangout, humming to herself, 'Thyme on my hands, you in my arms. . . .'

I really thought I had a winner in Norm, the delinquent Gnome. Original, dramatic, suitable for all age-groups. But I was wrong. He is useless to me, as I found out when I telephoned a publisher.

I telephoned the best publisher in London. I cannot, of course, mention his name but he was out so I spoke to his wife, Mrs Eyre Methuen.

'I've thought of this wonderful character for a book,' I said. 'He's a bent gnome called . . .'

That was as far as I got.

'A gnome?' she cried. 'A *gnome?* You can't write books about a gnome! That's Enid Blyton's territory. You might be able to get away with writing about a gnome if you were another Enid Blyton, but that is what you will never be.'

And so it has all been for nothing. I still have my beautiful little character, the crooked Norm, but I have to face facts:

'What's the good of a gnome if you're never Enid?'

Frank Muir

While Dennis was given:
'Discretion is the better part of valour' (Proverb)

I was watching a blue movie the other night – it wasn't meant to be that colour, but my TV set hasn't been the same since I turned it over on its side to watch more comfortably while lying in bed – and it was one of those wartime flying stories.

My mind immediately snapped back to that summer of 1941 when I was a Lab. Technician in the Photographic Unit of an RAF Training Station up in Northern Scotland. Our task was to teach budding Intelligence Officers how to 'read' Aerial Reconnaissance photographs. (Oh, you remember what they were – those photos of enemy terrain which were taken from a great height by our reconnaissance planes.)

My part in this training was boring but simple. Whenever we received an A.R. photo ('Aerial Reconnaissance'; come on now, don't make me have to explain *everything*), I would inspect it, select an appropriate square of it, blow that square up into a ten-by-eight glossy, then pass out several copies of this enlargement among the I.O.s. They would study their ten-by-eights through magnifying glasses, then each would take his turn interpreting the significant topographical features suggested by the photo: reservoirs, high ground, railway lines, wooded areas, etc.

Got the hang of it now? I hope so, because I now have to explain some of the handicaps under which I worked.

The principal one was that I never *received* any Aerial Reconnaissance photographs. Oh, Reconnaissance Command posted them to me all right, but as they were somewhere down in the Home Counties and the part of Northern Scotland we were in was really excessively Northern, the mail never reached us. Consequently I was obliged to obtain my supply of A.R. photos from whatever alternative sources I could find.

Well, at that time and in that place, there was only one alternative source – elderly back-numbers of the *National Geographic Magazine*, which the Dental Officer kept in his ante-room, presumably because anaesthetics were also in short supply. Several of these contained Aerial Photographs which were quite adequate for my purposes. As they were usually of places like The

Great Barrier Reef or Popacatapetl, I must admit the trainees didn't get that many marshalling-yards or heavy-water factories to recognise. Still, in wartime, improvisation itself becomes a virtue.

The other handicap I had to surmount was that as, in this remote corner, there was little else but scenery available in the way of off-duty pleasures, the Station had a thriving Camera Club. This meant that every moment of my spare time was taken up in developing and printing snaps for an entire squadron of keen amateur photographers.

It was this keenness which precipitated the awkward incident. For some time, the Flight Sergeant in charge of our Cookhouse had been paying court to a crofter's daughter named Ella McGivern. The only female in twenty-five square miles, she was an unprepossessing girl with a skin like a water-biscuit and legs like two vacuum-cleaner bags. Nevertheless, because of the sheer lack of competition, she functioned as our neighbourhood sex object.

For that reason, excitement ran high when it was announced in DROs that, on the following Friday evening, Ella had agreed to act as a live female model for the Camera Club. Fever pitch was reached when it became known, through less official channels, that the Flight Sergeant had persuaded her to pose in the nude.

In those days, of course, the word 'nude' was hardly the absolute term that it is today and Ella was insisting on retaining a pair of P.T. shorts below and a square of transparent net-curtaining up top. But when you've been the best part of eight months in a remote corner of Northern Scotland, even that is a fairly heady prospect.

Accordingly, come Friday, not only was the entire Camera Club to be seen clicking away at her but also a neighbouring platoon of Pioneer Corps, the complete intake of Intelligence Officers, all the sentries and two German parachutists.

For me, however, it meant only a virtually insuperable workload. For in addition to the task of developing single-handed all the figure studies of Ella that were snapped that evening, I also had to make ready an adequate supply of ten-by-eights for the official Aerial Photograph Interpretation Test which the C.O. had laid on for the Intelligence Officers the following morning.

The aerial photograph which I'd selected as the subject of the Test was of an area that, again, could hardly be described as a raging battleground. As time was short and the copies of the *National Geographic Magazine* were dwindling, I'd chosen a picture of a place called Karakorum, which is a mountain range in Tibet. As was my practice, I squared it off, selected an appropriate square and placed it under the enlarger.

At least, I think that's what I enlarged. To this day I can't be really sure. Bearing in mind that I also had in my Lab at the time three hundred or so Art Poses of Miss McGivern, the possibilities of error were considerable.

Mind you, the thought that I might have erred did not strike me until the following morning when the Test was already under way. I wandered in and watched the Intelligence Officers scanning their ten-by-eights of what they'd been told was 'mountain terrain'. Only then did it occur to me that what they were all studying through their magnifying glasses might, conceivably, through sheer pressure of work and lack of sleep, be a monstrous enlargement of some section of Ella McGivern.

'Excuse me, sir.' I tugged at the C.O.'s sleeve. 'There's a possibility I may have made a boob.'

The C.O. was a man who could have given irritability lessons to Captain Bligh. 'Belt up, Corporal,' he said. Then, to one of the Intelligence Officers – 'Come on then, Pilot Officer Lacey. Make anything of it?'

Pilot Officer Lacey nodded confidently. 'It's at least five thousand feet high,' he said. 'And there's cart tracks leading up the lower slopes.'

'There's also traces of volcanic activity,' volunteered a fellow Intelligence Officer. 'And is that a small hut at the top?'

I could not, in all conscience, allow this to go on. I leant towards the C.O.'s ear and quietly confessed the possibility that I had submitted an error. Equally quietly he reduced me to AC2 and confined me to camp until 1957.

Then he turned to the officers. 'I'm afraid the Test must be aborted, gentlemen,' he said. 'A certain measure of uncertainty has arisen regarding its subject matter.'

With some distaste, he picked up a ten-by-eight. Surveying it, he said:

'This creation is Tibet, or part of Ella.'

Excerpts from 'UPON MY WORD'
Published by Methuen & Co.

The Daily Blooper

PEDROS
Back from Spain, invites you to his world-famous Night Club
Discotheque
AT UPP. DUNMURRY LANE
OPENING FOR THE SEASON
Friday, 17th May
10 p.m.—2 a.m.
Chicks—25 New pence
Fanciers—37 New Pence
see
- Exotic birds, being barbecued in the open.
- Switched on Groups boozed—fused
- Games—Chasing Fairies in the Moonlight

It's all happening at
PEDROS

Belfast Telegraph

"I am married to a sewage worker. My small son, aged four, pulls the chain after going to the toilet and announces with pride that its on its way to daddy."

Evening Mail

One person was arrested last night on suspicion of being concerned in this morning's murders.

Jersey paper

Copy typist require work at home. Anything awful considered.

Rochdale Observer

SMITH & NEPHEW RESEARCH LTD.
TWO PLASTIC TECHNOLOGISTS
FOR
POLYMER RESEARCH & DEVELOPMENT

Grauniad

Violence-Judge Hits out

Nottingham Evening Post

As the war faded and peace loomed Vera Lynn was able to advise her husband and business manager Harry Lewis that she was going to have a baby. It was a symbolic and logical climax to five gruelling years as a forces' Sweetheart.

Evening Standard

Lesotho Women Make Beautiful Carpets
By Gordon Lindsey

Bangkok World

Mrs do-as-you-would -be-done-by
Another mother of 10, Mrs. Lavinia Nicholson, aged 37 blamed immigrants for the rise in population.

Yorkshire Evening Post

FIVE SCHOOL *BROADS* APPROVE SEX EDUCATION
The recently inaugurated state-wide sex education program has now been okayed by five of the twelve district school boards.

—Dewmore (Ariz.) Daiily

We have often in the past had Wimbledon wobbles with nervy players so shaky that their boobs have sometimes made park club players blush.

Scottish Daily Express

SPOTTED MAN WANTED FOR QUESTIONING

Hackney Gazette

NEASDEN HOSPITAL AFFAIR
We regret that owing to a typographical error the closing sentence of Sir David Llewellyn's article "Blessed are the merciful, for they shall receive money." 'Money' should have read 'mercy'.

Reading Evening Post

SCUTINEER: The job of a scrutineer is to check all advertisements before insertion in the newspaper for spelling, accuracy and legibility. Applicants must be able to work fast and accurately.

QUEEN TOASTED BY AMIN

Daily Telegraph

☆☆

From the best of MORECAMBE AND WISE by Eddie Barben

THE BANK MANAGER

☆☆

Scene: Bank Manager's office: Manager is seated behind his desk. Intercom on desk buzzes: Manager presses a button and speaks into it.

Manager Yes, Miss Dunn.

Ann (*distorted*) There's a Mr Wise and a Mr . . . Ooh!

Eric (*distorted*) Sorry.

Ann (*distorted*) A Mr Morecambe to see you, Mr Biggs, sir.

Manager You can show them both in.

Ernie Good morning, sir. Eric, this is Mr Biggs.

Eric Mr Biggs. That's a good name for a bank manager.

Manager Will you both take a seat, gentlemen.

Ernie Thank you. (*Sits at desk*)

Eric (*looking around*) So this is where you do it.

Manager This is where I do it?

Eric Good for you.

Ernie Why don't you sit down and shut up!

Eric (*to Manager*) He's talking to you. (*Sits*)

Manager I have your files here, Mr Morecambe and Mr Wise. I'm a very busy man and I would appreciate it if you could tell me what it is you want to discuss with me. (*Looks at wrist watch*) I can let you have two minutes.

Ernie Very well. (*Rises and struts about with some importance*) My rich Aunt Agatha has passed over and left me a substantial legacy.

Manager (*sudden change of attitude*) A substantial legacy . . . a rich aunt . . . A cigar, Mr Wise? (*Offers Ern a cigar*)

Eric I have an auntie who isn't feeling too well – perhaps half a cigar?

Eric reaches for cigar: Manager shuts box quickly. As Ernie lights cigar, Eric takes it.

Eric Can I have a light?

Manager Now then, Mr Wise, you would like some advice on investments.

Ernie I was thinking about overseas investments.

Eric Swiss banks.

Manager Swiss banks?

Eric Better rate of exchange in Switzerland – you get sixteen yodels to the pound.

Ernie Will you keep out of this?

Manager (*opens Ern's file*) Let's see what business interest you have at the moment, Mr Wise.

Ernie I am a playwright of considerable note. For my first business venture I am going to start the Ernest Wise Publishing Company.

Manager What a talented man you are, Mr Wise, I didn't know that you wrote plays.

Eric He only wrote twelve yesterday.

Manager *Twelve* plays?

Ernie There's one I'm not really happy about.

Eric But he'll finish it today before he has his tea . . . (*To Ern*) . . . won't you.

Manager So your aunt has died and left you this money.

Ernie I'm her only living relative.

Manager You're quite certain of this?

Eric Positive. I just saw his leg move.

Manager Mr Morecambe, I am trying to discuss business with Mr Wise. (*Looks at file*) I see that you have quite a large annuity.

Eric You can see it from there, can you. He's got a belt at home. I don't know why he doesn't wear it.

Ernie Stop butting in and mind your own business.

Eric Certainly. (*Takes out comic and begins to read*)

Ernie Do you see what I have to put up with, Mr Biggs? A grown man reading comics.

Manager Yes. Let's see how best we can invest your legacy, Mr Wise. (*Looking at file*)

Ernie (*aside to Eric*) Reading a comic in a bank manager's office.

Eric They're all in here, good they are.

Manager There's International Chemical, Amalgamated Tin . . .

Eric Desperate Dan.

Manager (*still looking at file*) United Steel . . .

Eric Pansy Potter.

Manager Bonnie Bluebell . . . International Computers . . .

Eric Bonnie who?

Manager (*realising*) Bonnie Bluebell – character from a comic many years ago.

Eric Don't remember that one.

Manager Bonnie Bluebell was a fairy, she broke her wing and a kind lady found her crying underneath a gooseberry bush.

Eric Do that a lot fairies, always breaking their wings, especially when there's a bit of frost.

Manager Now I suggest you invest your legacy in United Steel and Amalgamated Tin and possibly the rest in Unit Trusts. How much exactly have you to invest?

Ernie Twelve fifty.

Manager Twelve hundred and fifty pounds.

Ernie No. Twelve fifty.

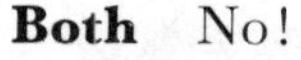

Manager Twelve pounds . . .
Ernie and fifty pence.
Eric It would have been £15 if she'd taken the empties back. She was going to leave it to the Cats' Home but he needs the milk more than they do.
Manager I don't see how we can talk about investing twelve pounds 50p. (*Rises*)
Eric Are you going?
Manager (*with sarcasm*) I suggest you put it in a tin box under the bed.
Eric I told him that. I could have been a manager.
Eric and Ernie go to leave.
Manager Just one moment, gentlemen. I would like to have a word with you Mr Morecambe. In private?
Eric Anything you say in front of me can be said in front of him, as long as he leaves.
Manager Please sit down. (*They sit*) It's about your overdraft. I see that you owe the bank £10.
Eric I've no further interest in the matter. If you look at my statement you will see that I have to my credit the sum of one thousand three hundred and seventy-three pounds.
Manager (*long suffering*) Mr Morecambe, that's the date!
Eric The date?
Manager The first of the third, '73. The important figures are these here printed in red.
Manager Looking at your statement, you don't seem to have regular money coming in.
Ernie Well, we don't get paid regularly. We work for the BBC.
Manager The British Broadcasting Corporation?
Eric No, the Birkenhead Brick Company.
Manager What exactly do you do for a living?
Ernie We're just entertainers.
Eric We used to be on the stage before we closed all the variety theatres. We used to do jokes.
Manager Wise-cracks?
Eric I'm afraid he does these days. It's his age.
Manager How very curious. I write a few jokes myself.
Eric and Ernie have a horrified reaction.
Manager Would you like to hear one or two?
Both No!
Manager But possibly you could use this one in your act –

> Judge in court to prisoner – 'Have you ever been up before me?'
> Prisoner – 'I don't know, what time do you get up in the morning?'

He chuckles and looks up, laughing, at the boys. There is no reaction from them and the Manager's face becomes serious.
Manager Could I send this to any other comedian?
Ernie Send it to Jimmy Tarbuck.
Manager Jimmy Tarbuck? Would he use my material?
Eric Why not. He uses everybody else's.
Both exit rapidly.

Eric It's amazing how much you can learn from one of your plays.
Ernie Learn?
Eric Tutenkhamen.
Ernie What about it?
Eric I always thought it was Tooting Common.
Ernie Had to do a lot of research to write that play about Egypt.
Eric Must have done.
Ernie Spent days at the British Museum.
Eric No problems getting out? Sorry about that, Ern.
Ernie I thought Robert Morley almost did quite well.
Eric Fair comment.
Ernie Quite well considering he had such a big roll.
Eric Kept catching me with it every time he turned a bit sharpish.
Ernie That's not a very gracious thing to say.
Eric I must be honest – a superb actor and one of the nicest men it's ever been my pleasure to work with.
Ernie Yes, I suppose I must be.
Eric I meant Robert Morley.
Ernie Oh him! A great actor.
Eric Like twelve Glenda Jackson's in a trouser suit.

Published by The Woburn Press

Encyclopaedia Pottanica

from MICHAEL BENTINE'S 'Big Potty Fun Book' Published by Robson Books

MARCO POLO. The world's best-known and first *commercial* traveller. Starting from Venice, his home-town, he took his goods – Italian tomato sauce, stinky Gorgonzola cheese and Chianti wine – all over Asia and the Far East, exchanging them for all sorts of things: curry powder and spices from India; Persian cats from Persia; lemon curd from Kurdistan; Afghan hounds from Afghanistan; and of course, spag-het – or, as it came to be known in Italy, 'spaghetti' – from China.

The Great Khan of China (not to be confused with his brother, the Great Khant, who wasn't much good at anything) invited Marco and his friend, little Giuseppe, who kept the accounts, to stay at his Imperial Palace in Peking.

Marco and Giuseppe enjoyed their stay immensely, except that they didn't get much sleep at night because of the yapping of the Pekingese dogs. They learnt how to make and fly Chinese kites, and had great fun trying to eat with chopsticks. In exchange for Marco's tomato sauce, the Great Khan offered him fireworks and spag-het. Unfortunately he explained what to do with them in Chinese, which Marco didn't understand. However, cleverly figuring that you ate one and set fire to the other, he poured tomato sauce over the fireworks and lit the spag-het. The fireworks didn't taste very nice and the spag-het took ages to catch fire, but Marco took them back with him to Venice. There they soon realised that it was the other way round, and took to cooking spaghetti with as much care as they set light to the fireworks.

But what a sight met Marco's eyes on his return to Venice! He had left his bath taps running when he went away on his travels to China, and Venice was now flooded. Still, as Marco said to Giuseppe, 'It's gonna be a big attraction for the tourists.'

QUEEN ELIZABETH I. Popularly known as 'Good Queen Bess', she spent most of her life trying not to get married. This was because she was too busy ruling Elizabethan England, and going to 'first nights' of new plays by William Shakespeare, and running England's biggest business, which was waylaying Spanish galleons and taking off them the gold and silver that the Spaniards had stolen from the South American Indians, and – well, anyway, Queen Elizabeth was just *too* busy to get married. King Philip of Spain wanted very badly to marry her so that he could get back his gold and silver, but the Queen flatly refused him. 'Never in the history of England,' she announced, 'shall an Elizabeth marry a Philip.' In the end Philip became so furious that he built a huge fleet of ships, called the Armada, to invade England.

Luckily Sir Francis Drake and Sir Walter Raleigh were back from one of their 'business' trips (pinching the Spaniards' gold) and were able to stop the invasion. This made Philip madder than ever, and to get even he left instructions in his will that all English tourists holidaying on the Costa Brava should be charged double. (Of course, that was years later, but then, Philip was a very nasty King who always bore grudges.)

KING ARTHUR. Everyone used to think of King Arthur and his famous Knights as dashing men in shining armour who led a leisurely life surrounded by beautiful damsels in fancy silks and satins with long pointed hats. But in fact King Arthur was the head of a band of working-class knights who worked their fingers to the bone killing off dragons, rescuing young ladies and foiling ogres. Over-worked and underpaid (just like most of us today), King Arthur and his knights eventually became fed up with their 'knightly' working conditions and formed themselves into a Union – or 'Knights of the Round Table' as they called themselves. King Arthur was elected shop-steward, and he called all the distressed damsels and fiery dragons and wicked ogres to a meeting and told them bluntly that his Knights were not working more than a 40-hour week rescuing and slaying and foiling, and that Sundays and week-ends would be double-overtime, and if they didn't like it the Knights would go on strike and have a sit-in round their Round Table, and all the distressed damsels, dragons and unfoiled ogres could jolly well go and jump in the lake!

Naturally there was a big row and the Knights picketed Camelot, which was where they worked, and beat up errant knights who tried to break the strike, and oh, there was a heck of a to-do! In the end the damsels and dragons and ogres grew tired of being distressed, unslain and unfoiled and agreed to King Arthur's terms and everyone lived happily ever after – or at least, until the next election.

Actually it's less of a battle – which suggests a beginning and an end and *sometimes* a few elementary rules and even first-aid for the wounded. Inter-sex strife has no such gentility. No, definitely not a battle, rather more a very long-running series of guerilla attacks and counter-attacks which seem to go on long after the arteries and hormones and adrenalin ought to have given out.

Money and sex are the major weapons, of course, though little matters like burning the toast, picking your ears, refusing to cut toe-nails, smashing the car's back brake lights for the second time in a week, and hanging your smalls across the bath – all and much much more are the small arms fire. And you can depend on it, this sort of warfare was going on way, way back – though it's difficult to be quite sure what ammunition was used before the advent of bathrooms, manners, mothers-in-law and all the rest of the exciting paraphernalia of more modern mate-baiting. HE could always have refused to bring home the bacon – literally – I suppose, but then he'd have felt rather foolish lurking round in the undergrowth with far too much raw animal for one on his hands. SHE could have denied him access to the conjugal cave, of course, and specifically the bit of dried grass and leaves that stood in as the marital couch. But then . . . HE was almost sure to be bigger and totally lacking in the finer gentlemanly attitudes, and much given to hitting anything that threatened him.

Divorce was not invented – and I suppose the only way to break out of the situation was to arrange for your boyfriend to put up a show of strength and drag you out by the hair – screaming of course. HIS best bet would have been to bring the Other Woman into the cave, and it was clouts all round if anyone objected. It really must have been back to basics then, and stay alive if you can, mate.

Come to think of it, give or take a few details, its not so different now. . . .

"Leave the dishes until tomorrow, Albert. It's your birthday today."

"Yes, I still can remember where and when I got married. What escapes me is why."

from the "Weekend Book of Jokes No. 17" Published by Associated Newspapers.

Marriage, which is what we seem to have started out with, is only one of the innumerable partnerships between the sexes where these deadly battles go on – and on and on and on until (one might say without being misunderstood) you are safely under the sod. Even when the connection is negative and virtually wordless, the fight is still on, the seduction must be tried, the experience had, points scored, wrongs righted – and rights wronged. An endless web being spun by the spider and wandered into by the fly (though who is which at any given time is anyone's guess):

From "Sick, Sick, Sick" by Jules Feiffe
Published by Wm. Collins Sons & Co. L

It appears to men that their spouse's disposition, changes shortly after the wedding. As a wife, her interest in him is not as deep as it appeared before marriage. Even her polite inquiries-as, for example, when he comes home in the evening - have a different ring to them now.

HER STATEMENTS 	HIS THOUGHTS (as a bachelor) 	HIS THOUGHTS (as a husband) 
How was your day in the office, dear?	She is interested in my career.	How much does she know about Mabel?
I like your friend	She likes my friends.	I wonder why she likes him.
You look tired, darling	So kind, so understanding.	All right, so the lines in my face are showing, She is not getting any younger either.
You are a wonderful dancer.	She is kind enough not to tell me the truth.	The liar
Would you like a cup of coffee?	That's just what I need.	Too lazy to mix a cocktail, eh?
Let's make love.	Hallelujah!	Can't she see I had a hard day in the office?
Don't forget your overcoat, dear.	She cares about me.	Nag, nag, nag, nag, nag, nag, nag.

ANDY CAPP

By Reg Smythe

Published by Mirror Group Books

Honour and Obey ?

MARRIAGE LICENCE

●● I consider it wise to include in the probation order that you impregnate no further females,' he said. 'Does the order apply if Martin marries?' asked the defence lawyer. 'Yes, He will have to get written permission.'

Daily Mail

ODD FELLOW

But a man who had five authenticated suicide attempts, who is separated from a wife he married knowing that she was pregnant by another man, who is the father of two children by different women, who is about to become a father by yet another woman, and who admits that he is a homosexual, cannot be regarded as entirely normal.

Court report in *Western Daily Press*

MARRIAGE-A DOGS LIFE

A Canadian divorce court heard that for two years Drew Sunley and his wife, Rosemary, did not speak to each other in their Toronto flat.

They communicated by tying notes to the tail of their golden labrador, Bondy. The dog spent its evenings trotting from one bedroom to the next.

Titbits

"No, I can't take a joke, David!"

Moral Support?

We noticed for example that John Simpson, who sued his wife for desertion, had his suit held up by affidavits.

Egyptian paper

"He asked your father to smile, not to laugh his head off."

The bride was given away by her father, who wore a white ballerina length dress of rose patterned lace, over taffeta, and shoulder length veil over head-dress of roses and lily-of-the-valley, and carried a bouquet of red roses.

Cambrian News

Wag

'Later he went to his home, packed some things and went. He said goodbye, made a short explanation to the dog and left,' said the Judge.

Yorkshire Evening Post

Dirty Weekend

Visiting a newly-wed friend, I asked how she liked married life. 'It's real hard work,' she said, 'you wash the dishes and make the beds, then two weeks later you have to do it all over again!'

Letter in *Woman*

FOUR IS A MOB

By PATRICK CAMPBELL

It's got to come to all of us sooner or later, and I got mine in a cupboard on the top floor of a house belonging to people called Cartwright, in the early spring of 1932.

Daphne Oakes was her name, a strapping girl from the sunlit beaches of Sydney, Australia, and she looked upon love as healthy exercise.

We were members of a house-party, gathered to celebrate a hunt ball in the Cartwright's home. Major Cartwright was the M.F.H., and the house was packed to the roof with human horses and hounds.

As soon as I arrived I found I had to bunk in with the Master himself.

Mrs Cartwright said, 'I'm afraid you'll have to bunk in with Bob and Daph will bunk in with me.' She gave a light, screaming laugh. 'It would never do,' she cried, 'if Daph were to bunk in with you!'

Daphne Oakes came bounding up. I'm afraid I'll have to come right out into the open here, and admit that she was not exactly a girl. Rising thirty-five, I should say, but as strong as a kangaroo. She looked, indeed, quite like a kangaroo, bleached and sunburned, with her longish nose, short, compact arms, and powerful springy legs.

It was easy to picture Daphne, startled, leaping away through the bush, except that nothing, save a sudden explosion, could possibly have startled Daphne Oakes.

She was in favour of my bunking in with her. The others seemed to know that this was humorously intended, for they laughed loudly as she wound her arms around my neck. I backed away, being only seventeen, and they laughed more loudly than ever. Except one of them – a human horse who had been introduced to me as Maxwell Crump. Mr Crump glowered. He had black, crinkly hair coming down almost to his eyebrows, and black, crinkly hair on the back of his hands. I had already marked him down as a slow starter in conversations not dealing directly with things on four legs.

Crump took Daphne away, and then gradually the party broke up, to change for dinner and the ball.

I accompanied Major Cartwright to our room. There was a small camp-bed in the corner, and on this I laid my suitcase.

Major Cartwright cleared his throat. He blew several times, and harrumphed, and then he said, 'Bathroom's down the passage. Better nip in before the ladies get powder all over the shelf.' Powder on the shelf seemed to be a grievance with him, for he added a moment later, 'Stinkin' stuff – gets up your neb.'

I was as clean as a new pin, but I went down the passage and waited in the bathroom for ten minutes. When I came back the Major was wearing underpants, a boiled shirt, and a pair of astoundingly red, bare feet.

I dressed quickly – we were continually getting in one another's way – and left him to it. He was having difficulty with his tie, but I thought it wiser not to make an offer of help.

The others were already gathered in the drawing-room – Daphne Oakes in electric-blue, convulsed with laughter, and slapping people on the back. We went in to dinner; then the band arrived; and the other guests; and the ball was under way.

For the first couple of hours I kept clear of Daphne. I was a reserved boy, and contented myself with partners in pink taffeta, as young and modest as myself.

I couldn't have been thinking when I let myself in for the Paul Jones, because there in the inner ring was Daphne, doing an aboriginal war-dance, pawing the ground, and shouting for music.

She nailed me on the first lap. I was about to join hands with a young lady carrying a bead bag when Daphne shot between us. 'Come on, Tommy,' she cried, 'let's go!'

I had no idea why she thought my name was Tommy. And a moment later I found I had no idea what she thought she was trying to do. We flayed our way round the ballroom, jerking and leaping, making hay of the other couples.

I tried to steady her by taking a firmer grip. Daphne, assuming this to be a sign of ripening friendship, tried to get inside my shirt. Her eyes were bright. A fine flush mantled her powerful cheek.

Near the door I rode her into a pillar, and brought her to a halt. 'Shall we,' I said, 'sit this one out?'

Daphne looked at me. Her eyes narrowed. 'Certainly,' she said, and dragged me into the hall.

The staircase was jammed with dancers eating ice-cream, and fanning themselves with programmes. We threaded our way through them, and came out on the first landing.

'Up here,' said Daphne. We mounted the second flight of stairs.

'Come on,' said Daphne. We reached the top floor.

It happened like lightning. There was a door under the stairs that led up to the attic. Daphne threw it open. She shoved me in. Then she fell upon me like a ton of bricks.

It was like nothing I had ever known before. I had previously been conducting a delicate courtship with a young lady in Dublin called Brenda Poole, but that had been a matter of sighs, and hand touching as if by accident. This, however, was murder, pure and simple.

There was no gleam of light in the cupboard, but I tried to fight her off. I sprang back and fell over a vacuum cleaner. Daphne Oakes came after me. I'd never struck a woman before, or even thought of doing so, but now I doubled my fist and let her have it, hoping to catch her in the eye.

I must have struck a bedroom jug on the shelf above her head, because there was a crash and a shower of broken china. Then I found the door. I leaped out on to the landing, and fled for my life. I got as far as Major Cartwright's room, shot into it, and wedged a chair against the door. Then I sank back, trembling, upon my bed. I'd lost my tie. All the studs had burst out of my boiled shirt. So far as I was concerned the ball was over.

I was still sitting on the bed an hour later when Cartwright came rattling at the door. In that time all manner of thoughts had seethed through my mind. Should I become a monk? I didn't know. But one thing was clear. I should have to tell Brenda Poole about what had happened, and, at the least, emigrate to Australia, in the hope of picking up a job. I made a rapid emendation — China. The thought of being cooped up in Australia with Daphne Oakes brought me out into a cold perspiration all over again.

I jumped up and took the chair away from the door. Major Cartwright blundered in. He looked at the chair, and then he looked at me, but it clearly meant nothing to him. He was a broken man. 'By God,' he said, 'I'm glad that's over.'

He wrenched off his tie. His collar burst open and writhed round the back of his neck. 'Pack of gabbling' wimmin,' said Major Cartwright. Then he cocked an eye at me. 'Better cut along to the bathroom, boy,' he said, 'before they mess it about with their fol-de-rols.'

I was getting tired of being sent to the bathroom by Major Cartwright, but I did as I was told. He was hot and peevish. He was not a man to be argued with.

I opened the door of the bathroom, and there was Daphne Oakes. I gave a scream, and tried to jump out into the passage. She slammed the door with her foot. 'Come here,' she said, 'you mad, mad boy.'

I snatched up a backscrubber. I told her I was dead beat. I told her I was engaged to be married. I said I was getting a glass of water for Major Cartwright. I announced I was going to be sick. Daphne Oakes advanced upon me, showing her powerful teeth.

I kicked her on the leg. I threw open the door, and tore down the passage to the Major's room. But Daphne beat me to it. She slipped past me, turned the key in the door, and dropped it down the front of her dress. 'Now,' she said, 'come and get it if you want to go to bed.'

I walked away, making for the head of the stairs. Daphne followed. She stopped at the door of Mrs Cartwright's room. 'I'll be here if you want me,' she said. 'The bed next to the door. Good night, Romeo.'

I made no reply. I walked straight down the stairs and into the sitting-room. I locked the door and put the writing-desk against it. Then I lay on the sofa and tried to go to sleep.

By 2.45 a.m. I'd had enough. I'd left my dinner-jacket in the Major's room, and my boiled shirt offered no protection against the draughts of the night.

I decided to go and get the key. I decided that, whatever the consequences might be, I would creep into Mrs Cartwright's room in the hope that the awful Oakes had left my key on the table beside her bed. It was a wild plan, but it had been a wild night.

I waited for another hour, trying to keep warm under a pile of satin cushions, and then I climbed the stairs. I removed my shoes outside Mrs Cartwright's door, opened it stealthily, and crept into the darkness on hands and knees. All reason had left me. It didn't matter any more what happened. I only wanted to be safe in my own camp-bed, with the Major watching over me, and our door locked on the inside.

I crept straight into something large and hot and solid. I shot out my hand and touched a face – a leathery, whiskered face, and a mass of crinkly hair. Maxwell Crump!

I felt my hand imprisoned in a vice. 'Who the hell,' hissed a hoarse voice, 'are you?'

Then I heard Daphne Oakes. 'By damn,' said Daphne, 'it's Tommy!' I heard a gasp of laughter suddenly smothered by a pillow

The grip on my wrist tightened. 'What's he doing here?' hissed Maxwell Crump.

Daphne subdued another paroxysm. 'Perhaps,' she whispered, 'he wants me to come for a walk!'

At that moment Mrs Cartwright turned on the light. Mr Crump and I pressed ourselves into the floor. The side of Daphne's bed came down to within an inch of the carpet. There was nowhere to hide.

'Sorry to wake you, Daph,' said Mrs Cartwright – 'I've got frightful wind over the heart.'

A series of despairing noises proved this to be true.

'It must have been the claret cup,' said Mrs Cartwright.

Daphne sat up. 'I've got some bicarbonate on the dressing-table,' she said quickly. 'Let me get it for –'

Mrs Cartwright jumped nimbly out of bed. 'You stay right there, dear,' she said, 'I'll get it myself.'

Crump put his head under Daphne's counterpane. I saw he was wearing tennis-shoes and a dressing-gown. I tried to get under the bedside table. Then Mrs Cartwright sailed across the room. On her head was a slumber-cap, tied with pink ribbon under her chin. Her face was thickly coated with cold cream. She wore only the top part of a pair of striped pyjamas that must have belonged at one time to her husband, the M.F.H.

She padded swiftly to the dressing-table, picked up the bottle of tablets, turned round, and then obtained a grip of the situation.

Mrs Cartwright was a heavy woman, but she tried to leap into the air. She screamed. She was still screaming when she came down. With a galvanic bound she reached the curtains, threw them round her, and brought the whole lot crashing down on her head.

Crump and I tried to get out of the door. We got tangled up in one another and came down again.

There was a loud, splintering crash at the other end of the passage. A bull's roar, the thunder of feet, and suddenly in the entrance to Mrs Cartwright's bedroom stood her husband, holding a broken chair.

He stopped, seeing his wife's room filled with people. He examined us minutely, one by one. Then he said, in a low voice, 'Some damn fellah locked me in. Couldn't open me door.' He looked at his wife in her slumber-cap and cold cream, draped in the curtain.

'Heard you screamin', Effie,' he said. 'Thought I could lend a hand.'

Mrs Cartwright made a splendid effort. She took a deep breath.

'It's all right, dear,' she said, 'go back to bed. We're only – only playing a game.'

Major Cartwright looked at her heavily. The world, as he knew it, had come to an end. No rhyme, no reason anywhere. No recognizable sequence of cause and effect.

'I see, m'dear,' he said. Then he added, 'Don't get cold.' He looked at the broken chair in his hand, and set it carefully against the wall. 'G'night, all,' he said. We heard him go down the passage. He stopped for a moment outside his own door, and then went in, closing it gently behind him. Then there was silence.

'Well,' said Mrs Cartwright brightly, looking at the ceiling, 'I suppose we'd all better get off to bed. I'm sure Daphne will be able to explain everything quite satisfactorily in the morning.'

Crump and I rose to our feet. We kept our eyes on the floor. We stepped aside to let the other out first.

I kept on walking. I walked down the stairs, I took someone's overcoat off the peg in the hall, I put it on over my boiled shirt, and walked a mile and a half to the station. I caught a milk train to Dublin soon after dawn.

A week later my suitcase arrived. It was neatly packed with the clothes I'd left behind. But there was no covering note. No communication from the Cartwrights. Nothing.

I sent back the overcoat by parcel post. I didn't bother to write a note either.

There didn't seem to be anything to say.

Excerpt from '35 Years on the Job'
Published by Blond & Briggs.

The Daily Blooper

The Tories have been under some pressure to toughen up their party political broadcasts. Mr. Heath, Mr. Macleod, and Mr. Peter Walker accordingly reached for their choppers.

From the Gruniad

SHELL SHOCKED

A prime cause of the poultry industry £5 million a year loss on cracked eggs wa explained yesterday by Dr. T. C. Carter director of the Poultry Research Centre in Edinburgh: Some hens stand on tiptoe to lay —and consquently their eggs drop harder to the floor.

Daily Express

FUNERALS

Parking for clients only

Notice at Surrey undertakers

Confrontation

★ A mother slapped her little boy hard after he had demolished a display of canned foods in the supermarket. Facing the hostile stares of assistants the mother said in a loud voice: 'If I don't correct him now he might grow up to be a student.'

Sunday Mirr

Long-term Forecast

— Mr. John Davies, a North London sandwich board prophet of doom, has been predicting the end of the world for 15 years. I've never given up hope that it will happen sooner or later.' he said.

Daily Express

Students who marry during their course will not be permitted to remain in college. Further, students who are already married must either live with their husbands or make other arrangements with the dean.

Syllabus of an Ohio College

Mr. Anthony Chenevix Trench, head of Eton, said the system provided for a great deal of participation by the boys. "I'm always available to boys of any age who want to see me. I've been put on the mat by quite young boys."

Grauniad

FARMER'S EIGHT-HOUR VIGIL IN BOG

All that night Sharkey remained in the bog without refreshments or food of any kind.

The conference's attitude was indicated by the almost total lack of applause after Mr. Wilson's 30-minute speech while engineering Union leader Bryan Stanley was greeted with sustained crapping when he put the anti-common market case.

Times of Zambia

MILK RACE

It's a strong strategic base for nex week's operation, but unfortunately Bayton, who would have been Edward's natural deputy, is still suffering from his fall. He finished at New Brighton with the bunch, but his back still pains, and he felt every bum in the road.

It was Havelka, a Czech of whom we know very little, who opened

Observer

Another member of the gang, 44-year-old Mr. John Drake, of Oldfield Grove, Rotherhithe, said: "When I saw the stowaway I told the other lads to keep him hidden while I went to our security office."

"We had discovered him when he grabbed the leg of one of my mates. He didn't seem to understand any English. When we asked him with signals how long he had been in the hold he indicated four days by holding up four fingers. The only English words he spoke were National Assistance."

Evening Standard

NOTICE

Will Mrs. Hargreaves, of 13 Coates Avenue, and all persons in it with her, please return Mrs. S. Hogarth to her own home at 2 Apple Tree Cottages, Salterforth, or legal action will be taken.

Signed, S. HOGARTH
2 Apple Tree Cottages
Salterforth.

God is always at Hand To Help in Adversity. Please write Box 3092

Border Counties Advertiser

Among the 20 guests was Mr. Sellars old friend and fellow Goon, Spike Milligan.

The couple have known each other two years but have always denied they would marry. Mr. Sellars has been married twice before.

From the Grauniad

TAKE YOUR MADICINE!

Judging by the fees they charge their private patients, doctors and more especially psychiatrists (psychoanalysts, psychotherapists, the lot) don't seem to realize that they are on their way out. The machines are going to take over, Doc. There are already reports of medical examinations that can be conducted by computer, and I'm sure it won't be long before the psychs. – worn down by the grind of listening on and on and on to the same old weary problems – hand over to a nice bland soothing robot. It may be a rather odd experience at first, being told by a computer to put out your tongue or lie on a couch – but I've an idea that after a bit it'll be a relief to be able to be absolutely self-centred when we go to be cured. At present you are too aware of the doctor or the analyst – it's too easy to notice that they too are looking tired and depressed or have bad breath and flat feet. This means, inevitably, that some of our energy is being spent on feeling sympathetic with them instead of being able to concentrate till we're cross-eyed over our own psychic aches or physical pains.

The telephone – a machine that puts a merciful distance between caller and called, and removes all but one of the senses from the encounter – is already used extensively as a therapeutic agent. Think of all your friends whose ears you weary with your troubles; think of all the 'Dial a' – services at your fingertips; think, too, of what can go wrong:

LINEBLOCK

by BARRY NORMAN

The French have just installed a telephone line in Paris so that 'Worried' of St Tropez or 'Overdue' of Aix-en-Provence or, indeed, 'Jilted,' 'Kinky,' or 'Abandoned-with-Child' of anywhere in Europe can call and discuss their sex problems with a panel of doctors, psychiatrists, family planning experts, and the like.

We have a similar system here, of course. 'Desperate' of Cheltenham or 'Frantic' of Harrogate can simply dial a number and an anonymous voice will tell him the latest Test score. Thus does each country deal with its national anxieties.

Interesting how this new French connection underlines what everyone believes to be that country's obsession with sex, just as our own telephone services reflect Britain's preoccupation with the weather, cricket, and the time. None of these services is interchangeable because the French are as little interested in, for example, Test matches as the British are, generally speaking, in sex.

But if, as seems likely, such 'dial-an-expert' telephone schemes are catching on, what would, I think, be popularly received here is some kind of gardening advice bureau The only trouble there is that, Paris being on STD and our Post Office being what it is, the chaos resulting from crossed lines and misdirected calls could be rather catastrophic. . . .

'Hello, is that the, you know – what's it called – sort of advice service?'

'Oui, m'sieur, à votre service.'

'Oh, Frog, are you? Funny, I was expecting Percy Thrower. Still, never mind. Look, what it's about . . . well, actually, I wanted to talk to somebody about the size of my cucumber, know what I mean – cucumber?'

'Oui, m'sieur, je comprends. It does not matter what euphemsim you care to give it. Speak freely.'

'Eh? Oh, right-ho. Well, it's like this: last year mine was the biggest cucumber for miles around. I had the tiniest King Edwards you ever saw but my cucumber was a whopper. Well, I'll tell you – I showed it to the vicar's wife one day and she was right flabbergasted. Said it was two inches thicker than the vicar's and he'd been expecting to win a prize with his . . .'

'M'sieur, please, one moment. I do not understand. You mean zat en Angleterre ze men show zair, er, cucumbaires to ze clergymen's wives?'

'Certainly. Show 'em to anyone, don't we? How else can we find out who's got the biggest?'

'And zis is important to you, to 'ave ze big, er cucumbaire? Tres extraordinaire 'Ow do you compare zem?'

'Well, we all go down to the village fete, slap our cucumbers on the table, someone comes along and measures 'em and the bloke with the biggest wins the cup.'

'Mon Dieu!'

'So, anyway, like I said, last year mine was the biggest in the county. Won prizes everywhere, it did. But this year, well, I dunno – maybe it's the cold weather but it's such a tatchy little thing I'm ashamed to show it to anyone. They'd all laugh.'

'You mean it 'as shrunk – ze, er, cucumbaire 'as *shrunk*?'

'No, 'course not! It's a different one, innit' I grow a new one every year, don't I? Blimey, don't you do that in France?'

'Non, m'sieur, grace à Dieu we do not. We cling to ze same, er, cumcumbaire all out lives.'

'Strewth, funny bloody lot, you are. Must be shrivelled up old things, hardly worth exhibiting. Anyway, what I want to know is: what shall I do about this puny one I've got? Shall I cut it off and hope a new one will grow in time or . . .'

Non, m'sieur, absolument non! Do not cut anysing, I implore you. Ecoutez, give me your address and I will send an ambulance round at once . . .'

And so the conversation ends with a distinguished psychiatrist and an Englishman in Surbiton staring gloomily into his cold frame and wondering whether some new vegetable resuscitation scheme had replaced the pay beds in the National Health hospitals.

Frank Taylor
"Try to avoid all forms of excitement . . . don't even glance at them in the street!"
At a London Clinic, a doctor was overheard providing this definition of a neurotic as opposed to a psychotic:
A neurotic builds castles in the air.
A psychotic lives in them.
A psychiatrist collects the rent.
Doctor: 'Why do you have HLM 391N tattooed on your back?'
Patient: 'That's not a tattoo. That's where my wife ran into me when I was opening the garage doors.'
I had a medical check up yesterday. My doctor wouldn't tell me how I was but he suggested that I didn't get too interested in radio and television serials.

DOCTOR NO! NO!

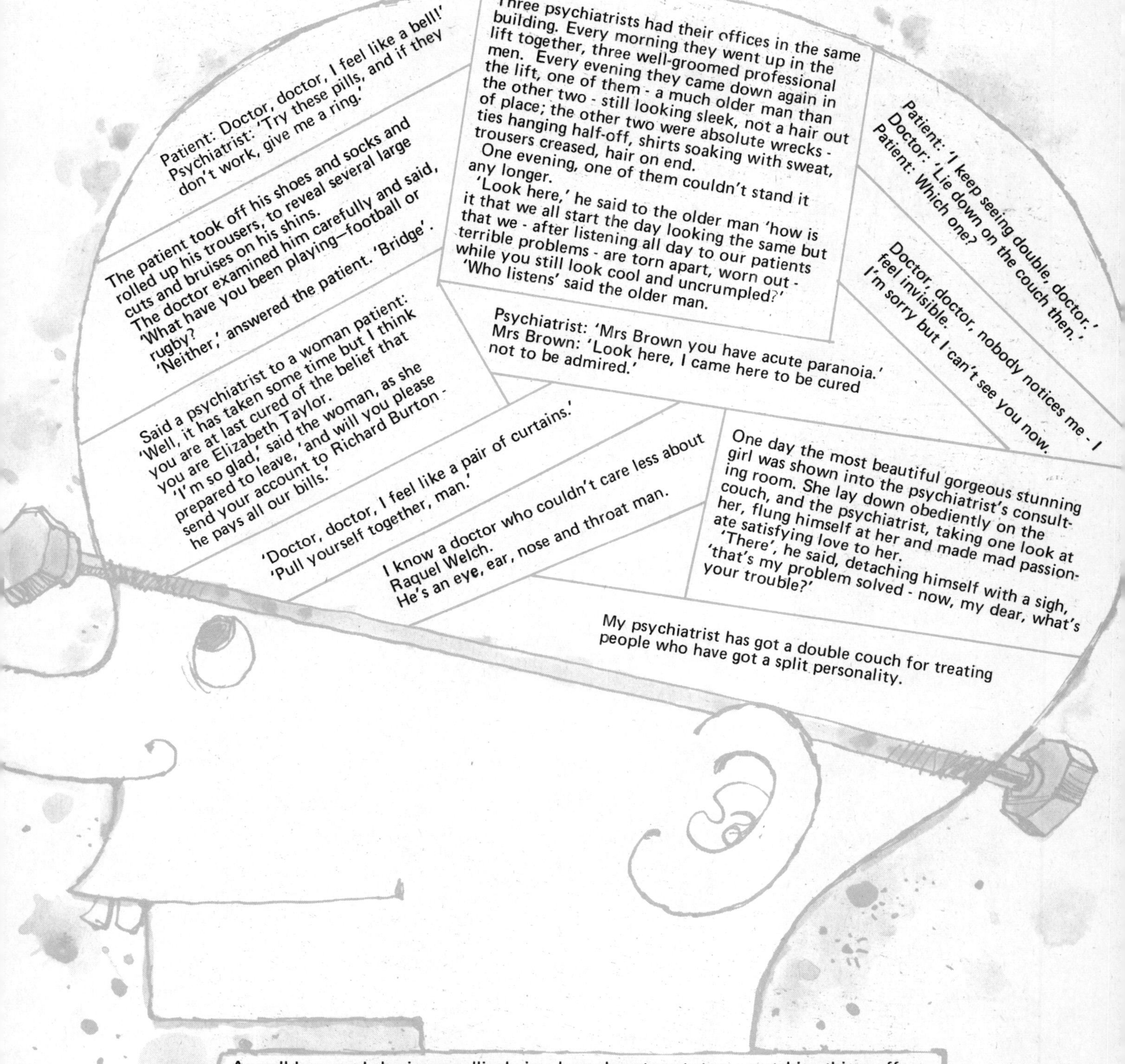

Patient: Doctor, doctor, I feel like a bell!'
Psychiatrist: 'Try these pills, and if they don't work, give me a ring.'

The patient took off his shoes and socks and rolled up his trousers, to reveal several large cuts and bruises on his shins.
The doctor examined him carefully and said, 'What have you been playing—football or rugby?
'Neither,' answered the patient. 'Bridge'.

Said a psychiatrist to a woman patient: 'Well, it has taken some time but I think you are at last cured of the belief that you are Elizabeth Taylor.
'I'm so glad,' said the woman, as she prepared to leave, 'and will you please send your account to Richard Burton - he pays all our bills.'

Three psychiatrists had their offices in the same building. Every morning they went up in the lift together, three well-groomed professional men. Every evening they came down again in the lift, one of them - a much older man than the other two - still looking sleek, not a hair out of place; the other two were absolute wrecks - ties hanging half-off, shirts soaking with sweat, trousers creased, hair on end.
One evening, one of them couldn't stand it any longer.
'Look here,' he said to the older man 'how is it that we all start the day looking the same but that we - after listening all day to our patients terrible problems - are torn apart, worn out - while you still look cool and uncrumpled?'
'Who listens' said the older man.

Psychiatrist: 'Mrs Brown you have acute paranoia.'
Mrs Brown: 'Look here, I came here to be cured not to be admired.'

Patient: 'I keep seeing double, doctor.'
Doctor: 'Lie down on the couch then.'
Patient: Which one?

Doctor, doctor, nobody notices me - I feel invisible.
I'm sorry but I can't see you now.

'Doctor, doctor, I feel like a pair of curtains.'
'Pull yourself together, man.'

I know a doctor who couldn't care less about Raquel Welch.
He's an eye, ear, nose and throat man.

One day the most beautiful gorgeous stunning girl was shown into the psychiatrist's consulting room. She lay down obediently on the couch, and the psychiatrist, taking one look at her, flung himself at her and made mad passionate satisfying love to her.
'There', he said, detaching himself with a sigh, 'that's my problem solved - now, my dear, what's your trouble?'

My psychiatrist has got a double couch for treating people who have got a split personality.

A small boy was behaving appallingly in a large department store - snatching things off counters, flipping clothes on display, sticking out his tongue at people, rushing up the down escalator, yelling and shouting and waving his ice-cream around. Finally, the store manager was fetched.

"I'm sorry," said the boy's father frantically, "but I can't do a thing with him."

"Don't worry, sir," said the manager, "we have a resident psychologist for this sort of emergency - I'll fetch him."

He returned with a tall bearded grey-haired man who went straight over to the boy who was swinging on an expensive garden seat, bent over and whispered in his ear. The boy stopped swinging instantly, slid off the seat, and trotted over to his father good as gold. When they got home, the father couldn't resist ringing up the store psychologist to ask him how on earth he'd effected such a miracle.

"Oh," said the psychologist, "I told him if he didn't belt up I'd wring his ruddy neck."

Yes, well, perhaps we're not quite ready for the machines to take over yet. But we are just as surely not ready for the do-it-yourself technique to be applied to surgery; and playing doctors and nurses is still not on, even for adults:

How to get Surgery All Sewn Up

by *ALAN COREN*

I make no apology for the unnerving nature of this week's column. Any apologies due should be requested with a stamped/addressed envelope, from Dr Eric Gibson, who this week told the Society of Health Congress in (where else?) Eastbourne that the strain would be taken off Britain's medical services if more patients treated their ailments themselves instead of rushing round to their GPs' surgeries every five minutes.

Well, Doc, surely the best way of passing on the necessary tips to do-it-yourselfers would be through the columns of our great newspapers?

Hello, again, Readers! Well, so much has happened since last week, that I really don't know where to begin, but I've had a very nice letter from Mrs Alice Lovibond of Hornsey who has written to thank me for my new week-by-week series on appendicectomy.

Dennis, her youngest, came home from school on Tuesday complaining of severe stomach pains, so, without further ado, and using my handy wall-chart and the free Lobby Lud scalpel given away with last week's issue, she immediately cut him open, following the instructions given in *Part One: Incision.*

Everything went without a hitch, I understand, and both she and Dennis are looking forward to this weeks' instalment, *Part Two: Removal*, which she'll find on page seven.

Hold on Dennis, help is on the way, and good luck with the sewing up Alice!

Lionel Kemp, a reader from Slough, has sent me a useful tip for all you home dentists; as I'm sure you'll agree, one of the problems is keeping your pliers dry, and Lionel has found that by wrapping ordinary absorbent kitchen towel around the pincers, he can get a far better grip on the tooth.

It also prevents unsightly marks on the instrument, and Lionel says he has used the same method for protecting his hammer against impacted wisdoms with spectacular results.

His entire family, he tells me, will soon be up and gumming their food happily!

On the exchange front, I've heard from a gentleman in Wisbech who has a 1937 kidney for sale, immaculate condition, one titled owner, teetotal, with its original nephrons intact.

Are you one of the medical handymen whose family's always nagging him for this or that pill on the slightest pretext? If you are, how's this for a bargain?

Dr R. G. Thurmold of Luton informed me that he has just been lucky enough to be allowed an American visa, thus becoming the 17,348th doctor to emigrate this year.

In consequence, and as a result of the fall in sterling against the dollars he needs to set up over there, he is having to dispose of vast quantities of valuable pills, medicines, and other quality items, most of them unlabelled and therefore on offer at an incredibly low price.

Round pills are 35p per gross (please state colour preferred when ordering), medicine is a mere £1.50 per gallon, available in pale brown, light brown, brown, dark brown, and extremely brown; and sticky yellow paste is going at £5 a firkin.

And many beginners among you, I know, often find that they've launched themselves into a piece of D-I-Y just a teeny bit early on in their career, and aren't sure where to turn for professional help at short notice. For you, good news! A new service, Rentaquack, of Surd Villas, Bermondsey, is offering the skills and opinions of several trained but unluckily struck-off experts.

So if you've inadvertently sewn a patient to his blanket, why not give them a ring, or write enclosing pieces where convenient?

And one last point this week, since it is, after all, spring! I've had a card from a lady amateur surgeon with what she describes as an interesting nodule on her head who would like to meet a gentleman with Murchison's Tremble.

She says she's interested in fast cars and Chinese food as well, so let's hope there's some handsome trembler out there who's reading these heartfelt words, eh?

That's all for this week, friends, so till next time, look after yourselves! And, naturally, after anyone else you can get those nimble hands on!

First Published in The Daily Mail 30/4/76

Come Home Sieggymund all is Forgiven

Excerpt from 'Getting Even'

by WOODY ALLEN

Published by W. H. Allen & Co. Ltd.

The following are a few samples of conversations taken from the soon-to-be-published book *Conversations with Helmholtz*.

Dr. Helmholtz, now nearing ninety, was a contemporary of Freud's, a pioneer in psychoanalysis, and founder of the school of psychology that bears his name. He is perhaps best known for his experiments in behaviour, in which he proved that death is an acquired trait.

Helmholtz resides on a country estate in Lausanne, Switzerland, with his manservant, Hrolf, and his Great Dane, Hrolf. He spends most of his time writing, and is currently revising his autobiography to include himself. The 'conversations' were held over a period of several months between Helmholtz and his student and disciple, Fears Hoffnung, whom Helmholtz loathes beyond description but tolerates because he brings him nougat. Their talks covered a variety of subjects, from psychopathology and religion to why Helmholtz can't seem to get a credit card. 'The Master', as Hoffnung calls him, emerges as a warm and perceptive human being who maintains he would gladly trade the accomplishments of a lifetime if he could only get rid of his rash.

April 1: As Helmholtz reclined in his leather chair, I asked him about the early days of psychoanalysis.

'When I first met Freud, I was already at work on my theories. Freud was in a bakery. He was attempting to buy some tarts, but could not bear to ask for them by name, Freud was too embarrassed to say the word "TARTS" as you probably know. 'Let me have some of those little cakes,' he would say, pointing to them. The baker said, "You mean these TARTS, Herr Professor?" At that, Freud flushed crimson and fled out the door muttering, "Er, no-nothing – never mind." I purchased the pastries effortlessly and brought them to Freud as a gift. We became good friends. I have thought ever since, certain people are ashamed to say certain words. Are there any words that embarrass you?'

Talk turned back to Freud, who seems to dominate Helmholtz's every thought, although the two men hated each other after an argument over some parsley.

'I remember one case of Freud's. Edna S. Hysterical paralysis of the nose. Could not imitate a bunny, when called upon to do so. This caused her great anxiety amongst her friends, who were often cruel. "Come, Liebchen, show us how you make like a bunny." Then they'd wiggle their nostrils freely, much to the amusement of each other.

'Freud had her to his office for a series of analytic sessions, but something went amiss and instead of falling in love with Freud, she fell in love with his coat stand, a tall wooden piece of furniture across the room. Freud became panicky, as in those days psychoanalysis was regarded sceptically, and when the girl ran off on a cruise with the coat stand Freud swore he'd never practice again. Indeed, for a while, he toyed seriously with the idea of becoming an acrobat, until Ferenczi convinced him he'd never learn to tumble really well.'

I could see Helmholtz was getting drowsy now, as he had slid from his chair to the floor under the table, where he lay asleep. Not wishing to press his kindness, I tiptoed out.

April 5: Arrived to find Helmholtz practicing his violin. (He is a marvellous amateur violinist, although he cannot read music and can play only one note.) Again, Helmholtz discussed some of the problems of early psychoanalysis.

Once Freud had some toffee in his pocket and gave a piece to Jung. Rank was infuriated. He complained to me that Freud was favouring Jung. Particularly in the distribution of sweets. I ignored it, as I did not particularly care for Rank since he had recently referred to my paper on "Euphoria in Snails" as "the zenith of mongoloid reasoning."

'Years later, Rank brought the incident up to me while we were motoring in the Alps. I reminded him how foolishly he had acted at the time and he admitted he had been under unusual strain because his first name, Otto, was spelled the same forwards or backwards and this depressed him.'

After dinner there were mints and Helmholtz brought out his collection of lacquered butterfles, which caused him to become petulant when he realized they would not fly.

Later, in the sitting room, Helmholtz and I relaxed over some cigars. (Helmholtz forgot to light his cigar, but was drawing so hard it was actually getting smaller.) We discussed some of the Master's most celebrated cases.

'There was Joachim B. A man in his mid-forties who could not enter a room that had a cello in it. What was worse, once he was in a room with a cello he could not leave unless asked to do so by a Rothschild. In addition to that, Joachim B. stuttered. But not when he spoke. Only when he wrote. If he wrote the word "but," for instance, it would appear in his letter "b-b-b-b-b-but." He was much teased about this impediment, and attempted suicide by trying to suffocate himself inside a large pancake. I cured him with hypnosis, and he was able to achieve a normal healthy life, although in later years he constantly fantasized about meeting a horse who advised him to take up architecture.'

Helmholtz talked about the notorious rapist, V., who at one time held all London in terror.

'A most unusual case of perversion. He had a recurring sexual fantasy in which he is humiliated by a group of anthropologists and forced to walk around bowlegged, which he confessed gave him great sexual pleasure. He recalled as a child surprising his parents' housekeeper, a woman of loose morals, in the act of kissing some watercress, which he found erotic. As a teenager he was punished for varnishing his brother's head, although his father, a house painter by trade, was more upset over the fact he gave the boy only one coat.

'V. attacked his first woman at eighteen, and thereafter attacked half a dozen per week for years. The best I was able to do with him in therapy was to substitute a more socially acceptable habit to replace his aggressive tendencies; and thereafter when he chanced upon an unsuspecting female, instead of assaulting her, he would produce a large halibut from his jacket and show it to her. While the sight of it caused consternation in some, the women were spared any violence and some even confessed their lives were immeasurably enriched by the experience.'

April 12: This time Helmholtz was not feeling too well. He had got lost in a meadow the previous day and fallen down on some pears. He was confined to bed, but sat upright and even laughed when I told him I had an abscess.

We discussed his theory of reverse-psychology, which came to him shortly after Freud's death. (Freud's death, according to Ernest Jones, was the event that caused the final break between Helmholtz and Freud, and the two rarely spoke afterwards.)

At the time, Helmholtz had developed an experiment where he would ring a bell and a team of white mice would escort Mrs Helmholtz out the door and deposit her on the curb. He did many such behaviouristic experiments and only stopped when a dog trained to salivate on cue refused to let him in the house for the holidays. He is, incidentally, still credited with the classic paper on 'Unmotivated Giggling in Caribou.'

'Yes, I founded the school of reverse psychology. Quite by accident, in fact. My wife and I were both comfortably tucked in bed when I suddenly desired a drink of water. Too lazy to get it myself, I asked Mrs Helmholtz to get it for me. She refused, saying she was exhausted from lifting french beans. We argued over who should get it. Finally, I said, "I don't really want a glass of water anyhow. In fact, a glass of water is the last thing in the world I want." At that, the woman sprang up and said, "Oh, you don't want any water, eh? That's too bad." And she quickly left bed and got me some. I tried to discuss the incident with Freud at the analysts' outing in Berlin, but he and Jung were partners in the three-legged race and were too wrapped up in the festivities to listen.

April 18: Arrived to find Helmholtz trimming some rose bushes. He was quite eloquent on the beauty of flowers, which he loves because 'they're not always borrowing money.'

We talked about contemporary psychoanalysis, which Helmholtz regards as a myth kept alive by the couch industry.

'These modern analysts! They charge so much. In my day, for five marks Freud himself would treat you. For ten marks, he would treat you and press your pants. For fifteen marks, Freud would let *you* treat *him*, and that included a choice of any two vegetables. Thirty dollars an hour! Fifty dollars an hour! The Kaiser only got twelve and a quarter for being Kaiser! And he had to walk to work! And the length of treatment! Two years! Five years! If one of us couldn't cure a patient in six months we would refund his money, take him to any musical revue and he would receive either a mahogany fruit bowl or a set of stainless steel carving knives. I remember you could always tell the patients Jung failed with, as he would give them large stuffed pandas.'

We strolled along the garden path and Helmholtz turned to other subjects of interest. He was a veritable spate of insights and I managed to preserve some by jotting them down.

On the human condition: 'If man were immortal, do you realize what his meat bills would be?'

On religion: 'I don't believe in an afterlife, although I am bringing a change of underwear.'

On literature: 'All literature is a footnote to Faust. I have no idea what I mean by that.'

I am convinced Helmholtz is a very great man.

In a way, politicians serve the same sort of purpose as 'the royals'. None of them has anything whatever to do with ruling or running the country, of course – we all know that *that's* done by the faceless few who only flash briefly into the daylight when they get their OBEs on the way to retirement.

No, politicians and royals are here to satisfy our need for scandal, because – (so the psychologists tell us) – our own lives are so drab and lacking in inner meaning that we have to look for a prototype, an archetype, any old sleazy type, on which to project all our dreams of riches and power and leisure and naughty goings-on. Heaven help us, should we ever do anything so silly as vote in a set of serious politicians (how's that for a contradiction in terms?) who just got on with the job, practised monogomy (dirty beasts) and actually tried to keep *out* of the headlines.

Unfortunately, today's royals simply don't measure up to their predecessors when it comes to providing the rip-roaring bawdy scandal-packed lives they got through, legitimately or illegitimately.

So we've got to depend on the politicians for our essential scandal and fun;

Mr. Quintin Hogg

Mr. William Whitelaw

Mr. Reginald Maudling

Mr. Anthony Barber

Mr. Iain Macleod

Lord Balniel

Sir Keith Joseph

Sir John Eden

Mr. Geoffrey Rippon

Mrs. Thatcher

Ten are arrested near Leeds Town Hall

KING SAUD TAKES 30 WIVES TO NICE

From Our Own Correspondent

NICE, Tuesday.

King Saud of Saudi Arabia arrived at Nice to-night from Geneva accompanied by an entourage of 84 for a convalescent holiday. People who saw the King leaving his special aircraft said that he looked "very tired."

Questioned about Kissinger's whore abouts, Ziegler said the president's national security affairs adviser was in the White House Monday.

Nice to feel at home

"I SPENT several days in a mental hospital and felt completely at home" **Christopher Mayhew MP**, told a meeting of the Sheffield Branch of the Mental Health Association.

The Prime Minister: Interviewed by Robin Day on Panorama. (8 BBC-1).

. . . *followed on BBC-2 by* **Heart Attack** (8.50).

Sir Alec Douglas-Home

The right hon. Gentleman asked about the five principles. I have never seen any difficulty about those principles. The proposals were within the five principles that Mr. Smith and I made, and any future proposals must be within the five principles. I should not at this stage like to commit myself exactly to the method which should be used in regard to the fifth principle in future; we are looking at the matter entirely anew and completely blind. [HON. MEMBERS: "Oh!"]

A large piece of green blotting paper rested on the Prime Minister's seat in the House of Commons today. It was both symbolic and necessary.

'C

A

SIR.—
to expi
with M
the sub
What
for Bri
'ast!
in two
crimina
lant kit
If Ha
sute su
in this
display
much a
I say: I
grapple
conscie
no part
The
one o
decency
is typi
moral
this co
Whil
Hamilt
heir n
what s

The
N

The Thoughts of Chairman Alf on Royalty

By JOHNNY SPEIGHT

They don't appreciate the Royalty in this country at all. When the Queen put in for a rise, same as yer dockers, they turned it down. She didn't go on strike, she went by the Industrial Relations Court, but they turned it down. I dunno why she let 'em. I mean, let's face it, she's got 'em over a barrel, ain't she? It's yer law of supply an' demand, annit? 'Cos she's the only person in the world who can do the job, ain't she? I mean, she's laughing, she is yer Queen. I mean, if she turned it in – if she emigrated like, they'd all be after her. Yer only real Queen in the world she is. Yer only real Royalty that's left, she is. I mean, yer Charles is Royalty too, but if his Mum went, young Charlie'd go with her, wouldn't he? I mean, stands to reason, dunnit? He wouldn't blackleg. He wouldn't blackleg, an' duck past no pickets to get on yer throne. Not that lad. Too loyal to his Mum, he is. No. I tell, you what, yer bloody Americans wouldn't half like to have her. Eh? What? Blimey, if she went out there to that America, she'd be in that bloody White House in no time. There'd be no bloody Watergate affairs then, would there?

I mean, she'd *prefer* to stay in Buck House – well, it's more Royal, annit? I mean, better appointed all round. Got continual flush toilets up there, she has. The only continual flush toilets in the world, they are . . . I know. I know the bloke what put 'em in. He lives round the corner from us in Wapping. Even during a water shortage, he said, they have a continual flow. Oh yer, she don't have to pull no chains or nothing – no Royal ball-cocks to go wrong. Anyway, I mean, Buck House'd be nothing without her. I know bloody Wilson's after it if he ever gets in again. Always had his eye on Buck House, he has. But, blimey, look at the mess he made of Downing Street when he was in there – left it like a pigsty, he did. Heath had to have it all re-papered before he could move in, with Wilson's bloody kids an' their jammy finger-marks all over the walls.

No, look, what I'm saying is, when that lot up there got stroppy about her rise, she ought to have threatened to pack her bags an' go. Blimey, it wouldn't have been a brain drain – it'd have been a bloody *Royal* drain – an' serve 'em right. The British government should realize that she could get bigger money out there. She could live in Hollywood. She'd get a lot of TV time, out in America. They'd give her her own show, regular, at least once a week – The Queen's Hour. And she'd come on there and talk about her little problems, an' about her dogs and what to feed your dog on. Blimey, she could do advertisements – I mean, you get adverts on there about Chunkymeats an' all that, but the Queen could come on and say, I feed my corgis on whatever meat she feeds 'em on, and then you'd know that your dog could eat Royal food, just like a Royal dog. And she could give a few racing tips. I mean, she's got one of the finest racing stables in Europe, she must know when one's going to win. She could let the punters know.

I mean, blimey, yer Yanks would have paid *millions* to have her out there making 'em all Lords an' Sirs. Eh? There'd have been yer Lord Nixon right away. An' that Agnes Spiro – blimey, she'd rather go out with the Queen than Frank Sinatra, she would. And I tell you what, yer Labour lot would be the first to try an' buy her back, 'cos without her, where are they going to get all their bloody titles from, eh?

An' Philip, I mean, he should have a rise too, he should get a pay increase. 'Cos I mean, it stands to reason, dunnit, he can't afford to live up to her standards without a bit of money in his pocket, can he? I mean, the man's got his pride, an he? An' he's got to be able to call his shout, an he? I mean, he don't want people going round whispering about him not pushing the boat out, does he?

Excerpt from 'The Thoughts of Chairman Alf'
Published by Robson Books

One thing that all good practising pornographic politicians should write (or if illiterate, arrange to have written) are private diaries and/or memoirs. These should be racy and if possible so libellous that there's bound to be a law-suit before publication (to boost sales if nothing else). Now and again, however, a politicians *wife* (normally a mere smiling sketch of a woman in a flowery hat standing the regulation politician's wife two paces behind her husband on all public occasions) now and again *she* boldly starts a diary, and this can spell trouble for her mate:

Mrs Wilson's Diary

by Richard Ingrams and John Wells

14*th June* 1974

Harold, of late, has become more and more pre-occupied with a large chart which he has, with the assistance of Mr Haines, sellotaped to the wall of his den in Lord North Street. I first became aware of this when Mr Rees, the quiet-spoken Secretary of State for Northern Ireland, came round after tea one day with a harassed look on his kindly, bespectacled face, to ask Harold's advice about what to do next. As Harold had expressed the wish not to be disturbed, I chatted to Mr Rees myself over the gas-stove, and made a good strong pot of Old Baloghi Turkish Tea in an attempt to calm him, suggesting that perhaps the time had come for a reappraisal of the options in the light of the latest developments. Mr Rees listened with great politeness, writing my suggestions down on the back of an envelope, and promising to put them before Mr Paisley when next they met.

At this moment the door of the den was flung open, and Harold emerged, his face wreathed in smiles. 'My dear!' I cried, 'Here is Mr Rees, come to discuss the critical situation in Ireland.' 'Do not bother me with that, woman,' Harold riposted, leading us both into his sanctum with a proprietorial air. Allow me to introduce the distinguished editors of the world-famous Guinness Book of Records.'
'This is it! Harold cried, pointing to the wall-chart, still held in place by a wobbling Mr Haines, perched precariously on the upturned Roses of England wastepaper basket, itself balanced on a fragile gilt chair. 'Gladys! Rees! Examine this chart and tell me whose is the longest.'

I looked at the chart carefully, and saw the names of all the Prime Ministers of this country since 1900, neatly set out down the left-hand side of a large piece of graph paper. 'Note the lines,' Harold cried. 'Against each name you will observe a strip of coloured tape, denoting the length of tenure achieved by each incumbent. Heath's, as you see, is derisory. Likewise his predecessors': Home's, Eden's, Bonar Law's, all miniscule. Consider Clement Attlee, a little better perhaps, but nothing to write home about. Only three giants survive your scrutiny: Asquith, Churchill, and myself. Now, I ask you all, what advantage do I have over the two last-named?' Mr Rees assumed an expression of earnest concentration and looked at the ceiling whilst I racked my brains for the correct answer. 'I am sorry,' Harold remarked at length, slamming his fist down on a bell beside his blotter, and turning in triumph to us, 'your time is up. Tell them, Haines.' The factotum turned his head with an expression of eager compliance, and then unfortunately lost his balance and slid slowly down the wall with a cry, tearing a wide swathe of paper from the centre of the chart and disappearing behind the sofa. 'I will ignore that,' Harold observed with dignity. 'The answer is that I am still alive, and that in approximately two years' time I shall surge into the lead, thus meriting inclusion in the Guinness Book of Records under the category of Longest Serving Prime Minister of the Twentieth Century.'

There was a long silence, broken only by Mr Haines' low moans as he fumbled for his spectacles

beneath the tattered remnants of the chart. 'Ahem,' coughed Mr Rees at last, 'how very, very interesting indeed. And now, Sir, if you have a moment, I would be grateful if we could perhaps discuss our policies with regard to the new situation in Ulster . . .' 'Rees!' Harold cried in a sudden access of fury. 'If you have no concept of priorities, you have no place here at this moment in time. Get up Haines. You do not need your spectacles to show Mr Rees the door. Gladys, the Sellotape from the bathroom cabinet and some scissors. This chart must be repaired at once.'

I am glad to say that this has now been done, and it is Mr Haines' task to advance Harold's tape by a centimetre for every week that passes. No visitor is allowed to leave the house without having seen it, and every evening after dinner, Harold sits in front of it with a tumbler of Old Boney Cognac-style Wincarnis, watching it with a glazed expression of contentment on his rubicund face.
Note: Mr Wilson resigned almost 2 years later!

10th January 1975

Imagine our surprise, on the morning after our return from a brief and somewhat bleak British Rail Away-Break Middle of the Week Winter Excursion All Inclusive Tour of Manchester where we spent a quiet Christmas, to hear a wailing voice emanating from the tower of St John's, Smith Square, calling the Faithful to Prayer. At the same moment, the sound of soft Silver Phantom Rolls Royces drawing up outside the house sent Mr Haines scurrying to take his hair out of curlers and open the front door. There stood Mr Healey, dressed in a soup-stained ankle-length overcoat with a tea towel tied round his head, accompanied by a multitude of small friends, all bearded and with twinkling black eyes flashing from under their Old Testament style burnouses. 'Ah, Prime Minister,' exclaimed Mr Healey as Harold and I came forward to greet our unexpected guests, 'Your Sublime Highness, Sheik Yamani Oryalife, allow me to present our managing director, Harold Pasha.'

Harold appeared somewhat nonplussed as the men of the East inclined their heads, and taking the initiative I cried, 'Come in, come in, and let me take your towelling.' Soon the ground floor of Lord North Street was filled with the aromatic smoke of bubbling hookah pipes, while Haines and the Inspector were busy arranging cushions on the floor in obedience to our new friends' silent gestures. Fortunately, my Aunt Betty had given us a box of crystallised grapefruit segments from W.H. Smith for Christmas, which I was able to pass round the host of seated potentates, and the Inspector obliged by pouring out from a good strong pot of Lyons' Instiblend Goolagong. 'Now', said Mr Healey at Length, lowering himself into Giles's inflatable Whoopee Cushion, 'let us get down to brass tacks. Harold, these Gentlemen have a very interesting proposition to make which I believe could make a substantial difference to our economic situation.'

'Well, I think I should make it quite clear at the outset,' began Harold, puffing at his pipe, 'that we are not beggars. There has been a flood of loose talk, particularly in the Tory press, about so-called collapses of the system and so forth. Nothing of the kind has occurred. As you see' – here he waved a hand at the Kosiglo fire – 'all public services are functioning normally. We are not interested in charity. What I am sure my colleague is talking about is a medium-term loan of say five hundred billion dollars, interest-free, to be paid back at the end of some reasonable period, let us say for the sake of argument, a hundred years.' 'Now, now Harold,' Mr Healey soothed. 'That is not what these gentlemen are offering. What is proposed, Prime Minister, is that our friends should make us a reasonable cash offer for the British Isles, to be obtained by a compulsory purchase order. I think on the face of it that this is a very attractive proposition.'

Mr Healey looked around the circle of bearded sheiks, who nodded and smiled. Anticipating any

possible reservations on Harold's part, the Chancellor continued, 'You may rest assured that your own position, at least as far as the appearances are concerned, will remain unchanged, and in perpetuity following the abolition of elections.' At this Harold's face brightened. 'Now gentlemen,' Mr Healey continued, 'are there any further points to be cleared up?' There was silence for a moment, and much benign shaking of heads, but then, to my surprise, one wizened Emir delved deep into his flowing robes and extracted a tattered press cutting which he proceeded carefully to unfold. As he passed it around for our perusal, I saw that it was a photograph of Harold being clasped to the ample bosom of Mrs Golda Meir, while tears streamed down her face. 'This is not good,' remarked our oriental guest succinctly. 'This very naughty. We not like.' All his companions craned over to see, and nodded vigorously, expressing marked distaste for Mrs Meir's figure and personal attributes. 'Bad vibes, man,' observed another Elder. 'Golda bad chick. No more of this, we pray.' Harold seemed irrationally annoyed and, snatching the photograph from the gnarled hands of a Bedouin who was examining it upside down with clucks of disapproval, he tore it to shreds.

'Healey!' he shouted. 'This is insufferable. My private life is my own affair. It is no business of the gutter press with whom I choose to spend my leisure hours.' 'Bad woman, bad woman,' muttered the Elder obdurately. 'And you belt up, Goat Features!' Harold snapped, at which a growing hubbub of outrage filled the room, and it was not long before our visitors were elbowing their way towards the door, ignoring the despairing pleas of Mr Healey to consider a reduced offer.

'Well, that's torn it,' the Chancellor vouchsafed as the last Rolls Royce purred from the kerb. 'Bang goes your chance of staying on top for 20 years. I'm afraid it will have to be Callaghan and a National Government.' 'Oh, come on, Denis!' Harold cried defiantly, slapping Mr Healey on the back and leading him into the Den for a Wincarnigrog and Twiglets. 'You are wasting your time with these camel-dung wallahs. Just wait till I have sorted Schmidt and Giscard out, and when the oil is flowing the Market will soon look up. We will sell, but when the time is right. Which reminds me, Haines, be sure to cash in my Post Office Savings Bonds, will you, before they become entirely worthless. I want to buy some socks from Marks and Spencers.'

Published by Private Eye Productions Ltd.

Blackburn Times reporter Valerie Seaton will not forget the night she danced with Prime Minister Edward Heath at a Young Conservative Ball — and ended up in the maternity ward of the local hospital

UK Press Gazette

Fugitive is arrested in swoop on cliff villa

Western Daily Press Reporter.

DETECTIVES swooped on a luxury villa on top of 300-ft. high cliffs near Dover before daybreak yesterday, and ended the six-month freedom of Harold Wilson

MR. WILSON.—Members on all sides have deprecated that those found Guilty can then obtain large sums of money by selling their members to the press. Proprietors generally have expressed their abhorence of this practice, and I think it would be better left in the hands of the Press Council, who are perfectly capable of dealing with it.

Times

Shepherd to paint new royal portrait

AT 69 years of age, the Queen Mother is to sit for another portrait. And this time the artist is David Shepherd, who has made his name as a wildlife painter.

'I'm delighted,' he says. 'It's a great chance to get away from painting elephants.'

Daily Mail

These extracts and many of the misprints in our "Daily Blooper" series are taken from "The Private Eye Book of Boobs"

De Chrissermuss Broadcast

from 'The Collected Bulletins of President IDI AMIN by Alan Coren

Dis de point where we steppin' into de worl'-wide role good an' proper, on account of dis bein' de tex' o' de pop'lar Xmas Broadcast, goin' out f'om de famous Radio Uganda station in de trendy downtown Kampala to ev'ry corner o' de worl', always provided we gittin' de plugs in proper an' not leavin' no bare wires hangin' out o' de skirtin' in Studio B, which is wot happenin' durin' de birfday broadcast an' it blowin' all de valves out o' de transmitter, had to wait six weeks fo' a new one f'om Hamley's, also all de wattles comin' off of de roof.

De broadcast goin' out at three o'clock pee em on Xmas day, an' de whole popperlation o' Uganda gonna be lissenin' in wid de love an' loyalty an' devotion, on account of we got de detector jeeps out an' anyone still guzzlin' de mince pies at 3.01 gonna find hisself havin' de brandy balls stepped on, not to mention bein' arrested by de ear an' taken down to HQ fo' a touch o' de seasonal goodwill, such as bein' worked over wid a lead-filled turkey. Now, here de scrip', hot f'om de miraculous four-colour Biro:

Hallo worl' an' all de loyal subberjecks, especially all those on de Wolf Rock Lighthouse an' sim'lar, dis here are President Idi Amin speakin' f'om de centre o' de known universe an' hittin' you wid de Peace On Earf bit, which is jus' us DJs' way o' sayin' dat de time come roun' again fo' gittin' de matchin' socks an' hankies an' turnin' our thoughts to de loved ones wot sendin' dis sort o' junk, can't even be bothered gittin' de size right; jus' as a example, an' showin' dat even de top heads o' state human bein's like anyone else, de fust present I got dis year comin' f'om de Finance Minister an' it takin' de form o' de barf salts, an' wot I'd like to say is, it interestin' to learn he doan like de way I smellin' an' he got to de end o' de broadcast to clear out de desk an' git hisself down de car-park where he takin' up de noo duties, an' damn lucky it Yuletide, else he gittin' de head shrunk on top of it.

Turnin' now to de international scene, wot de hell happenin' to de Queen's Xmas card? I sendin' her de pussonal home-made job, wot I doin' wid de little bits o' sticky coloured paper, an' a damn fiddlin' job, too. If I ain't gittin' de recipperocation by de nex' post, de diperlomatic representative o' HM Gumment gonna find hisself on de inside lookin' out.

Dis natcherly bringin' me to everyone spendin' Xmas in clink: it de time when we got to think o' those less fortunate than ourselves, so all you in chokey start thinkin' about de ones wot buried in quicklime in de prison yard, still plenty o' room out there fo' de slackers, an' I gittin' de word where a lotta shoddy mailbags bin appearin' lately, an' dis de last time I mentionin' it.

De way I seein' it, Xmas is a time fo' de fambly, an' I lookin' upon de whole worl' as a fambly, i.e. anyone steppin' out o' line gittin' de head smacked, especially if Julius Nyerere lissenin', altho' I ain't namin' no names, also any o' de Asian brudders wot givin' me lip, all ex-colonial rubbish wot still hangin' about de place, any memmers o' de Ugandan judiciary wot still on de lam, an' any subberjecks goin' roun' mumblin' under their bref.

Wow, lisseners, I jus' catchin' sight o' de studio sundial, an' it 3.10 already, so I signin' off now an' gittin' back to de puddin'. I mean, I'm fo' de peace an' de goodwill stuff as much as de nex' man, but enuff is enuff!

Published by Robson Books Ltd.

PUSSYCAT, PUSSYCAT WHERE HAVE YOU BEEN?

by MICHAEL ASPEL

On 17 May 1967, I drove up to the gates of Buckingham Palace. The crowds of tourists parted and stared, unimpressed, at my Austin 1100. The car was dusty, but I was immaculate in gent's dark blue natty suiting with pale blue shirt and floral tie bought for *7s 6d* from the girl in the office who made them from the bits left over from her cushion covers.

I was bright, shining and ready to share roast beef and two veg. with my Queen.

I was ready, but I still didn't believe it, and I was fairly certain that the huge police sergeant at the gate would wave aside my forged invitation with, 'Oh, you've had one of those too, have you? Hop it.'

But he didn't. He touched his helmet and waved me through. It was on! The invitation was genuine, and I was expected. I drove into the inner courtyard, where several limousines were drawing up close to a red-carpeted glass portico.

'Would you care to park over here?' said a young army officer, peeping over the collar of his dress uniform.

I got out of the car, and locked the door. The young officer smiled bleakly. 'I think you'll find it still here when you come out,' he said.

Still dazed with disbelief, I was shown into the Bow Room and introduced to my fellow guests. There was Cardinal Heenan, Jack Scamp (the industrial troubleshooter), The Hon. E. D. G. Davies (Chairman of National Carbonising Co.), Malcolm Morris, QC, S. J. L. Egerton (Chairman of Coutts Bank), Dr Maurice Miller MP, Muriel Powell (the Matron of a nearby hospital), and me....

Everyone else seemed about seven feet tall. I stood in the valley formed by two enormous figures. One last moment of panic. How should I address her? 'Your Majesty,' and thereafter 'Ma'am', I decided.

A few minutes passed, and three corgis trotted into the room. I bowed deeply. 'Not yet,' someone muttered.

And suddenly, there they were, looking just as I'd seen them on the newsreels, although the Queen was smaller than I'd expected, more petite, and a lot more attractive.

When we were introduced, my intended 'Your Majesty' to be delivered Raleigh-style, came out as 'Smissyeam'.

The man next to me cracked his nose on his knee in a flamboyant bow, and then I was being introduced to Prince Philip, who smiled cheerfully and gave me a few moments to take in the cut of his suit for future reference.

Introductions over, the line broke up and we formed into small groups around the Royal pair as they wandered amongst us. It soon became obvious that although the Queen might appear to be a solemn lady who only really relaxed when she was out with the horses and dogs, she was in reality a charming person – with a quick wit, and far more easy in her manner than any of us would have expected. Of course, all the Royal Family are professionals at putting people at their ease, and at keeping up the pretence of being riveted by other people's company when in fact they must be bored out of their minds. I don't suppose we were the most scintillating lot they'd ever met, but if we didn't amuse the Queen, she certainly amused us. The day before, she had opened the new mammal house at London Zoo, a cavernous place where day was turned into night so that visitors could observe the nocturnal animals. The only trouble was that this meant there were dark passages, with obvious hazards.

'How did you like the new mammal house, Ma'am?' I ventured.

'I should think it's the perfect place for an assignation,' said the Queen.

And so it went. She told us of some friend of hers whose car had been sat on by an elephant, then mentioned a gift that Mr Kruschev, the Russian premier, had once made to Princess Anne – 'It was a bear,' she said. 'What a ridiculous present to give a child – all those claws.'

'You must get an awful lot of stuff you don't want,' I said, getting more self-confident.

'Yes we do,' said the Queen.

'What happens to it all?'

'Oh, people in the house take it. Billiard tables are difficult to get rid of.'

Just then a helicopter landed in the grounds, and her Majesty looked a little irritated. 'I wish they wouldn't do that,' she said, 'it makes the windows so dusty.'

Luncheon was served. I'd heard that they liked plain food. We started with fresh salmon. I took much too large a portion, not through greed, but because I couldn't co-ordinate my movements with the cutlery. 'Will you have wine, orange squash or beer?' enquired a flunkey. I didn't hear him mention beer to anyone else. Some things show through even the nattiest of gent's suiting. I chose wine – a hock.

After the salmon, and after clearing up the lettuce which had slipped from my plate, they served ham and peaches.

All this time we chatted quietly amongst ourselves. There was no shouting across the table, no cries of 'pass the salt' or 'anybody for the pickled onions'. The table was oval, and of course everything glittered and gleamed. Grandest of all, the fruit knives of solid gold, and plates decorated with gold leaf.

It seemed a pity to eat the fruit. I resisted the temptation to pocket a pear. That would have been the height of bad manners, and anyway the bulge would have been difficult to explain. . . .

Up until this point, the Duke of Edinburgh had said nothing to me. I was reassuring myself that he wouldn't let any guest go without saying *something* to them, even if to ask how the hell they'd got in there, when a voice from behind me said, 'Hello – you on tonight?' – and there was a beaming Prince Philip.

I explained that I wouldn't be reading the news that night as we hadn't had time to put up the 'By Appointment' sign over my desk. What impressed me most about the Duke was that he really seemed to be interested in what one had to say.

If he was amused, he didn't just smile politely and stroke his nose, he threw back his head an came back for more.

The only slight pang of disappointment I felt as I climbed into my car (it *was* still there) was that there was no memento, no souvenir of the occasion. It would have been nice to have a photograph 'seen sharing a joke' or linking arms with raised glasses. But they only do that sort of thing in the real world.

Excerpt from 'Polly wants a Zebra'
Published by Weidenfeld & Nicolson Ltd.

DAILY SKETCH Friday January 12, 196? 7

MOTHER-IN-LAW TROUBLE MADE A HUSBAND QUIT

Daily Sketch

Your M.P. writes...

LEGAL OBSCENITY

PHILIP GOODHART, M.P.

Beckenham Journal & Kentish Times

Sir Charles Clore Millionaire

He has just finished Mario Puzo's novel The Godfather (Heinemann £1·75) which describes methods used by the Mafia. He was most interested.

Evening Standard

Life with Powell

By Chris Moncrieff, of the Press Association

The woman behind the most talked about and controversial politician in British politics, spoke yesterday about being Mrs. Enoch Powell.

In an exclusive interview, Mrs. Pamela Powell told me about the man who is still nervous before he makes a speech in the Commons, who finds time, even during a general election, to graft dahlias and mow the lawn, and who reads aloud to his wife in bed every night.

When I asked Mrs. Powell, who is 44, what it was like to be married to such a man, she said: "I suppose you get used to anything.

Times

The Daily Blooper

QUEER TALE

[F]lags of all nations, that had been limp and [dro]pping all morning long, fluttered and danced [in th]e freshening breeze.

Lake Morris (Wash.) Herald

Tired of appearing in westerns, the film star said he wanted to try more dramatic or romantic *rolls*; something he could get his teeth into.

—Falmouth (Ore.) Advocate

An invitation

If you feel strongly about any particular subject why not write to the "Gazette" about it.

Or if you have a point of view to express, [dro]p a line to the Editor. We prefer dis[cussi]on on local, rather than rational, top[ics].

County Times and Gazette

Tell it to the Marines

● Led Zeppelin, the wild men of rock, have their own particular ways of escaping from the rigours of exhausting tours. There is a lurid tale of a young lady who is said to have been whipped with a live octopus. Bass-player and keyboard man John Paul Jones told me: 'I don't think that is entirely true. As far I can remember, it was a dead shark.'

Sun

Mr. Goodman expressed his appreciation, and said he did like to feel he could claim some little part in the development of the district. When he came the population was 22,500 and now it was 37,500.

Bromsgrove Messenger

SQUATTERS IN COURT AFTER SIEGE

The magistrate, Mr. Edward Vicarage, Leyton, was mounted on Saturday, with all the accuracy and timing of a military exercise.

Leyton Express & Independent

America's millionaire, pl[at]inum king' flew the Atlan[t]ic to watch Nijinsky con[]clude his business in England in a style which thrilled a huge crow on a warm, sunny afternoon.

Sunday Mirror

MAKE-UP HINTS

Hints on making-up were given to members of the Leeds branch of the British Sailors' Society today by Mrs. W. Toulson, of Bedale. Mrs. Arthur Beevers presided.

Yorkshire Evening Post

HUNT FOR CAR AFTER BEXHILL ACCIDENT

Police were searching for a car which failed to stop after a mini car [s]werved off the road and crashed into [a] lamp post in Magdalen Road, Bexhill. No casualties were reported, but [co]mmunications on the 155 mile rail[wa]y—only link between Addis Ababa [and] Djibouti have been disrupted.

Evening Standard

Major David Cotton of the Grenadier Guards was bidding on the Prince's behalf. His instructions apparently were to buy guardsmen.

Two lots were purchased: for £12 he obtained the mounted Band of The Life Guards in state dress, including drum-horse and director; for £9 he obtained six Somerset Light Infantrymen and an officer standing with binoculars, four marching Scots Guards with officer and piper, and seven Grenadiers in firing positions.

Times

Banas, who three minutes before had come on for Willim (he went off with an injured bootlace) stole the ball from the West Ham player, took it up the wing and crossed to Sadek who scored by the post.

Evening Post

War is not funny, and it probably never was. Not a lot of laughs, in the old days, being shoe-horned into several tons of armour, rope-hoisted up on to a dumb animal in a tablecloth, given a thumping great pit prop to balance in one tin-plated hand, and pointed in the direction of some other idiots in more tons of metal similarly mounted. Going over Niagara in a barrel must be a lot more fun than falling off in *that* get-up. And you'd think that nowadays, with all the lovely little extras we've made ourselves, like napalm, atom and hydrogen and heaven knows-what-next bombs, war would be even less laughable. And yet – and yet – whenever and wherever people are thrown together in shell holes, NAAFI canteens, munitions factory, stationary airfields, minefields – sure enough, they'll be making terrible jokes, writing rude words on the curved sides of what they only *think* is a dud bomb, singing unprintable songs. From the humorously acid comments of Old 'if you know a better 'ole' Bill of the First World War to Pilot Officer 'forever pranging' Prune in the Second, people have managed to laugh.

And maybe that's the highest form of bravery there is – though so far there's been no Victoria Cross for extreme hilarity in the face of the enemy – no solemn investitute at Buck House, of the Order of the Golden Chamber Pot (1st Class) for the man who cracked a joke as he went over the top, or exploded an appalling pun as he fell (or was pushed) out of his Dakota on a parachute drop on enemy guns, or scrawled Up you, Hitler, on the one remaining wall of her flattened home.

Of all the men who have recently managed to laugh – and to make us laugh, in the face of the insanity of war, Spike Milligan leaps (and bobs and ducks) to mind. One of the positions I would like least to have held in the last World War would have been Spike's commanding officer – or even NCO since the nearer you got to that inspired lunatic the harder it would be to keep proper Army attitudes.

'Major Chaterjack: I see Milligan is smoking a pipe.
Sgt. Dawson: Yes sir.
Major Chaterjack: He looks very good smoking it.
Sgt. Dawson: Yes sir.
Major Chaterjack: He looks manly.
Sgt. Dawson: Very manly.
Major Chaterjack: Unflappable?
Sgt. Dawson: Definitely unflappable!
Major Chaterjack: What's he like as a soldier?
Sgt. Dawson: Bloody awful sir.'

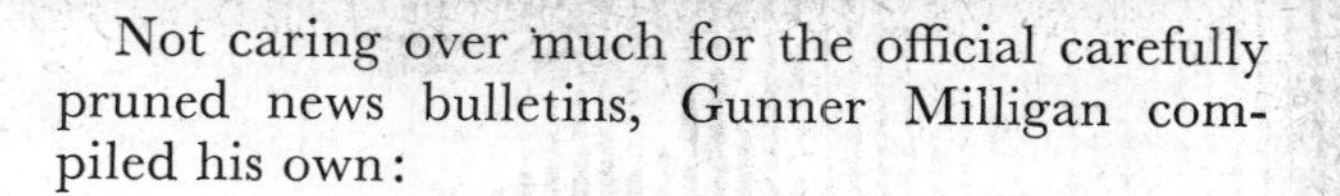

Not caring over much for the official carefully pruned news bulletins, Gunner Milligan compiled his own:

Bulletins ?*!*?

Hitlergram No. 1560934a

FÜHRER: Tea – zat is how ve will break der Britisher!

MESSERSCHMIDT: A great idea mein Führer.

FÜHRER: Zer Englanders, zey like make drink tea? – zis is vat I vant you should make, you vill build eine Tank – zis Tank vill inside a bladder have – in zer bladder ve have zer smell of zer NAAFI tea – we sneak zer tank up on zer Tommy Lines, at 4 o'clocken, zer gun barrel, we squirt zer NAAFI tea smell up zere trouser legs.

MESSERSCHMIDT: Squirt ze tea Schmell?

HITLER: Zen zer Tommy will jump up and run vid zer mug tovords zer tea-schmell-tank. Zen we shoot-bang-fire!

MESS: Zis vill finish zer Englanders.

U.S. BULLETIN

The scene: A highly camouflaged American Ice-cream refrigerator in the battle zone. A 'phone rings.

EISENHOWER: Who is that?

VOICE: I'm General Patton 2nd in line to John Wayne . . .

EISENHOWER: It's Ike here? We've taken a thrashing from the Germans at Kasserine.

PATTON: Germans? I'll put them on the list, but first we get rid of the Limeys!

EISENHOWER: Remember, form the Tanks into a circle – with women and kids in the middle.

X Camp 201 PoW

MILLI-NEWS

Libya: Last night, under cover of drunken singing, British Commandos with their teeth blacked out, raided an advance Italian Laundry, several vital laundry lists were captured, and a complete set of Marshall Gandolfo's underwear, which showed he was on the run.

China: Chinese troops are reported in the area with their eyes at the slope.

Syria: It is reported that Australian troops have taken Cascara. They are trying to keep it dark but it is leaking out in places and the troops are evacuating all along the line.

Rome: Il Duce told the Italian people not to worry about the outcome of the war. If they lost, he had relatives in Lyons Corner House, from whence he would run the Government in Exile.

Local: Sanitary Orderly Liddel takes pleasure in announcing his new luxury long drop Karzi*. Secluded surroundings, screened from the world's vulgar gaze by Hessian. Plentiful supply of Army Form Blank. Book now to avoid disappointment in the dysentery season.

*From the Zulu word M'Ķarzi, meaning W.C.

Life, death, heroics? Forget it. War, it seems, concentrates the mind wonderfully on the real essentials – like food, sleep, sex, smoking, sex, booze, skyvving, sex.

American Cadet: 'Look me over, honey. I'm a West Pointer.'

Girl: 'I don't care if you're an Irish setter, you're not my type.'

So some days you had to think about something else instead: *SPIKE AGAIN*

Our Cook, Gunner May, a dapper lad with curly black hair and Ronald Colman moustache was doling out Porridge. He spoke with a very posh voice and Porridge.

'Where'd you get that accent Ronnie?' asked Gunner Devine.

'Eton old sausage.'

'Well I'd stop eatin' old sausages,' says Devine.

With a flick of the wrist, May sent a spoonful of Porridge into Devine's eye. 'Good for night blindness,' he says ducking a mug of tea.

'The wireless truck will collect you at 19.00 hours.'

'19.00?' I said. 'That's a pity, my watch only goes up to 12.' He passed a damp cigarette. 'Ta,' I said. 'I'll have it valued later.'

We sat down to eat 'the unexpired portion of our rations,' 'unexpired' being a piece of bully beef that is gradually dying for its country. I grabbed my throat, staggered round gasping 'This bully's been poisoned with food. Ahhhh!' and fell to the ground.

'Bury me up a tree,' I said.

'You bloody fool,' said Edge, 'why?'

'After I die I want people to look up to me.'

As Devine reached for my cigarettes, I said 'Gord, you still scrounging fags, how many do you smoke a day?'

'As many as I can cadge, in civvy street I smoked sixty a day.'

'That's too many mate.'

'Yes, it was too many, but some days, it was just right.'

'They'll kill you in time.'

'*Something* kills *everybody* in time, take my grandmother, she died of deafness.'

'Died of *Deafness?*'

'Yes, there was this steamroller coming up behind her and she didn't hear it.'

Or, you set about getting yourself something eatable like Sergeant chef Harris who brought a live piglet back with him off leave, meaning to fatten it up for his mob for Christmas – and charge a nice fat price per portion for it:

'The keeping of pigs in barracks was forbidden, so Harris gave the creature two coats of white paint with patches of brown that near as dammit made it look like a Cocker Spaniel. The pig got bigger and had to be painted as a Great Dane. At night it went foraging. Lt. Budden awoke one night. He phoned the guard house. 'Am I drunk?' he enquired. 'No sir,' said the duty N.C.O. 'In which case,' said Budden, 'there's a pig painted brown eating my boots.'

We tried to tether the animal but it broke the chain . . . and dashed squealing over the football pitch. Seeing our Christmas dinner disappearing, We gave chase. Heading up the road to St. Leonards, it suddenly turned right. 'No! My God, no!' said Bombardier Donaldson as the pig rushed up the steps and through the front door of the 'Belgravia Guest House for Refined Gentlefolk'. Screams issued forth, crockery was breaking. Entering the hall we saw chaos! A bald man lying face down on his back with a grandfather clock across him. A fat bursting woman was clutching a gross of Pekinese: 'My darlings,' she trilled through a rouged hole. On the landing a fine old man with a rolled newspaper was flailing away at nothing and shouting 'Shooooooo'. A toothless crone issued forth stirring a saucepan of thrice-watered porridge. Behind her a blind man holding up sagging trousers appeared at the W.C. door. 'There's no paper, Mrs. Hurdle,' he said. 'In the cellar!' screamed a refined voice. Down we raced. Up we came, with the blind man bound hand and foot, still looking for paper. 'It's the wrong one,' said Harris. Down we raced again. A woman at the top stair kept shouting, 'Mind my bottled quinces.' At last we got the animal up. We were covered in cuts, bruises and bottled quince. The pig was unmarked. With a noose around his neck he was as quiet as a lamb. 'Who,' said a vast landlady, 'who is gwoing to pway for all this dwamage! eh?' Sergeant Harris, braces dangling, bowed low. 'That's no bloody good,' she said. 'Madam, every last penny will be repaid,' said Harris. He took her vile hand, kissed it, passing on his hereditary gingivitis.'

From Adolph Hitler 'My part in his downfall' by Spike Milligan, Published by Michael Joseph

WAR ACCORDING TO SPIKE MILLIGAN

Sleep came high on the list of priorities, if only because like all the rest you could never get enough of it – the great advantage of sleep being, as always, that it got you away, right away, from it all (wherever or whatever it happened to be in your particular bit of the war):

19 March, 1943. That night I slept Al Fresco, and there's nothing better, except sleeping Al Jolson.

I awoke in the wee small hours, but not for a wee, no! *something* was crawling on my chest, my first thought was it must be an eleven foot King Cobra, it was moving slowly down towards where women affect you most, if he bit me there, some twenty women in England would take the veil. I called very softly 'Harry . . . Harry . . . Harry . . . ' He moved and mumbled something like 'It's all right mother, I've known her three years.' 'Pay Parade!' I said. This got his eyes open. 'Now listen! There's something on my chest.'

'They're called blankets.'

'I'm serious, it's moving downwards, can you carefully take the blankets back and get it?' He lit the oil lamp, and very carefully peeled off the blankets, he gasped.

'Cor bloody hell!'

'Never mind that, what is it?'

'A black scorpion.'

'Rubbish, it's an eleven foot King Cobra!'

'It's a two inch scorpion. I'm going to knock it to your side.'

'What's wrong with yours.'

With a sweeping movement he whisked the scorpion off, smashed the tent pole, collapsed the tent, extinguished the light, spilled the paraffin, and set fire to the blankets. From then on the evening lost its splendour, we stood in the pouring rain amid smouldering blankets, trying to avoid the scorpion, and to retrieve our kit. The night was spent in the gay carefree interior of Kidgell's lorry, much to Wilson's disgust.

Wilson was a dour Scot, sporting pebble glasses only the British Army would make him a driver. I think he drove in Braille. In peace time he'd been a shepherd. He rarely spoke, but sometimes in his sleep, he bleated.

'I kept walking into things, falling down holes and treading on sleeping comrades. I had trodden on Gunner Maunders so many times he asked me, should he change his name to Axminster, but this night I didn't tread on Gunner Maunders, no, I just drove straight into a Minefield. 'Don't worry' I said 'It's one of ours.'

And if it actually came down to fighting (which is what war is supposed to be all about, only it isn't for a lot of lucky people) ' . . . every day was lunatic. What can you say when Gunners taking mobile showers get a sudden call to action? Imagine the result – the sight of a gun team in action, naked, in tin hats and boots, all save Bombardier Morton who holds his tin hat afront of that part which only his "loved one should see". As I stood there I thought "My God, what havoc one determined German could wreak on this lot with a feather duster."

Our guns were firing. What a bloody noise. What in heaven's name did they think they were doing—it was past midnight! What would the neighbours say? Soldiers needed rest. They have to get up every morning looking lovely for their Regiments.

We took the spindle from the drum and unwound by hand. More flares, suddenly a rapid burst of automatic fire. It was a Spandau, a return burst, the unmistakable chug, chug, chug of a Bren gun. A flare silhouetted us beautifully for the whole Afrika Korps to see. 'Freeze,' hissed Fuller. I had one leg raised when he said it. Somewhere a German O.P. officer was saying 'Himmel! zey are using one-legged soldiers.' The flares fade. Fuller says 'I'm lost.'

'I thought you'd never say it,' I said.

Rather than go back to the gun position we hung around at the foot of the O.P. hill yarning and smoking. Finally, towards evening, we started back.

'It was all a bit of an anti-climax,' Fuller said.

'Yes. I wonder which bit it was?'

I felt my chin. I had a three day growth. A dust storm was starting to blow up, I couldn't decide whether it was German or one of ours. In the middle of it, a staff car emerged from across the fields.

Me: Look Frank! In the middle of it, a staff car has emerged from across the fields!

It was General Alexander with some staff officers. They got out, pointed in all directions, leaped back in the car and shot off at speed. The rich have all the fun! Dusty and tired we arrived at the gun position. Lt Joe Mostyn had just returned from a meal with an Arab sheik. 'I had to eat three bloody sheeps' eyes!'

'Really?' I said, 'Bend down and you should be able to see out the back.'

Poor old Joe! He was not particularly good at Gunnery! On his first day at an O.P. he scored ten direct hits, – on a field. I pointed out there were no Germans in it.

'Ah,' he said, 'they may fall in the holes.'

'Of course,' I said, 'German Division surrenders with twisted ankle.'

"Rommel? Gunner Who?" first Published by Michael Joseph

War is good business while it lasts – all those lovely bombs and poison gases and imitation meat and synthetic shoes, how could you wage anything without them? But when its over, what then? No one wants to blow anyone up (for a while, anyway) or bury them alive, they just want to get somewhere comfortable and safe, sink their teeth into as much real meat with real blood in it and eat as much – do as much of everything as they want But there is one industry that comes very well out of the war – the business of War Memoirs. They pour out of the studies and the back parlours and the prisons in a torrent of print and paperback – rear-admirals, leading aircraftsmen (2nd class), generals, enemy chiefs of staff, even conscientious objectors ('Why I *Didn't* Win the War by Albert Tearaway') you name it, they've written it (except women, who seem to have kept remarkably quiet about their wars – discretion or good tactics?) One extraordinary set of reminiscences which hasn't had quite the audience it deserved are those of Friedrich Schmeed:

The Schmeed Memoirs

The best-known barber in wartime Germany, provided tonsorial services for Hitler and many highly placed government and military officials. As was noted during the Nuremberg Trials, Schmeed not only seemed to be always at the right place at the right time but possessed 'more than total recall,' and was thus uniquely qualified to write this incisive guide to innermost Nazi Germany. Following are a few brief excerpts:

In the spring of 1940, a large Mercedes pulled up in front of my barbershop at 127 Koenigstrasse, and Hitler walked in. 'I just want a light trim,' he said, 'and don't take too much off the top.' I explained to him there would be a brief wait because von Ribbentrop was ahead of him. Hitler said he was in a rush and asked Ribbentrop if he could be taken next, but Ribbentrop insisted it would look bad for the Foreign Office if he were passed over. Hitler thereupon made a quick phone call, and Ribbentrop was immediately transferred to the Afrika Korps, and Hitler got his haircut. This sort of rivalry went on all the time. Once, Göring had Heydrich detained by the police on false pretenses, so that he could get the chair by the window. Göring was an oddball and often wanted to sit on the hobbyhorse to get his haircuts. The Nazi high command was embarrassed by this but could do nothing. One day, Hess challenged him. 'I want the hobbyhorse today, Herr Field Marshal,' he said.

'Impossible. I have it reserved,' Göring shot back.

Himmler arrived in a frenzy. He had been in the midst of a tap-dancing lesson when the phone rang, summoning him to Berchtesgaden. He was afraid it was about a misplaced carload of several thousand cone-shaped party hats that had been promised Rommel for his winter offensive. (Himmler was not accustomed to being invited to dinner at Berchtesgaden, because his eyesight was poor and Hitler could not bear to watch him bring the fork up to his face and then stick the food somewhere on his cheek.) Himmler

'I have orders directly from the Führer. They state that I am to be allowed to sit on the horse for my haircut.' And Hess produced a letter from Hitler to that effect. Göring was livid. He never forgave Hess, and said that in the future he would have his wife cut his hair at home with a bowl. Hitler laughed when he heard this, but Göring was serious and would have carried it out had not the Minister of Arms turned down his requisition for a thinning shears.

I have been asked if I was aware of the moral implications of what I was doing. As I told the tribunal at Nuremberg, I did not know that Hitler was a Nazi. The truth was that for years I thought he worked for the phone company. When I finally did find out what a monster he was, it was too late to do anything, as I had made a down payment on some furniture. Once, toward the end of the war, I did contemplate loosening the Führer's neck-napkin and allowing some tiny hairs to get down his back, but at the last minute my nerve failed me.

At Berchtesgaden one day, Hitler turned to me and said, 'How would I look in sideburns?' Speer laughed, and Hitler became affronted. 'I'm quite serious, Herr Speer,' he said. 'I think I might look good in sideburns.' Göring, that obsequious clown, concurred instantly, saying, 'The Führer in sideburns – what an excellent idea!' Speer still disagreed. He was, in fact, the only one with enough integrity to tell the Führer when he needed a haircut. 'Too flashy,' Speer said now. 'Sideburns are the kind of thing I'd associate with Churchill.' Hitler became incensed. Was Churchill contemplating sideburns, he wanted to know, and if so, how many and when? Himmler, supposedly in charge of Intelligence, was summoned immediately.

knew something was wrong, because Hitler was calling him 'Shorty,' which he only did when annoyed. Suddenly the Führer turned on him, shouting, 'Is Churchill going to grow sideburns?'

Himmler turned red.

'Well?'

Himmler said there had been word that Churchill contemplated sideburns but it was all

unofficial. As to size and number, he explained, there would probably be two, of a medium length, but no one wanted to say before they could be sure. Hitler screamed and banged his fist on the table. (This was a triumph for Göring over Speer.) Hitler pulled out a map and showed us how he meant to cut off England's supply of hot towels. By blockading the Dardanelles, Doenitz could keep the towels from being brought ashore and laid across anxiously awaiting British faces. But the basic question remained: Could Hitler beat Churchill to sideburns? Himmler said that Churchill had a head start and that it might be impossible to catch him. Göring, that vacuous optimist, said the Führer could probably grow sideburns quicker, particularly if we marshalled all of Germany's might in a concentrated effort. Von Rundstedt, at a meeting of the General Staff, said it was a mistake to try to grow sideburns on two fronts at once and advised that it would be wiser to concentrate all efforts on one good sideburn. Hitler said he could do it on both cheeks simultaneously. Rommel agreed with von Rundstedt. 'They will never come out even, *mein Führer*,' he said. 'Not if you rush them.' Hitler became enraged and said that it was a matter for him and his barber. Speer promised he could triple our output of shaving cream by the fall, and Hitler was euphoric. Then, in the winter of 1942, the Russians launched a counter-offensive and the sideburns came to a halt. Hitler grew despondent, fearing that soon Churchill would look wonderful while he still remained 'ordinary,' but shortly thereafter we received news that Churchill had abandoned the idea of sideburns as too costly. Once again the Führer had been proved right.

After the Allied invasion, Hitler developed dry, unruly hair. This was due in part to the Allies' success and in part to the advice of Goebbels, who told him to wash it every day. When General Guderian heard this, he immediately returned home from the Russian front and told the Führer he must shampoo his hair no more than three times weekly. This was the procedure followed with great success by the General Staff in two previous wars. Hitler once again overruled his generals and continued washing daily. Bormann helped Hitler with the rinsing and always seemed to be there with a comb. Eventually, Hitler became dependent on Bormann, and before he looked in a mirror he would always have Bormann look in it first. As the Allied armies pushed east, Hitler's hair grew worse. Dry and unkempt, he often raged for hours about how he would get a nice haircut and a shave when Germany won the war, and maybe even a shine. I realize now he never had any intention of doing those things.

One day, Hess took the Führer's bottle of Vitalis and set out in a plane for England. The German high command was furious. They felt Hess planned to give it to the Allies in return for amnesty for himself. Hitler was particularly enraged when he heard the news, as he had just stepped out of the shower and was about to do his hair. (Hess later explained at Nuremberg that his plan was to give Churchill a scalp treatment in an effort to end the war. He had got as far as bending Churchill over a basin when he was apprehended.)

Late in 1944, Göring grew a moustache, causing talk that he was soon to replace Hitler. Hitler was furious and accused Göring of disloyalty. 'There must be only one moustache among the leaders of the Reich, and it shall be mine!' he cried. Göring argued that two moustaches might give the German people a greater sense of hope about the war, which was going poorly, but Hitler thought not. Then, in January of 1945, a plot by several generals to shave Hitler's moustache in his sleep and proclaim Doenitz the new leader failed when von Stauffenberg, in the darkness of Hitler's bedroom, shaved off one of the Führer's eyebrows instead. A state of emergency was proclaimed, and suddenly Goebbels appeared at my shop. 'An attempt was just made on the Führer's moustache; but it was unsuccessful,' he said, trembling. Goebbles arranged for me to go on radio and address the German people, which I did, with a minimum of notes. 'The Führer is all right,' I assured them. 'He still has his moustache. Repeat. The Führer still has his moustache. A plot to shave it has failed.'

Near the end, I came to Hitler's bunker. The Allied armies were closing in on Berlin, and Hitler felt that if the Russians got there first he would need a full haircut but if the Americans did he could get by with a light trim. Everyone quarrelled. In the midst of all this, Bormann wanted a shave, and I promised him I would get to work on some blueprints. Hitler grew morose and remote. He talked of parting his hair from ear to ear and then claimed that the development of the electric razor would turn the war for Germany. 'We will be able to shave in seconds, eh, Schmeed?' he muttered. He mentioned other wild schemes and said that someday he would have his hair not just cut but shaped. Obsessed as usual by sheer size, he vowed he would eventually have a huge pompadour – 'one that will make the world tremble and will require an honour guard to comb.' Finally, we shook hands and I gave him a last trim. He tipped me one pfennig. 'I wish it could be more,' he said, 'but ever since the Allies have overrun Europe I've been a little short.'

Excerpt from 'Getting Even' by Woody Allen
Published by W. H. Allen & Co. Ltd.

Of course, in the last little dust-up that Britain had much to do with, it was not only the boys in blue or khaki or whatever, who actually 'saw action' as they used to say when they meant fighting – or maybe they just meant standing behind a tree and watching Back home, it was often just as noisy and twice as dangerous especially during the blackout:

BUT I JUST TOLD YOU MISS UPLIFT, RECONNAISSANCE MEANS GOING OVER UNKNOWN TERRITORY.

"I'VE LEARNED A LOT FROM THIS BLACKOUT DRILL, MR POLLITT"

BECAUSE YOU'RE A FIRE WATCHER, MR. SMYTHE, IS NO EXCUSE FOR MEDDLING WITH MY HOSE

"STOP IT, BERT, IT IS BERT, ISN'T IT?"

BUT YOU PROMISED TO LET NOTHING COME BETWEEN US,-MISS SPOONER!

"Good heavens, I can't think why the warden hasn't been round to you about the lights."

From 'Run Adolph Run'
compiled by Denis Gifford
Published by Corgi Books.

In the end, though, you come back to the beginning – war (apart from the friends you make which are like no other friends you ever had before or since) war is mad; and the only – the bravest – thing to do – when you can – is to laugh at it, madly. Like Spike Milligan who found a clapped out old piano just about surviving in some wayout battle zone:

'. . . still playable but the floor adjacent had given way, so I made no effort to play my attractive version of Chopsticks, which is not better than any other version, except I do it blindfolded standing on one leg with my trousers down. Oh I know it would mean nothing at a Chopin recital, but it had been well received in the NAAFI Canteen on Christmas Eve 1942, and who's to say, during those long nights at the Carthusian Monastery in the Valedemosa, Chopin didn't drop his trousers to compose the E Minor Nocturne? It was common knowledge that when he played in the relative minor of C, his legs overheated, at one time George Sands' hands were a mass of burns.

One afternoon the line-laying truck (M2) halted by the door, and a long thing called Harry Edgington drew nigh, giving our special "choked scream", I greeted him in my draws cellular. (I was counting my legs to see how near to Chopin I could get.) "And why," he said, wriggling his fingers in the air, "are you in a state of dishabille?"

"I'm practising to be Chopin's legs."

"Good, I'm training to be George Sands' teeth." '

"Rommel? Gunner Who?" first Published by Michale Joseph

An unwilling conscript during the Second World War was undergoing his medical tests, as part of which he had an interview with an Army psychiatrist.

'And what might be your ambition in His Majesty's service?' asked the doctor.

'I'd like to parachute right into Berlin, right on top of Hitler's bunker, sir,' said the conscript fervently. 'All I want is a pistol and a pocket full of hand-grenades, and I'd finish this war all by myself!'

'You're mad!' said the psychiatrist.

'Can I have that in writing?' asked the conscript.

Jamie, a raw recruit, lost his rifle during his first week of service, and was sentenced to twenty-eight days' detention and £2 a week off his pay until the rifle was paid for.

'Do I have tae pay fer it as weel?' he said.

'You certainly do,' replied the C.O. grimly.

'Man,' groaned Jamie, 'noo I ken how a captain prefers tae gang doon wi' his ship!'

One Squadron-Leader who had just been promoted to Group-Captain was bursting with prode at his upgrading. He was sitting in his new office when there came a knock on the door.

'Come in!' he called, and as the door opened he picked up his phone and said, 'Very well, Air Marshal. Thank you, Air Marshal. Goodbye.'

He put down the receiver and said to the airman who had just entered, 'Well, what is it?'

And the airman replied, 'I've just come to reconnect you phone, sir.'

THE DAY WAR BROKE OUT

The day war broke out, my wife said to me, she said, "What are you going to do?" I said, "What about?" She said, "About the war!" So I joined the Home Guard. The first time I came home in me uniform, she said, "What are you supposed to be?" I said, "A Home Guard." She said, "What are you supposed to do?" I said, "Keep back the Germans if there's an invasion." She said, "What you?" I said, "Not just me. There's Charlie Evans and Tom Jenkins, oh, there's seven or eight of us altogether."

Robb Wilton (1940)

A recruit was ordered to stand at the end of the line by his sergeant. A minute later he returned.

'I told you to stand at the end of the line!' roared the sergeant.

'I went, sergeant' said the recruit, 'but there was someone already there.'

THANK GOD! THEY'RE CIVILIZED.

But the last word must come from Milligan.

'Even if we win the war, the bloody Germans won't admit defeat, they'll say, "Ve came second".'

The Daily Blooper

Weather checks

THERE WAS LESS weather than usual last month.

Bristol Evening News

Our own Bishop has promised to take the chair. There will be a very strong platform to support him.

Diocesan Magazine

Keep Death Penalty, Urges Clergyman

No-one Free From Killer if Deterrent Is Remove

Because of the dreadful crimes of which unregenerate man is capable the death penalty should be there to emphasise the sanctity of human life and protect it.

1.30 Colour: New series

WATCH WITH MOTHER

MR. BENN

Every week Mr. Benn dresses-up and finds himself in a new ad. venture.

From the Radio Times

WOMEN'S WRITES

Bowing to popular demand, landlor Bob Wass of the Baron of Beef, Cam bridge, has installed a graffiti blackboard— in the ladies' loo.

Financial Times

Golden Oldie

□ One example of the kind of case that merits a phone was an old lady living in Berkshire who could not speak.

Reading Evening Post

Mr. Griffin said last night: "I am very pleased after this long wait that we are now able to get married. It was worth every minute.

LONG WAIT

"The dispensation had to come from the Pope. Now what we both hoped for is actually coming true. Both my wife-to -be and myself were, and still are, true and active alcholics and we will continue to be so.

Yorkshire Post

Dropped Shot

○ Two men were shot, one in the foot and one in the leg, when police fired over rioter's head's in Londonderry. They were taken to hospital.

Evening News

The Nilotic race is remarkable for the disproportionately long legs of their men and women. They extend on the eastern side of the Nile right down into the Uganda Protectorate.

From a book by Sir Harry H. Johnson

Here is thy Sting

□ Dying is to cost more at King's Lynn, Norfolk. Higher Burial charges are being introduced at cemeteries. The increased cost of living is blamed.

Daily Telegraph

MIRACLE DRUG HITS SNAG

Among the side reactions of this mercurial drug the most important is the death of the patient shortly after the injection.

New York State Medical Journal

CUSTOMERS GIVING ORDERS WILL BE PROMTLY EXECUTED

Notice in Bombay tailor's

STOOPED TO CRIME

□□ Miss Giavollela had pleaded guilty to stealing goods worth £25 0s 2½d from Tesco Supermarket; to assaulting a policewoman; and to dishonestly handling a garden gnome.

Oxford Time

Change of Address

●● A City Stationer reports that a recent letter from a Surrey customer ordering 100 Christmas cards included the statement that: 'We would like 15 printed "From Mr. and Mrs. Sidney—," 25 "From Sidney and Angela," 20 "From Sid and Angie," 10 "From Uncle and Aunt ditto," 20 "From Stuffy and Blossom," and 10 "Guess Who?"

Evening Standard

Pushing On

Mr. Chris Richardson, county councillor for London Colney and Colney Heath, said the gipsies had been harassed for centuries and he saw no reason why they should not be harassed for a little while longer.

Herts Advertizer

London's new Lord Mayor goes for youth

Kentish Times

Personally Speaking....

There are certain famous people who, in addition to being good at what makes them famous, are also very clever *raconteurs* (which is French for making a good story even better). The best thing about these stories is that they are the sort of thing that didn't actually happen to us – but we wish we had; and some very funny reactions and cracks – which we like to *think* we'd have made *if* the whole thing had happened to us. Like these episodes from DAVID NIVEN'S book 'The Moon's a Balloon'; the first from his schoolboy days; the second from, quite definitely, some time later:

The musical success of each service (we suffered through two a day) depended entirely on my prowess behind the organ. This was a position of great trust, but the newly found clown in me could not resist the opportunities it offered. For a small price – two chocolate whirls, one Cadbury's Milk Flake or a brace of Turkish delights – I could be bribed to let the air out of the bellows on important occasions. The whole school, on the selected day, would be in the know and would sit through an endless sermon hugging itself with delicious anticipation.

It took careful preparation but I could generally arrange matters so that a rude noise could be subtly injected into the proceedings, usually just after an Amen. I could redress the situation rapidly by quick pumping and only the connoisseurs could detect that it was not a mistake . . . the boys were all connoisseurs.

Once I tried it when the Bishop of Ripon was in the middle of a special address. This was my masterpiece and also my downfall but the bribes were mountainous.

It was a highly technical job and involved surreptitiously and noiselessly keeping the bellows half-filled for several minutes after the end of the preceding hymn. I had intended to let this air out in a series of well-spaced small squeaks and trills thus keeping the boys happy during what promised to be a long, trying period, but something went wrong and it all came out at once and on a most unfortunate cue . . . a quotation from Proverbs 7, 'I have perfumed my bed with myrrh, aloes and cinnamon . . .'

It was as if the bellows could not contain themselves any longer – a tremendous fart rent the air. All was confusion.

Soon after we got back to the Pink House, my birthday loomed up and Hjördis, my wife, said, 'Let's go down to some little place on the beach and have lunch together.'

It was a Sunday and the weather was glorious, and dreading the bumper-to-bumper traffic, I advanced every excuse, but she was adamant. So I took my place resignedly behind the wheel and we headed out towards Malibu.

She pointed excitedly, 'Let's go in there . . . it looks sweet.'

'The Frigate Bird' was a well-known whore house with a very unsavoury reputation. I explained this to Hjördis.

'Oh, *please*,' she said. 'I've never been in one before. Please, do take me in there . . . and look . . . it says Dining Room!'

Still chastened by our short separation, I gave myself a good mark, for being attentive to my wife though luncheon in a brothel seemed a strange way to demonstrate it, and turned into the driveway.

As we entered, a parrot in a cage gave a wolf whistle and a sleazy madame greeted me with,

'Look who's here! Well, hullo there, Dave! . . . Long time no see' – a libellous and erroneous statement as it happened but I pretended not to hear and pressed grimly on towards the dining room. Then I froze. In the gloom, I saw the well-known back of a close friend. His arm was around a blonde girl's waist . . . Laurence Olivier.

'Quick!' I hissed to Hjördis. 'We've got to get out of here.' Then as my eyes became accustomed to the semi-darkness, I spotted another even more easily recognisable form . . . Peter Ustinov was pinning a dark girl to the wall. My head spun. My friends had gone mad – what a lunatic risk to take! I grabbed Hjördis by the arm and dragged her down the passage; the parrot whistled again, a peal of well-known laughter followed Patricia Medina!

Only then did I catch on. My surprise birthday party in surprise surroundings was a complete success.

We'd all like to have written (let alone received) the sort of letters GROUCHO MARX blessed his friends with from time to time:

TO ROBERT RUARK

June 26, 1963

Dear Mr Ruark:

Thanks for your piece on dirty comedians. It blew a fresh breeze across a smutty section of America.

Freedom of speech is one thing, but these gents are over-doing it. And when I say 'gents', this is where most of them should be doing their act.

Sincerely yours,
Groucho Marx

January 14, 1964

Dear Eddie:

Briefly (and quickly) the two biggest laughs that I can recall (other than my three marriages) were in a vaudeville act called 'Home Again'.

One was when Zeppo came out from the wings and announced, 'Dad, the garbage man is here.' I replied, 'Tell him we don't want any.'

The other was when Chico shook hands with me and said, 'I would like to say good-bye to your wife,' and I said, 'Who wouldn't?'

Take care of yourself.

Regards,
Groucho Marx

Here's one that was written to GROUCHO

Dear Julius:

The magazine on which your daughter now works wrote me for references. And I replied that I had known Miriam Marx for many years, and have always found her to be five feet six and a half inches tall, and that I know her to have the integrity and potential ability of her famous father, Karl. P.S.: She got the job. I haven't heard, but I suppose she's still there.

I would have answered your letter of a year or so ago, much sooner, had it not been that Jane and I got mixed up with a television show – or as we call it back east here, TV – a clever contraction derived from the words Terrible Vaudeville. However, it is our latest medium – we call it a medium because nothing's well done. It was discovered, I suppose you've heard, by a man named Fulton Berle, and it has already revolutionized social grace by cutting down parlor conversation to two sentences: 'What's on television?' and 'Goodnight'.

Love,
Goody

TO ALISTAIR COOKE

July 8, 1957

Dear Mr Cooke:

I was a little disappointed on receiving your rather lengthy letter, to find no mention of money. I am of course, an artist, with my head in the clouds. And I was very happy to be invited to appear, gratis or thereabouts, on 'Meet the Press' 'The Last Word', etc. But my business manager Mr Gummo Marx, has a passion for money that is virtually a sickness. I am constantly being embarrassed by it. Still, he is my brother, and rather than upset him, I have to bow to his wishes.

I hope you and your charming wife are happy and as gay as the weather permits; and that this note will not end our fragile friendship.

Regards,
Groucho

TO PHIL SILVERS

November 15, 1951

Dear Phil:

I won't bore you with the details of how happy I am over your success. You've had it coming.

But I must warn you. In a musical, as you know, there are temptations. Thirty or forty beautiful babes in back of you kicking up high – so high that they frequently display sections of their anatomy that in other circles are carefully reserved for the man they ultimately marry. Phil, steer clear of these man-traps. Marry, if you must, but don't marry a chorus girl. As the years roll by you will discover their high kicks grow proportionately lower, and their busts sag just as much as the busts of girls who have never seen the inside of a dressing room.

You may ask then what is the difference? As a veteran of three Broadway musicals, I can quickly tell you chorus girls are notoriously pampered and insolvent. No matter where you take them, they order champagne and chicken a la king. This can be very embarrassing if you are in the Automat.

However, if you must marry, I suggest you look in other fields. In a city as big as New York I am sure there are pants manufacturers, wholesale delicatessen dealers, and various other merchants who have daughters who conceivably have virtues even more indispensable to a near-sighted major comic than a talent for high kicking.

So steer clear of these coryphées. Under no circumstances shake their hands, for the slightest Physical contact can lead to disaster.

So look smart, be smart, and remember . . . in Union there is alimony.

Love,
Groucho

In his line of business JIMMY SAVILE must meet thousands of people – and he must like them too, because his anecdotes are kindly as well as very funny. Like the story he tells in his book about his mother:

Her naivety was monumental. About to go off on a trip to Spain she trots to the doctors. 'No Mrs Savile, you won't need anything, you're remarkably fit.' That wasn't good enough for her. She needed pills of some sort or the trip would lose its flavour. Surrendering, the doctor suggested she buy some water-sterilizing tablets in case the local Spanish water was off. Satisfied, the Duchess left him and marched to the chemists. It was full but my mother was small and appeared at the counter.

'Yes Mrs Savile?' asked the chemist.

'I want some sterilization pills,' quoth the Duchess.

This brought the shop to a standstill. The chemist coughed and leaned over the counter.

'Er, who for?' he said.

'Me,' announced the Duch.

Chemists are not used to being confronted by eighty-year-old ladies who fear they may become pregnant.

'You,' croaked the started man.

'I'm going to Spain,' announced the Duchess grandly, 'and the doctor has advised that I take some sterilization pills.

'He says the water may be contaminated . . .'.

And the one about his show:

Once on our panel of experts we had a titled lady of over eighty. Wanting to smoke a cigar but not wishing to distress her (sitting next to me), I leaned across and whispered, 'Will my cigar smoke bother you?'

A little hard of hearing, she replied, 'It's very good of you but I'll have one of my own.'

I nearly fell off the chair as this darling eighty-year-old pulled out a cigar case and had hers lit while my mouth was still open.

* * *

Like all good comedians grounded in music hall, CHARLIE CHESTER learned the hard – and impecunious way; he was often out of work and

On one occasion I was so fed up I rang Moss Empires and spoke to Val Parnell, the boss under old George Black. I said: 'Mr Parnell, this is Charlie Chester, look, I'm a young man and I want to work!'

'Well buy yourself a pick and shovel!' came the reply. That piece of advice cost me the only twopence I possessed in the world!

Once on his way up, though, Charlie could afford to relax and find humour not only in his act, but in life around him. There was his landlady:

Hettie, bless her, was the grey-haired retainer, four years older than God, and when she carried a plate of soup to the table, you only got what was left after she'd finished spilling it.

After our first meal there, I went out to do some shopping, and from that moment onwards, every meal for me was purgatory. Each time Hettie served me anything, she kept staring at my neck. She would slowly walk round the back of me looking at it with deep concern. If I noticed her doing it she pretended that I'd been mistaken and wait for a further opportunity.

Every course, every meal, this happened and I began to wonder if I'd got a permanent tide mark. It began to get on my nerves. In fact it ruined the week for me.

It wasn't until some time after I learned that during my shopping expedition after the first meal, she must have said to one of the boys what a nice young man she thought I was.

They replied: 'Nice young man? Young? He's sixty-eight?'

'Oh don't be so ridiculous,' she countered. Whereupon they insisted that I was indeed that age and that I'd had my face lifted three times. They also added: 'If you look closely on his neck, you'll see the join marks!'

'Humour' Charlie says in his book 'is not only a deep subject, but also a delicate one'; and he tells of some unexpected reactions he's had from his audiences:

People, I discovered, are emotionally concerned over a great many things. Workmanship, religion, politics, loved ones, physical defects and so on. This came to me forcibly when doing a routine with Arthur Haynes in my radio show. I happened to say: 'That's a lovely shirt you're wearing Arthur. Do you send it to the laundry, or do you tear the buttons off yourself?'

I had a letter, written in furious terms, from the head of a laundry in Streatham, saying: 'We don't tear buttons off, we take a pride in our work.'

On another occasion I joked, 'My brother has been very ill and the doctor told him he must sleep in the open air, so he joined the Police force!' Before I was off the air, I had a policeman from Edgware Road ring up and shout: 'You can do my bloody night duty any time you like!'

Soon after the war, when we still had to queue up for petrol coupons, had bread units, and orange juice was rationed along with meat. Mr Attlee was then Prime Minister, and I made my usual topical gags about the situation.

'All this queueing up for bread and petrol, meat and stuff . . . things wouldn't be like this if

Mr Attlee were still alive.' Some people asked me if Mr Churchill wrote my scripts after that one.

My only answer was to follow it up the next week saying: 'Last week I was a bad boy, I said a joke about Mr Attlee not being alive . . . and he heard me. He jumped up, looked in the mirror, and boy, was he relieved!'

FAMOUS SHORTS about FAMOUS PEOPLE

It is said that Wilfrid Lawson and Robert Newton, two fine actors noted for their addiction to the bottle, were once appearing in *Richard III*. Newton, as Richard, lurched on stage patently under the influence, which provoked the outraged shout from the gods, 'You're drunk!'

'You think *I'm* drunk!' responded the King, 'Wait till you see the Duke of Buckingham!'

Wilson Barrett, the popular late-Victorian matinee idol, was having his house redecorated. He invited all the workmen to the Princess's Theatre to see him in *The Lights Of London*, his current success. The artisans took advantage of his generous offer of complimentary tickets, but at the end of that week on the pay-sheet, Barrett saw the following item against each man's name:

Saturday night. 4 hours' overtime at Princess's Theatre . . . 8s.

Mrs Patrick Campbell, when asked what she thought about homosexuality, famously replied: 'I don't care what they do, as long as they don't do it in the street and frighten the horses!'

When asked whether his life was insured, Jack Benny replied, 'That's my own business, but I will tell you this: when I go – the Prudential goes!'

Bob Hope for many years visited American troops every Christmas in South East Asia. On one occasion he also did a show for South Vietnamese troops, who didn't understand a word of English, but a local Major volunteered to translate Hope's wisecracks as he went. The performance was a fantastic success, and when it was over, Hope said to the Major, 'You were great! I haven't had such a reception like that since I started coming over here. You did a great job.'

The Major looked embarrassed and finally said, 'Well, Mr Hope, I'm afraid that you talked so fast I couldn't keep up with you, so after your first couple of jokes I just started telling the boys some of my own!'

Dame Edith Evans, when asked about her famous role of Lady Bracknell in *The Importance of Being Earnest* replied, 'I've played it everywhere except under water.'

A woman in Bolton fell madly in love with Cary Grant, to the extent that she spent all her time buying photographs of him, watching his films, and attending meetings of Cary Grant fan clubs all over the country. Her husband not unnaturally became concerned with her behaviour which bordered on the obsessive, so he went to ask advice from a psychiatrist.

'All I can advise you,' said the doctor, 'is to model yourself on your wife's idol, and then she may begin to pay some attention to you and transfer her affections back. You might start by having a hair-cut like Cary Grant.'

So the husband, who sported long hair round his shoulders, made the supreme sacrifice and went to the barber's shop and asked for a cut like Cary Grant. As the locks began to fall to the floor, the husband began to get worried about the competence of the barber. Eventually he had a crew-cut which would have satisfied the most exacting of regimental sergeant majors, and the husband began to get very concerned indeed. The last straw came when the barber picked up a razor and shaved a bald patch across his head from ear to ear.

'Hey, wait a minute!' he said in panic. 'Are you sure you know what Cary Grant looks like?'

'Of course I do!' said the barber. 'I saw *The King and I* fourteen times!' ●

From "Best Showbiz Jokes" Published by Wolfe Publishing Ltd.

A London couple decided to go and see a concert at the Royal Festival Hall where Yehudi Menuhin was giving a recital. That particular day was freezing cold and thick fog. There was a tube strike, and with no buses or taxis running because of the lack of visibility, they had to walk.

After an hour and a half they arrived at the Festival Hall frozen to the marrow, but triumphant. They took their seats, and discovered that they were the entire audience – no one else had arrived. The manager then came and told them that due to the poor turnout, the concert would be cancelled and their money refunded.

'That's not good enough, mate,' said the music-lover. 'The wife and me 'as walked all the way from Shepherds Bush to be 'ere. We don't want our money – we want our concert! I'm goin' to see Mr Menuhin meself.'

And so he did just that; he went round to the great man's dressing-room and put his case.

'After all,' he said. 'If the wife and me 'as taken all this trouble to get 'ere on a perishin' cold night, you might at least give us *one* song!'

And after Mr Menuhin had duly obliged with one song, the East Ender remarked, 'Blimey! No wonder no one else turned up . . .' ●

Cecil B. de Mille was so impressed with the amount of money he made with his epic film *The Ten Commandments* that he hired a team of writers to come up with ten more. ●

Ronnie Carroll (according to Billy Connolly) once called over a waitress and said 'I'd like a steak, grilled not fried. No potatoes. And some carrots and asparagus tips.'

Off she goes and comes back twenty minutes later with his dinner. There's the steak, sure enough, and the carrots, but no asparagus tips.

'Er . . . where's the asparagus tips?'

'Oh, I'm very sorry – we've only got Benson and Hedges.' ●

Excerpts from:-
Moon's A Balloon by David Niven. Published by Hamish Hamilton
The Groucho Letters by Groucho Marx
Published by Michael Joseph
As it Happens by Jimmy Savile. Published by Barrie & Jenkins
The World is Full of Charlies by Charlie Chester
Published by The New English Library

★★★

Another great star (in every sense of the word) is HARRY SECOMBE who, like all the Goons, is a great teller of tales, tall and otherwise. Such as this one, which has another Goon playing a small supporting role, and is called

Milligan's Overcoat

I think it was the overcoat that sparked the whole affair off. It was Milligan's overcoat, and as I was at that time much slimmer than my present shape would have you believe, we shared clothes. We also shared a bedsitting room, which has now become, in the recounting of various anecdotes from the past, a flat. But believe me it was a bed-sitting room – and the only sitting room was on the bed.

The phone rang on the landing early one Monday morning and I was informed by my agent, who for more than six weeks had been unobtainable, that I was working at last. A comedian due to appear at the Opera House, Belfast had fallen ill, and as all the good comedians were at this time fully engaged in pantomimes, I was reluctantly chosen to take his place.

'You'll have to catch the plane at ten o'clock for Belfast,' said my agent breathlessly. The shock of anyone actually offering me work was almost too much for him. 'The ticket will be waiting for you at the Air Terminal where you will have to be in an hour's time. And for God's sake don't forget your evening dress trousers this time.'

I had once appeared at Finsbury Park Empire on an Easter Monday night first house wearing a dinner jacket and a pair of brown tweed trousers. I had sent the evening trousers to the cleaners on the previous Friday, and when I went to collect them Monday morning I found the place closed for the Bank Holiday. My appearance that night had given my agent a violent heart attack and ruined my chances of a summer season at Skegness.

'Of course I'll not forget them, Mr Hardman,' I said and put the phone down.

It was now nearly nine o'clock and I had to shave, pack, borrow money off a sleeping Milligan and catch the airport bus at the Terminal. I bounded up the stairs and shaved very quickly. I was still doing the act in which I mimed the way people shaved, and my hair and my pores contained a permanent supply of shaving soap. Once, waiting for a bus in a shower of rain, my hair acquired a halo of fine bubbles – a sight which was greeted with superstitious awe by the other members of the bus queue.

Milligan turned sleepily in his bed. 'Can I borrow your overcoat Spike?' I said quickly, knowing that he had a nearly new black crombie which fitted me nicely, and acutely aware that my own demob overcoat was gracing the back room of the second-hand clothes merchant around the corner. He grunted. It could have meant anything, but I chose to interpret it as 'yes'. Then, picking up a couple of quid from the mantelpiece, I said 'Pay you back next week – I'm off to Ireland.' His nose became alive over the sheet, nostrils twitching as they always did when he began to wake – but I was off down the stairs before he could collect himself.

On the bus from the Terminal I caught sight of myself sideways in the side window. The black spectacles and the black overcoat gave me a sort of mysterious look I thought, and I slipped easily into my secret agent mood. Eyeing the other passengers keenly, I stepped off the bus at London airport, already playing the part, handling my brief case with my band parts, pyjamas and toilet articles as if it contained state secrets.

I half smiled in a conspiratorial way at the uniformed official behind the ticket desk and padded stealthily into the passengers' lounge. Feeling thirsty I went to the bar, which was being patronised by some loud American tourists, and putting my brief case carefully on the floor I asked in clipped English for a drink. 'What?' said the lady behind the bar. I had obviously clipped my words too short, so in an unnaturally loud voice I repeated 'A dry martini'. The American nearest me turned at my shrill plea, and at the same time I moved to fish out some money. The impact of our meeting sent his gin and tonic cascading down his sharkskin suit. I stood aghast and then acting swiftly I whipped out a grubby handkerchief, and began mopping him down. 'Terribly sorry', I said, rubbing bits of lemon into his suiting. He stood, saying nothing, looking down at his ruined lapels, and in my confusion the handkerchief dropped to the floor. I bent to pick it up and on straightening, hit his American jaw sharply under the chin with my solid Welsh skull. The blood flowed freely down his chin joining the alcohol on his lapel. He brushed aside to move away from the bar and fell over my briefcase. 'Goddam clown,' muttered the American.

My vision of secret agent was by now completely dissipated and I slunk into a chair away from the rest of the passengers. Then I saw him. He sat facing me, eyes expressionless behind thick lenses, a seemingly sardonic smile on his sharp, foreign face. Obviously a continental, probably German by the cut of his black leather coat. He watched me malevolently. Had I played my part too well? My insistence on keeping my briefcase in my lap on the bus and my over-exaggerated caution at the airport may have been too realistic. Could he be a counter-agent?

I looked down nervously at my crossed legs and was chagrined to see a big hole in my sock. The gents toilet was behind me and smiling desperately at the other fellow I nipped smartly inside and adjusted my sock so that the hole was not visible. By the time I had finished the flight had been called and I was the last to board the plane.

The only seat available was the one next to the German. I sat down, clutching the briefcase, aware of his eyes on it and believing by this time that it really contained something valuable. 'Fasten your seat belts,' said the air hostess taking the case from me and putting it in the rack. As it was my first flight, I became terribly involved with the seat belt until my companion, still saying nothing, sorted out my confusion. 'Thanks,' I said awkwardly. He nodded, chilling me with a gold filled smile.

The rest of the journey was uneventful except for the fact that I was ill in a paper bag, and I was glad when we arrived safely at Knutts Corner. As we sorted our luggage from the rack I saw the German reading the label on my briefcase. He nodded, his spectacles gleaming when I snatched it from him. This is getting out of hand I thought when I found that his taxi was following mine all the way into the city. We pulled up outside the stage door of the Opera House, and he drew up behind. I entered the theatre hurriedly and ran straight to my dressing room. His footsteps hesitated in the corridor then went on. I breathed a big sigh of relief and began to unpack.

Later, standing in the wings I saw the German sitting on the stage playing a zither. He nodded cheerily to me. It was Anton Karas of *The Third Man* fame. I nodded back, then went to my dressing room and was sick in the sink.

Excerpts from 'Goon for Lunch'
Published by Michael Joseph Ltd.
in association with M. & J. Hobbs

On the American scene (from his companion Carlotta Monti), some frank but sympathetic anecdotes about the late W. C. FIELDS, the red-nosed, rasping voiced American comedian – who drank and didn't care who knew it. As one studio executive found out when he said one day to Woody (as he was known):

'Having you in a picture is not without certain risks, Mr Fields. If I may be very frank, let me say that it is repeated around Paramount that you drink all the time.'

Woody jumped to his feet and pointed his cane at the executive. 'That, sir, is a damned lie!'

The executive backed down by saying, 'It's only a rumour.'

'Such charges are preposterous, ridiculous, and slanderous,' Woody scoffed. 'I certainly do not drink all the time. I have to sleep you know.'

Persuaded by friends to consult the medical profession about his drinking, Woody apparently gave the doctors more than they bargained for:

Doctor: 'When did your drinking first start, Mr Fields?'

Woody: 'With a glass of beer.'

Doctor: 'Have you ever considered giving up drinking?'

'Why try to improve on happiness?'

Doctor: 'How often do you get drunk?'

'I've been drunk only once in my life' (adding *sotto voce* to Carlotta) 'But that lasted for twenty-three years.'

Another doctor once warned Woody:

'Mr Fields, if you don't stop drinking you'll be dead within six months.'

'Why, that's exactly what a German medico in Baden-Baden told me twenty-five years ago. I'm glad you doctors agree on something' retorted Woody.

Then there was the doctor who tried very persistently to stop Woody drinking, and, as this story illustrates, came out very much second-best:

Young, energetic, and sharp as he was, it proved a hopeless task for the doctor to ferret out all of Woody's hiding places for liquor. Should he discover one and destroy the stock, Woody simply conceived another. His tricks and subterfuges were too much for the physician. When Woody offered to teach the doctor how to play golf, the medico was jubilant. Here, he thought, was one place Fields could never sneak a drink.

Woody appeared for the game dressed in baggy tweed trousers that appeared about two sizes too large. There was a valid reason for his poorly tailored appearance. His pockets were filled with small bottles of whisky, the miniature kind served on trains even today. To protect them from breaking or making a tinkling sound that might arouse the doctor's suspicions, Woody had packed them in cotton wadding.

They started playing. Woody constantly coached the doctor, emphasizing that he should stare at the ball, slowly counting to ten before taking a swing. This gave the coach ample time to sneak a bottle from his pocket and down the contents. A steady stream of instructions kept flowing from teacher to pupil, such as:

'Slower, Doc . . . slower, don't look up . . . keep your head down . . . eye on the ball.'

After eight days of golfing, the doctor commented, 'Mr Fields, you've been without a drink for quite a spell and you're looking fine.'

'Do you really think my health has improved?' Woody asked the doctor.

'One hundred per cent,' was the answer.

'I'll drink to that,' Woody said, forgetting himself and pulling out a bottle.

When it came time to settle the bill, Woody, with his usual business acumen, deducted the golf lessons.

Woody's own assessment of drinking was typical:

The worst disease known to man, and one neglected by medical science, is 'Martini Elbow'. It's a cousin to 'Tennis Elbow' but more severe. Painful calcium deposits make it impossible for the unfortunate drinker to lift his cocktail glass. He must, therefore, either have an assistant with him to perform this duty, or he must himself bend his face down to the glass – a dangerous procedure, as the glass rim may cut his proboscis.

Everything else having failed to divorce him from liquor, I even did the childish thing of having him raise his right hand and solemnly swear never to take a drink again. The time of this historic event was four o'clock on a summer afternoon in 1945. Two hours later I saw him downing a martini.

'You swore off,' I accused. 'You took a sacred oath.'

He admitted such had been the case. 'But,' he said childishly, 'I didn't say for how long.'

All Woody's stories and ripostes weren't about drink, of course, and Carlotta records a mass of other tales, long short, tall – and funny. Like the time they were at a show-biz party in Hollywood:

The first voice we heard belonged to an actor who had managed to land a fair part in a movie two years before, and had been at liberty ever since. He was dropping names right and left. They rolled easily off his tongue, and in rapid succession we heard mention of Louis B. Mayer, Lana Turner, Greer Garson, and Bing Crosby. 'All good friends of mine,' he added.

Before the actor managed to mention another

celebrity, a tight-skirted, buttock-swaying starlet wiggled across the room. He followed the undulations of her torso, and gasped, 'My God!'

Woody rushed up to him, demanding, 'How well did you know *Him*?'

Of course, he was famous for his declared dislike of children, and these are some of the many stories of his encounters with them:

'Woody was auditioning a flock of kids at his Toluca Lake house, along with a director ... Woody lined up eight children – one of them called Marlowe – who, for some reason were standing at semi-attention, like troops being reviewed. After a cursory inspection of the group, he pointed at Don Marlowe. He beckoned him over to a desk where he had seated himself.

Marlowe did as Woody wished and stood prepared to furnish his background, his name, the parts he had played, or perhaps read a few lines. Instead, Woody filled a martini glass nearly to the rim with his favourite drink (years later Marlowe said he thought it was water) and handed the glass to him.

"Here's what I wish you to do" Woody instructed. "Run around the room as fast as you can, and hand me back the glass."

Marlowe, somewhat puzzled but obedient, did just that. Woody inspected the glass, turning it around slowly in his hand. Then he showed it to the director. "Not a drop spilled" he said in a complimentary tone. "Did you ever see such talent?"

The director nodded his approval.

"You're hired" Woody told Marlowe ... and intoned "What a talent ... what a talent".'

Asked what was his most unpleasant experience ever:

Woody hesitated five or six seconds, then snapped his fingers. 'That's easy to remember. The time a hot, sticky baby jumped onto my lap and called me "Daddy"!'

'What did you do, Mr Fields?'

'What did I do, son? Why, I did the only thing I could do – the only course any red-blooded man could pursue to keep his honesty and integrity and standing in the community. I simply opened my legs and catapulted him on his head. Never forget the sound – brings back a flood of wonderful memories. Sounded like a ripe melon squashed by a sledgehammer.'

'What happened to the child?'

'Grew up to become one of the most important men in Hollywood. Now the brains of a giant studio,' Woody rasped.

And in San Francisco, he left a woman with her eyes popping out:

He'd given her an autograph and then politely inquired about her offspring. The woman said pridefully 'He's a tough little one.'

'Madam' Woody commented, 'there's no such thing as a tough child – if you parboil them first for seven hours, they always come out tender.'

And to another women who'd ventured to say to him:

'Somehow, Mr Fields, I feel that you aren't overly fond of children.'

'Only in an experimental way,' he said.

'Experimental?' She was puzzled.

'Yes, I have invented something I'd like to try on them.'

'Would you care to tell me about it?'

'Gladly, my good woman,' he said. 'I have invented a permanent gag, adjustable to any size of mouth, to fit all children until they reach the age of puberty.'

'But how could they eat with their mouths covered?' the neighbour asked.

'They couldn't,' Woody stated. '*That*, Madam, is the object of the device. Slow starvation.'

And a last round-up of his famous short snappy come-backs – often to dumb questions:

On lawyers:

'The only thing a lawyer won't question is the legitimacy of his own mother.'

On whether there is intelligent life on other planets:

'There damn well better be, because there's none on this one.'

On wine:

'A wonderful drink, wine. It has unexploited values. Did you ever hear of a barefooted Italian grape crusher with athlete's foot?'

On marriage:

'Marriage is better than leprosy because it's easier to get rid of.'

'In marriage a man must give up many of his old and pleasant habits, even if it means giving up the woman he married.'

'Marry an outdoor woman. Then if you throw her out into the yard for the night, she can still survive.'

'Never trust your wife behind your back, even if she claims she only wants to wash or scratch it.'

'An ideal start for matrimony would be to have a drunken rabbi perform a Catholic ceremony in an Episcopalian church. Then it could be declared illegal in the courts.'

On presents, when he was ill in bed:

'If you really want to cheer me up ... Bring money. And never mind the gift wrapping. A large rubber band will do nicely.'

from 'W. C. and Me' by Carlotta Monti and Cy Rice
Published by Prentice Hall Inc.

But not all the stories about famous people can be easily attributed – OR really proven true. Here's a selection of some that we can't vouch for but are worth repeating!

A certain English singer, renowned in Britain for his singing of lieder, was persuaded by his agent to accept an invitation to give a recital in Vienna. With the greatest of trepidation the singer accepted, but was very nervous about singing in German to a German audience – and singing lieder at that. However, after his very first song there was great applause and shouts of 'Encore! Encore!' To his gratification, the demands for him to sing his very first offerings were so insistent that he could not continue with his programme.

Accordingly, he had a brief word with his accompanist, and sang the song again. And still they roared and yelled out 'Encore! Encore!' The singer was overwhelmed at such a reception – surely this must be a unique event in musical history – and so again he sang the first song. And yet a third time he had to repeat it, and still a fourth.

And after the fourth rendering of this lied, to his astonishment his audience still demanded that he repeat it. But he felt that he must press on with the rest of his programme, and so in very halting German he told his audience that he really could not sing the same song all the evening. At which a voice from the fifth row shouted: 'You will sing it again. And again – until you get it right.'

*

A Hollywood film star was delayed by a traffic accident on the way to his wedding to a much married screen goddess. He sent her a telegram which read: 'AM DELAYED FOR THREE HOURS STOP DON'T MARRY ANYONE TILL I GET THERE.'

*

A young actor decided to impress his new girl friend by taking her to dine at the most exclusive 'pro's' restaurant in London. Having arrived, the girl went to the powder-room, and the young actor found himself standing by Frank Sinatra.

'Excuse me talking to you,' said the lad, 'but my girl friend will be out in a moment – would you do me a great favour?'

'Do you want my autograph?' said Frank.

'No, actually, sir, I wondered whether – it's an awful cheek my asking you this – but when my girl comes back, could you pretend you know me? Just walk up to me and say "Hello, Jack" or something like that. She'd be terribly thrilled to think that I know you.'

'All right,' said the star. 'I was young myself once – I know how it is.'

Just then the young actor's girl-friend returned, and as they began to walk into the restaurant the Famous Actor came over and said, 'Hello, Jack – how are you these days?'

'Get lost,' came the reply. 'Can't you see I'm busy.'

*

There was once a man in America who suffered constantly from his remarkable similarity to Mario Lanza. Everywhere he went he was pestered, and his constant denials were more often than not disbelieved, which made the whole thing even more exasperating. In addition his job was as travelling salesman, which could hardly have been more unsuitable.

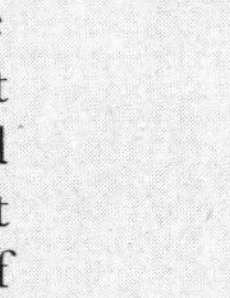

He arrived at one hotel and asked the desk-clerk whether he might have a room for the night. 'Certainly, Mr Lanza,' came the reply. 'For you Mr Lanza – anything.'

'I am not Mario Lanza!' yelled the unfortunate individual.

'No, sir,' said the clerk, with a wink. 'Boy! Take Mr Lan – take this gentleman's bags up to room 313.'

At the door of the room, the bell-boy said, 'Here you are, Mr Lanza. I hope you like the room.'

'I am not Mario Lanza!' roared the traveller, thoroughly offended and upset. He ordered breakfast to be sent to his room at seven o'clock, and went to bed, angry and disgruntled.

At seven in the morning there came a discreet tap on his door. 'Come in!' he called sleepily.

The door opened and in came the most luscious, sultry little brunette he had ever seen in his life, carrying his breakfast on a tray. She put the tray on a table in the centre of the room, smoothed her dress down tightly over her hips and shimmered over the side of the bed, where she stood very close.

'Would you like me to serve you in bed, Mr Lanza?' she purred softly.

'Be My Looove . . .!'

*

A beautiful and well endowed blonde was trying to get a break in films, so at a Hollywood party she sidled up to an important producer and said: 'Tell me, if I were a Genie and could grant you just three wishes: what would the other two be?'

Perhaps the same producer was bemoaning the fact that he couldn't find a beautiful redhead to play the lead in a new musical he was planning.

'Hold everything!' said an agent within earshot, 'I have the very girl you're looking for – a client of mine.'

'Have you?' asked the producer dubiously. 'All right then – get her over to my office in one hour and I'll see her.'

'Oh, she won't be able to see you today,' said the agent. 'She'll have to get her hair dyed red . . .'

THE WIT OF

Tony Blackburn

In London the Police are trying to stop gambling.
It has got such a hold over them they can't seem to give it up.

Do you realise that with the rising cost of living, you are now starving on the income you once dreamed about.

Sampson would have made a good actor. He'd have brought the house down.

Would an acrobat in love fall head over heels?

A small town is a place where everybody knows what everybody else is doing, and the local paper tells you who was caught doing it.

I went to a wedding the other day where the bride was 82 and the groom 88. Instead of confetti, the guests threw vitamin pills.

I took an optician's daughter to a party last night. Two glasses and she made a spectacle of herself.

I don't think it's fair to say that British workmen are idle. Only the other day I came across a workman with two spades in his hand — plus the ace of diamonds and a king.

I've decided to go into the cement business. I've always been a good mixer.

Definition of a taxpayer — the cross section of the British public.

Two birds were perched on the same branch. One turned tp the other and said: 'Have you bred any good rooks lately?'

Judge: 'I've taken all the factors into consideration, and I'm going to award your wife five pounds a week.'
Defendant: 'That's very kind, Your Honour. And I might even slip her a few pounds now and again myself.'

Did you hear the rumour about the watchmaker? He's just wound up his business.

And now I'd like to mention something off the top of my head. — Dandruff.

Did you know the liquor improves with age? The older you get the more you like it.

Sign inside a restaurant:
OUR TONGUE SANDWICHES SPEAK FOR THEMSELVES.

If a woman's intuition is so good, why do they always have to ask so many questions?

If magicians do not feel very well, do they have to go away for a spell?

I met an architect the other day who bought his wife a girdle and put it down on his income tax claims form as a structural improvement.

A bachelor is a man who doesn't have a better half. So he's always got better quarters.

They call our language the mother tongue because father seldom gets a chance to use it.

A man never knows the value of a women's love until he starts paying alimony.

Definition of a clerical error — a vicar putting his collar on back to front.

Men do make passes at girls who wear glasses — if they've got rhe right frames.

I know a photographer who specialises in taking portraits. He's in prison now. He took one from the National Gallery.

The way to strengthen sterling is to add starch to £1 notes.

Someone asked me if I liked bathing beauties yesterday. Ridiculous. I've never bathed one.

Sign in London Pub:
'REMEMBER THE CUSTOMER IS ALWAYS TIGHT!'

Excerpt from 'A Laugh in Every Pock
Published by W. H. Allen & Co. Ltd.

THE GOONS

ROBIN'S POST

from 'The Book of the Goons'
by Spike Milligan
Published by Robson Books Ltd.

THE CAST
Peter Sellers
Patsy Hagen
Major Dennis Bloodnok
Grytpype-Thynne
Henry Crun
Bluebottle
Spike Milligan
Fred Fumanchu
Throat
Moriarty
Minnie Bannister
Eccles
Harry Secombe
Chief Commissioner Neddie Seagoon
With The Ray Ellington Quartet, Max Geldray, and the Orchestra conducted by Wally Stott.
Script by Spike Milligan.
Announcer Wallace Greenslade.
Producer Peter Eton.

Wallace
This is the BBC. It feareth not, and holdeth forth not, but it keepeth friends with alleth.
Ned
And a ripe twit thou soundest. What's all this 'thim them thou' chat?
Wallace
Chat? Well, we felt that in strict contrast with the coming brisk clinical commercial radio, we might introduce an olde worlde atmosphere.
Ned
A good answer, now read the statues on this Monogrammed Water Buffaloo.
Wallace
In the absence of entertainment we present –
Peter
The Great Brown, all the way from mysterious Upper Dicker. No question is too difficult.
Jim
First question?
Harry
My name is Gladys Clutt.
Jim
There is no cure. Next!
Harry
No, my name is Gladys Clutt spelt with a Masculine G as in Gee Whizz.
Peter
I'm his friend.
Jim
Just stand in this open crocodile and wait for the first spring swallow.
Ned
Who won the Battle of Waterloo?
Jim
Tom Kretch.
Ned
Wrong! It was Lord Wellington.
Jim
It's only your word against mine, Jim.
Peter (*gushing BBC twit announcer*)
And this week's 'Workers Playtime' came from a cake-bottling factory in Burton Wood. Now, here is the foreman's name –
Ned
Tom Hopkin.
Roars of Laughter. Goats and Cows
Wallace
That was the sound of the human race – resignation forms are now available. Now, to certain things –
Peter
Aye to that, sirr.
Wallace
The part of the Cornish idiot was played at short notice by a very well-known Cornish idiot player.
Peter
Harr . . . narnnnnnnnnnn.
Wallace
Ta. We present a tragedy – the story of Lord Seagoon, playboy of the Western Approaches, great lover, man of action, athlete, slob – and great wit.
Ned
Who's a great twit?
Old Time Orchestra playing The Lancers in the distance. Murmur of the dancers
Spike
Jove, you look lovely tonight, Daphne.

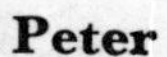

Peter
Oh, you're just saying that.
Spike
Let's go into the garden.
Ned
Hear that maddening sound of gaiety, music and acting? Huh huh huh . . . It took place in Robin's Post, my ancestral home at Hailsham, Sussex, S.W.3. Now, it's all gone. G-o-n-e pronounced – '*Goneeeeeeeeee*'
Ned
I was rich, as you will now hear.
Ned
This is me now speaking, a ruined, broken, crumbling man, going to pieces.
Length of the tubular bell falls from the tubular bells.
Ned
There goes another bit.
Peter
After her, men.
Ned
Her? Yes, it was a woman who brought me this low – that and short legs.
Duck quacks
Ned
Duck's disease, the curse of the Seagoons. Anyhow, we met years ago. Her name was Penelope, mine was Ned. Why, I can hear her now.
Peter (*old dear*)
Hello, Ned dear.
Ned
There she is!!!!!! But let's go back to when it allllll started. It was 1901 and I was holding a masked ball.
Thynne (*approaches laughing*)
Ha ha ha, tell me Lord Seagoon, why are you holding that masked ball?
Ned
This is no ordinary ball.
Thynne
Don't frighten me, Ned.
Ned
This man was the powerful Lord Thynne, power behind the throne, owner of *The Times*, Peer of the Realm and relief pianist at the Hackney Empire.
Moriarty
Tell me, Neddie, what is that ball made from?
Ned
Oh, silly old gold.
Moriarty screams and yells about gold
Thynne
Steady, Moriarty, it's only gold. Come, lets weigh it on this set of scales I happen to have handy . . . there.
Squeak of scales
Thynne
Fourteen carrots, three turnips and a mango – gad, it's worth its weight in greens.
Ned
But what does it mean to me, Lord Thynne, me, a man of means?
Eccles
Hello Neddie, Hello Neddie. Ho, phew, I've danced every dance since it started, Lancers, eightsome reels, tango, waltz.
Ned
Who was the lucky girl?
Eccles
I didn't bother about them, I did it on my own. I'm not the idiot you think I am.
Thynne
Oh, which idiot are you then?
Eccles
Ummmmmm, what I mean is, I'm a great thinker.
Thynne
For instance?
Eccles
For instance, I think . . . er . . . I think . . . I think I'll go home.
Thynne
You thought of that all by yourself?
Eccles
Well, if you put it like that – yes.
Thynne
Mmmmm – time for Conks Geldray.
Max and Orchestra: Music
Max
That was the music of Conks Geldray, folks. Conks lets in the air.
Wallace
Mr Geldray wishes it known that the Conks Anonymous Club is now open for membership. Part Two of our Tragedy.
Sound of Old Time Music as before. Music stops – polite applause. Laughter of dancers leaving the floor
Ned
Between dances we sat on the balcony smoking port and drinking sherry.
Thynne (*aside*)
Moriarty – stand by the light switch. Now, Ned, let's have a look at the golden ball.
Sound of crackling of electricity
Ned
Don't panic, folks. It's only the gas mantles fused – carry on dancing.
Peter (*Geraldo*)
What do you mean, man? The boys can't see to play in the dark.
Ned
Come now, you can busk.
Peter
Only from music. In the dark we're strictly a load of schmose.

Ned
Nonsense. Hand me an instrument, I'll play. Waltz, please.
Orchestra: Plays Waltz Tempo
Ned
And so the magic of my waltz rhythm rang through the hall (*Sings*) Fertang, fertang, fertang tang tang – but in the rosy light of dawn, I discovered myself sitting in the middle of a field in full evening dress playing the drums. I took immediate action – I stopped playing –
Mate (*to self*)
Hello, we got a right twit 'ere.
Ned
Ah, good morning, Constabule.
Mate
Hello, sonny, lost the band?
Ned
No, someone has stolen Robin's Post, my ancestral home.
Mate (*slowly*)
'Ere, you haven't escaped from anywhere, have you?
Ned
What do you mean?
Mate
You know – one of them. (*Puts finger in mouth – wobbles*) Wo wo wo wo.
Ned
I say, how do you do that?
Mate
Wo wo wo wo.
Ned
Here, let me try . . . Wo wo wo wo . . . ha ha ha ha . . . Let's do it together.
Ned and Mate
Wo wo wo wo.
Ned
I say this *is* fun.
Mate
And it's tax-free, mate. Now, come along, off to the station.
Orchestra: Plays soft sad long dull chord
Wallace
Very puzzling. Part Two
Sound of rattling iron door
Ned
Let me out of this place! Take this jacket off. (*Interrupts behind Wallace*)
Wallace
Lord Seagoon had been incarcerated in a gentlemen's rest home in Sussex on a charge of going 'Wo wo wo wo wo', illusions of grandeur, and duck's disease. Wow wo wo wo wo – I say, it's not difficult – wo wo wo wo wo.
Mate
In you go, too.
Iron door slams
Wallace
You can't lock me away, I'm from the BBC – wo wo wo wo wo wo.
Mate
Oh, you're just the right type, mate. Wo wo wo wo 'em, mate.
Ned
It's no good, Wal. We'll plot to get out of here – I'll bake a cake, put a file in it and post it to myself –
Jim
Parcel for you!
Ned
It's arrived!
Sound of rapid ripping open
Ned
And here's the file. Now, while I claw a hole in the wall with my bare hands, you cover up the sound by filing through your teeth.
Sound of filing
Bloodnok
I say, are you filing your teeth?
Wallace
Yes.
Bloodnok
Well put 'em under 'T'.
Ned
Bloodnok! How did you get in here?
Bloodnok
I have the OBE and a parcel of steamed squids.
Ned
Shut up man – help me dig a tunnel.
Sound of digging up rocks by hand
Bloodnok
Ohhhhhhhhhh . . . Ohhhhhhhh –
Ned
You've *got* to get rid of these rocks –
Bloodnok
I'm eating them as fast as I can!
Ned and Bloodnok (*grunting*)
Sound of rocks being piled
Wallace
What are you doing, Mr Seagoon?
Ned
Twit! I'm trying to tunnel out.
Bloodnok
Now, Ned of Wales, Bloodnock of Anywhere will get you out of this home provided you sign the contract on this boiled egg.
Ned
Is this contract binding?
Bloodnok
A real eye waterer. Now, let's have your deposit – this set of drums will do – gad, they look in fine military condition. I'll do a parrididdle on 'em.

Ned
Don't you dare!!
Orchestra and drums play a military beat
Bloodnok (*over orchestra sings his favourite military melody. All fade into distance*)
Ned
He's escaped by military drums. Thank heavens – he's gone.
Bloodnok
And thank heavens – he's back again. 'The Return of Bloodnok', Part Three. Hello, Neddie of Wales. Look, we've all been imprisoned here for wo wo wo and unlawfully detained as retired stud horses.
Ned
Yes, why should we spend the rest of our time here?
Bloodnok
True. I mean, I can still pull a cart and whistle the Queen. (*Whistles tunelessly*)
Ned
Look, this is *my* plan.
Sound of series of electronic sounds
Bloodnok
Oh. It sounds infalliable, when do we start?
Ned
Now. First we must contact a solicitor. Contact.
Crun
Contact.
Propeller-engined plane roars into life then slurs to a stop
Crun
Contact made. Welcome to Whacklow, Futtle, Crun and Bannister – Solicitors for Oaths, Thin Oil and Certain Thingsssssssssss.
Minnie
Thingssssss!
All join in 'Thingssssssssss'.
Crun
Thingssssssssss are catching onnnnnn, Min. Now Sir, what, apart from your plasticine nose, is the trouble?
Ned
My wife left me.
Crun
Where did she leave you?
Ned
At home.
Crun
What was her name?
Ned
Mrs Seagoon.
Crun
So, she's a married woman? There's a clue. Have you a description of her?
Rustling of plans
Ned
Here's a complete set of plans of her.
Crun
These are the plans of a house.
Ned
She's inside.
Door opens
Ned
Anybody in?
Ray (*off*)
Yes, there is.
Crun
What is your name, Madam?
Ray
I can't see, the lights are fused.
Door closes
Ned
You see? All we've got to do is find that house and there she'll be.
Crun
Krermunck. Thingssssss . . . of Mongolia?
Minnie (*off*)
I won't be a second.
Crun
Good, there's no money in the boxing game. Min of Mongolia, this man in the mosquito net hat is a new client.
Ned
How do you do.
Minnie
I didn't catch the name.
Ned
I haven't dropped it yet.
Tubular bell dropped on stage with a telegraph pole clang
Ned
That's it.
Minnie
Mr Steel, he's coming, he's coming nearer, he's almost here, he's arrived.
Ned
Who?
Minnie
Ha ha ha ha.
Crun
Now, Ned, that will be a pound. Come and see us in ten guineas' time.
Ned
Have you got change of a hern – no? Then to hell with you.
Sound of wolf howling
Ray
Man, that sounds like my cue and I don't like it, I don't like it at all.
The Ray Ellington Quartet: Music
Wallace
That was Ray Ellington who is seven feet tall and covered in ginger hair, known in Woodside Park as – 'Gor, look at 'im!'. Part Three of 'Certain

Thingssss'. Mr Thynne – will you summarize?

Thynne

The secret of Ned's missing home is simple. We have lifted it lock, stick and birrle on the back of a tank transporter. The dance inside continues. We intend to ransom the more important guests to Eastern Potentates, to be held as political hostages who will become the centre of international political tension at a reduced fee of ten guineas a day until World War Three, or the price of avocado pears is reduced to the ore fourteen minimum. Now for my next impression –

Sound of tank transporter rumbling along the road

Moriarty

Driving along the king's highwayyyyy.

Thynne

Happy, Moriarty?

Moriarty

Owwwwww.

Thynne

Look, there's something in the road ahead.

Moriarty

It *is* a head, with a body attached.

Bluebottle

It's mine, Bottle of Finchley. Can you give me a lift to London Town?

Moriarty

Go on, hop it.

Bluebottle

It's too far to hop it.

Eccles

Hullo, Bottle.

Bluebottle

Cor, look, look at him, in brown evening dress. Eccles of Lengths.

Eccles

He's OK, Moriarty, he's a friend of mine. Come on.

Bluebottle

Ta, Eccles. Here's a cigarette card of Newt, and here's one of a King Edward potato at two months old.

Eccles

Oh, just what I need for lunch (*Gulps*) Ohhhhh ...

Bluebottle

I been doing life-guard duties on the Splon beach at Ratsgate.

Eccles

I didn't know you could swim in water.

Bluebottle

I had to learn to swim at two weeks old.

Eccles

Why?

Bluebottle

The vicar dropped me in the font.

Splash and bubbles –

Bluebottle

– I went. My next impression will be of a goose.

Peter screams

Bluebottle

Ohhhhh, hello everybody, I didn't see you there. One – two – three ... oh, not such a big crowd tonight. (*Thinks, panic*) Is – is poor Bottle losing the public that has kept him in liquorice and long shorts for all these years? Am I a fallen idol? Another has-been? Noooooo! I shall go on from triumph to triumph.

Bluebottle

Oh, my trousers have come down! Never again will I trust knitted string from Freda Milge.

Eccles

Never mind, have a brandy.

Sound of long pouring from a three gallon tin into a glass. Then a long syphon of soda

Bluebottle

No thank you. Ringgggg-ringgggg-ringgggg – the phoneeeeee. Hello?

Ned

Hello, Bottle, help me, where is Robin's Post?

Bluebottle

It's on a lorry going down the Great North Road.

Ned

You will be rewarded for this with a twill nightie and a spare sock. Gid up!

Dick Barton theme – then Paul Temple theme – then the Archer's theme – then Mrs Dale's Harp

Ned

It's pick of the flops! With that music behind me and my horse underneath –

Lone Ranger – William Tell theme –

Hern

Yes, a fiery horse, a flash of light, two pounds of potatoes, a sack of knees and ho Silver and the Lone Ranger.

Coconut shells

Ned

Gid up, proud beauty.

Peter (*old dear*)

All right, dear.

Thynne

Ring ring ring in the direction of Ned.

Ned

What's that? It sounds like a telephone. (*Tastes*) It tastes like a telephone. What number does it taste like?

Bloodnok

Hastings 1066.

Ned

That's us. Hello?

Moriarty (*distorted*)

Listen, Neddie, I'm warning you not to follow us. We've had beans for dinner.

Ned
What what what? Arrest that phone, the man on the other end is a criminule.
Sound of handcuffs and chains on telephone
Ned
There! Hello? Hello? Blast, he's escaped, this phone is empty. Tarara!
Bloodnok
It's near enough for jazz.
Ned
We'll never catch them on a horse. But, just as I said that, folks, an old Indian hooker drew up on a nearby canal.
Lalkaka
Hello hello hello hello, Mister Man.
Banajee
Yes, Hello. We are Hindu bargees, Lalkaka and Banajee Limited. Here is our card.
Ned (*reading*)
Jim Jones and Tom Squat, Printers.
Banajee
Yes, they are the men we bought the cards from.
Lalkaka
We got them second hand.
Ned
Right. Cast offffff.
Now then, who's our navigator?
Eccles
I am.
Ned (*panic*)
Man the boatssssss! Neddie and children first.
Eccles
Wait a minute . . . Major.
Bloodnok
Let me explain. This man is brilliant at cartography and astral navigation – ask him any question. Eccles, did you know that the mouth of the Amazon is one hundred miles wide?
Eccles
Oh, yer.
Bloodnok
And the coast of Albania is ten thousand miles long?
Eccles
Oh, yer.
Bloodnok
You see? He knew the answer to both questions.
Eccles
Yer, here's a map of the route.
Ned
What's the scale.
Eccles
Doh ray me far so la te dooooooooo.
Ned
Perfect. (*Calls*) Set course for Ferpudden.
Eccles
What's Ferpudden?
Ned
Prunes and custard.
Bluebottle
Wind's coming up.
Orchestra: Ta Raaaaaa
Bloodnok
Caught with their instruments down. Ohh, not long to the pay-off now, folks. Now, Neddie, pick a card – don't show it to me. What is it?
Ned
Jim Jones and Tom Squat, Printers.
Bloodnok
Correct.
Jim
Heloo, Jim, hello Jimmmmmm.
Ned
Helooooo Jim.
Jim
Look what I found floating in the canal – the pay-off.
Ned
It's the front door of Robin's Post.
FX: Door opens
Old fashioned orchestra – sound of dancers
Ned
Stop the music!
Music slows down to a blur
Ned
Where's my wife, Bulgarian Meg? Ahhh – Megggg – kis kis kis kisssss.
Ray
There *must* be some mistake.
Peter (*Meg the Bulgar*)
Neddie, Neddie darling, your back – your front – you brought them both with you.
Ned
I carry them for sentimental reasons – I –
Sound of great avalanche of rocks
Ned
She's fainted.
Peter (*doctor*)
Stand aside, I'm a doctor, I specialize in fainting. Groannnnnn.
Body falls to ground
Ned
So he does.
Thynne
Neddie, you disrespectful swine – standing there with two fainted people – take your shoes off.
Two small explosions
Thynne
Do you have to wear such loud socks?
Ned
Yes, I've got deaf feet.
Thynne
Yes, folks, exploding socks – it's the new noise clothes. Why not get your grannie a pair of red flannel drawers that go –
Great cackling of startled hens
Wallace
And with Lord Seagoon's wife safely fainted, and a good laugh on a pair of cackling drawers, we say farewell from page thirteen of another Goon Show.
Bloodnok
Is there no end to it! Ohhhhh!
Orchestra plays Old Comrades March

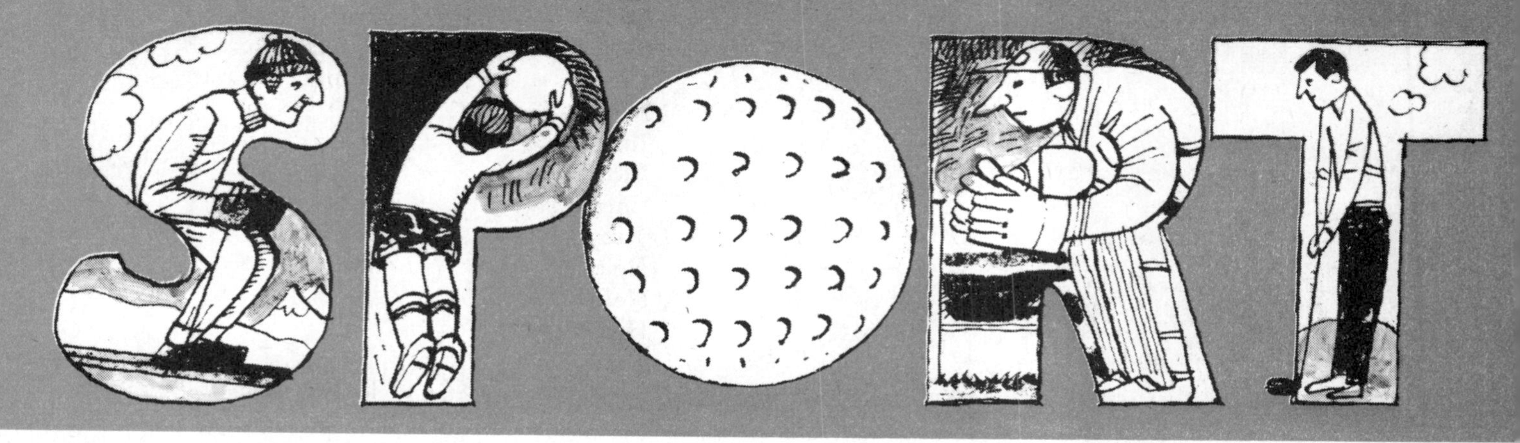

It's difficult to say much about sport without being ruder than one means (or is allowed) to be – mainly because so many of the games we take so seriously are concerned in some way or another with spheroids. These spheroids (known colloquially as balls – and having, thus described, some richly comic significance which the psychologists might give us a treat by explaining) – these spheroids are kicked, whacked, smashed or chased about on a stretch of carefully cut green grass of a specific shape and size, keeping them within laboriously marked white lines – the object being to get them into bits of netting slung between two poles, or into tiny holes in the ground, or over, under and through various other deliberately devious devices – at the same time, and better still, preventing other people from doing it first – or at all. If you can damage these people in the process, so much the better. And this extraordinary behaviour – for which yet more people will pay good money (and sometimes bad money, if tickets are short) to go and see – is carried on for the most part in weather totally unsuitable for it:

"This could save the match for England."

"Put it off? Because of a little shower?"

and is watched over by a small army of men and women crouching, running, sitting on step-ladders, squatting, leaping up and generally exhausting themselves in an attempt to see that the players are keeping to the rules. For this curious way of earning a living, they are assaulted, pelted with bottles, screamed at, and brought for reprimand before councils of other men and women (mostly retired from something or other and very fierce on that account) who apparently have something to do with the whole crazy show.

TEE BREAK

"I'm worried about you, Eric! Why not pop round to the surgery and have a word with Doctor Dixon?"

Two members were playing golf together and one of them seemed to be taking rather a long time in playing his next shot.
'What's the matter?' asked his partner.
'My wife came along with me today— she's watching me now from the clubhouse, and I want to make this next shot a good one.'
'Good lord,' said his partner, 'you haven't got a hope of hitting her from this distance.'

"What d'you think? A three iron or a four wood?"

Two members of an exclusive golf club had just reached the 12th when a funeral procession passed by. One of the players immediately put down his club, removed his hat, and stood solemnly with his eyes lowered while the cortege passed by.
As the procession disappeared from view, his friend said, 'Somebody you knew?' 'Yes,' said his friend, 'And she was a damned good wife to me too.'

They were watching television golf but but the fellow at the back of the hall could not hear the sound.
'Turn it up a little,' he called out.
'Ssh . . ' said a voice from the front.
'Not while Palmer is putting

'Prisoner at the bar — you have been found not guilty of stealing a set of golf clubs.'
'Please, your honour, does that mean I can keep them?'

The old fourball was heading down the sixth when Bill, who was at least 85 years old, dropped down in a bunker and appeared to have grounded his club. In fact he had died of heart failure.
Lofty, who had partnered old Bill for close on fifty years in these mid-week matches, was telling the story at the bar later.
'It was awful,' he said. 'Bill died at the sixth when we were two down. It wasn't the fact that we were losing the match that worried me but it was terrible playing in — picking up Bill, hitting a shot, picking up Bill, hitting a shot . . .'

Doctor: 'Who's the patient?'
Nurse: 'A man has had a golf ball knocked down his throat.'
Doctor: 'Who is the chap pacing up and down in the waiting room?'
Nurse: 'Another golfer.'
Doctor: 'Whats he waiting for.'
Nurse: 'His ball back!'

No matter how gentlemanly, unexciting and un-cricketlike the top ranks of the game may have become, there are still plenty of very rough and ready ways of playing it – some of them even out of doors – where anything really does still go:

STICKY WICKET

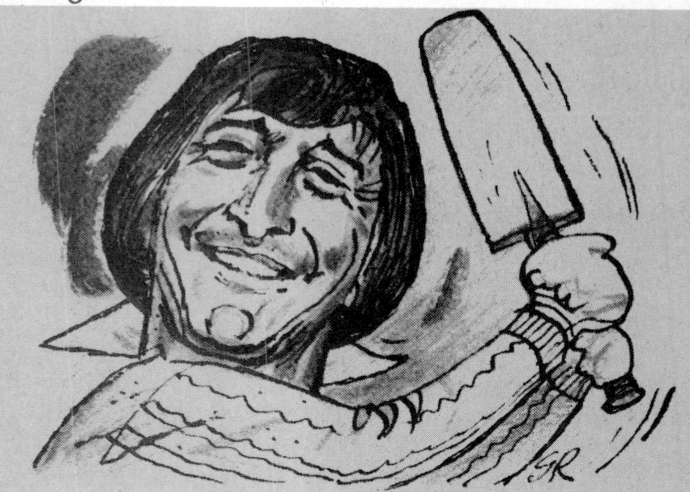

From CRICKET MAD

By

MICHAEL PARKINSON

To have played cricket and never taken part in a knock-out competition is like joining the Army and never hearing a shot fired in anger. Knock-out cricket is designed to bring the worst out of players and spectators alike. It gives off that most delicious of cricket perfumes: the heady whiff of crushed grass and skullduggery.

My old man adored knock-out cricket. Being the sort of player who could turn a gentle game of beach cricket into something resembling the landing at Iwo Jima he relished the tense and often violent atmosphere of knock-out cricket. Much of the excitement at these games comes from the spectators whose normal ration of pride in the local team is supplemented by the fact that they have ten bob on the game with the local bookie.

My old man tells a lovely story of the time he played his first knock-out game. His father was a big betting man and was well pleased when the opposition was bowled out for 42.

It seemed a walkover for my old man's team, so much so that when he went to look at the batting order his skipper had only put down four names and said to my dad: 'Off tha' goes Sammy. We shan't need thee.'

Fortunately he stuck around long enough to see his team collapse to the extent that when he went out to bat at No. 11 his side were 20 for 9 wickets and needed 23 to win. As he went down the pavilion steps he was the object of much excellent advice from the betting fraternity, none more pithy than that offered by his father, who said, 'If tha' gets out before we've beaten them I'll thump thee ear'ole.'

Basing his innings on this sound advice my old man managed to keep his end up while the batsman at the other end scored the runs to win the game.

The rejoicing was great and my old man was later downing a hero's pint in a nearby hostelry when he was approached by a local who said:

'Spending thi' collection money then, Sammy?'

'What collection?' said my old man.

'That what thi' father organised after tha'd won t'game for us. Collected about five quid on thi' behalf.'

Father swallowed his pint and dashed to the ground where he met his old man lurching gently away from the bar.

'Where's my collection then?' he said.

'Supped it' said his old man, burbing loudly.

It would be wrong to assume however that knock-out cricket only affects the spectators. It is beautifully designed to corrupt everyone who comes in contact with it.

In the knock-out cricket I used to play in, the right to cheat your way to victory was not written in the laws but it was certainly branded deep into the soul of every player. The rules allowed each team to play two professionals which meant that every team went to extraordinary lengths to play as many professionals as they could without their opponents finding out. As local professionals were well known the illegal ones had to be imported from nearby towns. When I played in these games they used to give the illicit professionals false names.

All this changed the year that the winning team was found to comprise of two Browns, four Smiths and five Jones. A subsequent inquiry revealed they were all professionals from the Lancashire League with names like Leatherbarrow and Strongitharm. After that the rules were changed and the teams had to declare the correct names of their players before the competition started. But there were ways round that. Once we arrived to play a team in the semi-final and the opposing captain popped into our dressing-room just before the game started to say he was a man short. 'Can I borrow a substitute, Fred,' he asked our skipper. 'No,' he replied, helpfully.

The opposing skipper then asked if he could pick a substitute from the spectators, and Fred agreed only if he had the right to veto. They set off round the ground together looking for likely prospects. Every time the opposing captain indicated a husky young lad, Fred, who was enjoying himself immensely, would shake his head and point to an old man in a wheel chair. They had made a complete circuit of the ground and reached the pavilion again when the opposing captain pointed to a hunched, wizened figure sitting on the grass. An Indian wearing a bus conductor's uniform. Our captain thought this was a huge joke.

'They've got Gunga Din playing for them,' he told us. Someone reminded him cautiously that Indians could play cricket. 'But he's a bus conductor not Ranjitsinhji,' he replied. He received the first inkling of the way in which he had been deceived when we batted. After a couple of overs the little Indian was asked to bowl which was a bit strange considering they had found him on the ground only ten minutes earlier. We had our suspicions confirmed in the Indian's first over which contained five leg breaks and one googly of a quality normally reserved for Test batsmen. From that moment we knew our captain had been tricked and that we were doomed. The Indian took eight wickets for less than 20 and we lost the match.

Our skipper was fit for nothing after the game. He wasn't angry, just disappointed that he had not been the first to invent such a stunning piece of twisting. He just sat in the bar downing pints of bitter and staring moodily at the floor. But his worst moment was yet to come. The little Indian, back in his bus conductor's uniform, was sitting across the room with the winning team when someone asked him, just to rub it in, who was the best batsman he had bowled to. Everyone on our side stopped talking and listened because we still didn't know who or what he was.

Our skipper burped wittily and said sarcastically, 'Bradman.' 'No,' said the Indian, 'I think Len Hutton was the best.' It was too much for the skipper. He gave all his gear away and swore he would never play again. We never did find out who that little Indian was.

What we did learn, however, those of us reared on knock-out cricket was that while it is perfectly true that the game can uplift the spirit and make men angels it can also stimulate the darkest corners of a man's personality and turn him into a criminal mastermind.

Published by The Hutchinson Publishing Group Ltd.

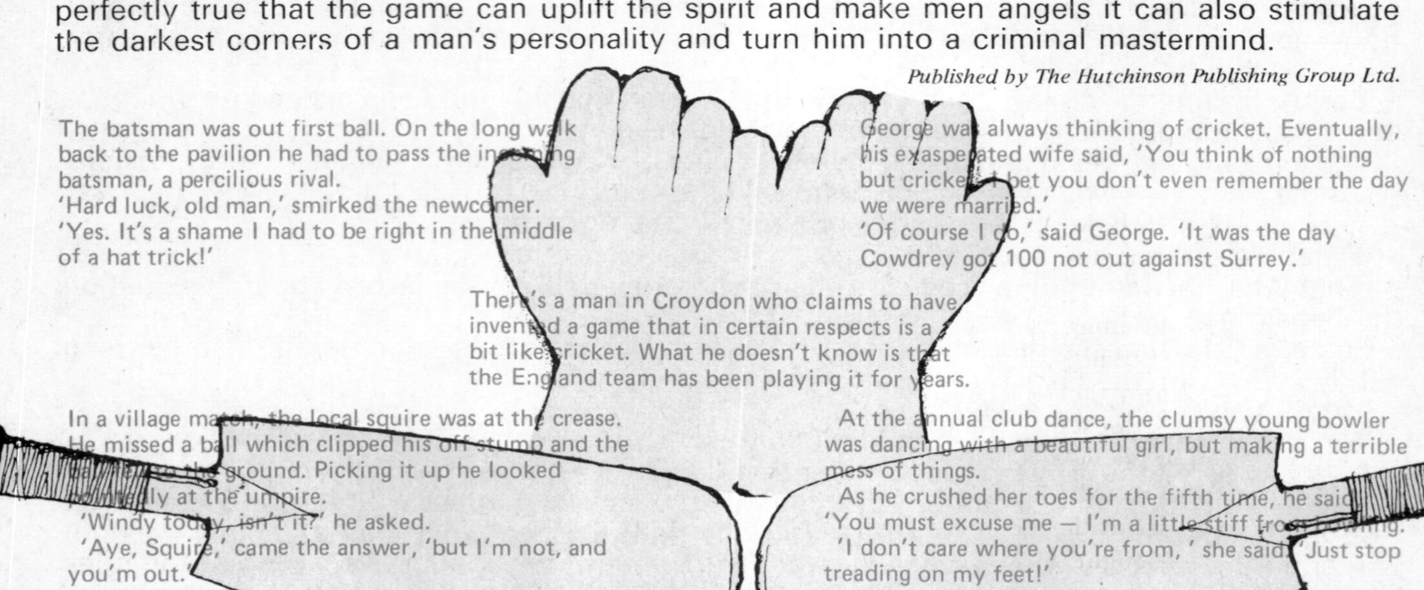

The batsman was out first ball. On the long walk back to the pavilion he had to pass the incoming batsman, a percilious rival.
'Hard luck, old man,' smirked the newcomer.
'Yes. It's a shame I had to be right in the middle of a hat trick!'

George was always thinking of cricket. Eventually, his exasperated wife said, 'You think of nothing but cricket. I bet you don't even remember the day we were married.'
'Of course I do,' said George. 'It was the day Cowdrey got 100 not out against Surrey.'

There's a man in Croydon who claims to have invented a game that in certain respects is a bit like cricket. What he doesn't know is that the England team has been playing it for years.

In a village match, the local squire was at the crease. He missed a ball which clipped his off stump and the bail fell to the ground. Picking it up he looked pointedly at the umpire.
'Windy today, isn't it?' he asked.
'Aye, Squire,' came the answer, 'but I'm not, and you'm out.'

At the annual club dance, the clumsy young bowler was dancing with a beautiful girl, but making a terrible mess of things.
As he crushed her toes for the fifth time, he said, 'You must excuse me — I'm a little stiff from bowling.'
'I don't care where you're from,' she said. 'Just stop treading on my feet!'

The cricket enthusiast was looking depressed.
'What's the matter?' asked a friend.
'The wife says she'll leave me unless I give up cricket.'
'That's bad.'
'Yes. I'll miss her.'

Take golf –

and in particular what it seems is known (correctly without doubt) as coarse golf:

Straight Down the Middle

By MICHAEL GREEN

It is a wet Wednesday afternoon not far from the North Circular Road. The United British Corsets Ltd. Golfing Society are holding their autumn meeting. There is some confusion as to the form this is to take. The first four players off understood it was to be a Stableford, but it has since been discovered that no one else knows how to score in a Stableford, and the society captain has told the others just to mark their cards up and they'll decide how to pick the winner in the bar afterwards. He is in a hurry for them to get on with matters as there are already loud complaints from club members at being held up by 'another of those damn society meetings'.

At the present moment, four players are waiting their turn to drive from the first. Three of them are respectively Fatty, Lanky and Blood Pressure. These, of course, are not their real names but they are fair descriptions and the details can be filled in as we go along. The fourth player is completely out of place and we shall call him George.

George has just joined head office as an executive trainee straight from university. He used to go round the Gog and Magog at Cambridge in the high eighties and back home in Hampshire his handicap is 19. It is his first game for the firm and after hearing the confident way everyone talked in the locker room he is very worried as to whether he will make the grade.

A pair are driving off in front of them. Lanky and Fatty are wildly swishing the air with their drivers, while Lanky voids himself of satisfied grunting noises and announces to all and sundry that he has at last cracked the game.

The player who is driving stops his address and looks round pointedly. Fatty and Lanky freeze into impossible positions of immobility. The player is aware out of the corner of his eye that two men are standing like something out of a cellar in the Louvre and wishes they would relax and let him concentrate.

As they show no signs of doing so he hopes for the best, takes a short backswing and sends the ball into a lateral water hazard on the left of the fairway. As he does so Fatty and Lanky relax with audible exhalations of breath, as if a couple of old cycle tyres were going down.

'Scrubbers,' says Blood Pressure fiercely, and they all nod in agreement, because Blood Pressure is greatly admired by them all, having once had a handicap of 23 with a golf club in Sussex. 'We'll go through them in a minute, never fear. I think it's your right to show us the way.'

They have not in fact tossed a coin, but in any case Blood Pressure is sales manager and his word is law. Fatty does not fancy letting himself down in front of the clubhouse, but he reluctantly drags himself forward, tees up his ball and peers hopefully into the distance

'Better let 'em get on a bit,' he mutters, 'I might hit 'em if I connect properly.' (The pair in front are three hundred yards away.) He waits until they are on the green, when a sudden and terrible change comes over him. His eyes widen in a ghastly stare, veins stand out all over his face and his whole body becomes completely rigid.

Still rigid he hunches himself forward, his legs wide apart, towards the ball. Four feet from it he stops, and slowly bends his legs until he is in a semi-squatting posture, with the seat of his trousers about two feet from the ground. He then stamps the ground twice like Rumpelstilskin. After remaining in this uncomfortable and slightly obscene posture for some moments he lifts the club back round his neck in a low, flat swing like a ruptured man lifting a heavy weight, and lets fly.

The ball travels 100 yards off the toe of the club and lands in a small copse on the right of the fairway, while Fatty staggers about the tee like a drunken man.

George, who feels he ought to get a reputation as a good fellow, murmurs 'Bad luck' sympathetically.

To his astonishment Fatty turns to the others in triumph.

'Beat that,' he snarls and takes up a position of easy confidence, casually leaning on his club at the edge of the tee and muttering to himself.

The others are by no means confident that they can.

Lanky now takes up his stance. This is slightly unusual, inasmuch as he is facing at right angles to the hole, and people at the side of the tee move away in alarm. Lanky, however, is merely compensating for his slice. After a good deal of twitching and shuffling he picks up his tee, moves it three inches to the left and starts again. Suddenly, without warning, he winds himself up like a cheap alarm clock, utters a half-human shout, and in a whirl of thin limbs puts his ball into a nearby back garden, via the handle of someone's trolley.

Blood Pressure's turn. He looks professionally towards the hole several times and then at the ball, as if he is afraid someone is going to steal it.

When he is apparently satisfied that nobody is, he cautiously approaches it and remains silent and still for some minutes. Then he lifts his driver back very slowly until it is level with his waist and pauses. Finally, keeping every fibre of his body rigid, he lowers the club on to the ball which reluctantly leaves the tee and travels thirty yards in a dead straight line.

'I'm getting them away today,' he says complacently.

Meanwhile George has been watching with astonishment. He is young and inexperienced and hasn't seen anything like this before. His address is spoiled by the constant noise going on behind him on the tee, where Fatty and Blood Pressure are arguing in a loud whisper about the love-life of Fatty's secretary. Just as he has accustomed himself to the row there are loud cries of 'Ssh . . . ssh . . . quiet everyone . . . give the lad a chance' and the whispering is succeeded by a painful silence, broken only by heavy breathing.

George tries to collect his shattered concentration and swings a little desperately. The ball curves precariously over the rough but at the last minute fades back on to the fairway after travelling about 170 yards.

He is just stepping back rather crestfallen when he is surprised by an outbreak of noise among the others, who are exclaiming: 'Brilliant! What a shot! You've played before' . . . and so on. Blood Pressure adds, 'And the lad says his handicap's nineteen. I don't believe it.'

The four go their separate ways. George's offers to help search for balls are turned down and he hits a nice five iron to the apron without waiting for Blood Pressure who is jerking around somewhere near the ladies' tee.

Having reached the green in three George leans on his putter and waits. After ten minutes two women arrive on the green and pointedly ask if they can carry on, as he apparently doesn't intend to putt out. George agrees and asks if they have seen any signs of three physically deformed men playing the hole.

The women say no, although as they were driving from the ladies' plateau tee a red-faced man stuck his head over the front and was nearly decapitated. But they thought he was a greenkeeper.

While the women are putting there is a terrible humming noise like a six-inch shell in full flight and a ball thuds near the stick and vanishes at high speed into the rough behind the green. From behind a distant bush is heard a faint, despairing cry of 'Watch it someone, for heaven's sake.'

George apologises on behalf of his colleagues, pointing out that the ball was obviously played from a point where the striker could not see the green. The women are not amused and ask acidly why George's partners are skulking about behind bushes as if afraid to show themselves.

At that moment Lanky rushes out of some trees to one side of the green like a sex maniac in hot weather and vanishes into the bushes the other side without a word of explanation. The women depart, looking apprehensively about them.

Blood Pressure arrives on the green and is followed by Fatty who has branches and twigs all over him. At las they can putt out.

George takes two for a five. Lanky, who is assailed by a terrible fit of jerking, putts into a bunker, takes three to get out, and then adds four more putts. Fatty takes one putt, which rolls six feet past the hole, picks up his ball and says, 'Never bother to take those tiddlers when I'm playing with friends.'

Blood Pressure, who is nine feet from the hole, promptly picks up his ball and says, 'Me neither.'

Without leaving the green, the three take out their cards and pencils, ignoring distant cries of impatient protest from the first round of the Knock-Out Cup behind them.

'Afraid I took a five there,' announces Fatty.

There is a moment's silence during which George wonders if he is going insane.

'How do you make that out?' says Blood Pressure severely.

'Quite simple,' says Fatty. 'One into the wood, two out, three on the green and two putts – five.'

The sheer effrontery of this takes everyone's breath away, but Lanky recovers sufficiently to say, 'But I saw you swishing away like mad as I was climbing the garden fence to get my ball.'

'I was trying to kill a wounded bird,' replies Fatty promptly. 'I couldn't leave the poor thing in agony, could I? Killed it cleanly with a three iron on the back of the neck. Just a touch of slice, though. Must have been bending the elbow again.'

He turns to George, who is looking anxiously at the players gibbering behind.

'How many did you take?'

'Five.'

'Then we halve,' says Fatty with an air of finality. 'If I may presume, I think you took the wrong line on that first putt. The borrow is very tricky on this green. All right, all right, we're going.' The last sentence is prompted by the thud of a ball on the green as the Knock-Out Cup at last lose all patience.

Three and a half hours later it is still raining and from the clubhouse, which stands on a hill, it is just possible to discern four wet and weary figures playing the last hole in deep gloom. The Knock-Out Cup have long ago passed through and are now sitting round the clubhouse fire.

Spurts of sand, like little fountains, from the cross-bunker announce that Lanky is in some difficulty. Beside the ditch what appears to be a small fat mole is creeping along on all fours, peering into the water with shrill cries of dismay. On the fairway a tiny earthquake is going on, where Blood Pressure is solenmly proceeding fifty yards at a time. There is no sign of George who is the other side of the hedge, looking for Fatty's ball.

Blood Pressure is first on the green, long experience having taught him the futility of trying to help the others. He is followed by Lanky (via the roof of the professional's shop) and surprisingly by Fatty. George is not only last, but his six iron, normally so reliable, lands him a good forty yards to the left of the green. He walks up the hill and on reaching his ball waves to the others to play.

'No, you play,' shouts Blood Pressure, 'we're on the green.'

George replies that he, too, is on the green. He modestly adds that being a conventional type of person he prefers to finish the course on the eighteenth and not the thirteenth.

After ten minutes' argument, during which Fatty has to be restrained from chipping off the green, it is agreed that George can play out on his green and the others on theirs. Having done so they hasten through the rain to the clubhouse.

In the bar there is a certain amount of confusion. The harassed secretary of the United British Corsets Ltd. has rashly undertaken to work out everyone's Stableford score from their cards, since most of the players cannot be trusted to do it themselves. Blood Pressure says he will work out his own and announces it as 48. Fatty demands a recount and the secretary makes it five, at which point Blood Pressure angrily denounces the whole competition as a fiddle.

The winner is eventually announced, with a score of 29 points. George, who knows perfectly well that he himself scored 33, does not bother to argue, but offers to buy Fatty a drink.

'Well,' says Fatty, his tongue loosened by the beer, 'I can't say I tamed the course, but I certainly showed it a touch of the whip, if I may put it that way. Ninety-four's not bad considering the conditions.'

According to George's private calculations, started at the second hole, Fatty had taken at least 115 strokes that he could see, not counting invisible and mysterious swishes in the undergrowth, and his Stableford total is one. But the last four hours have shown him a new world and he keeps quiet.

Blood Pressure and Lanky join the group.

'I thought our young friend here wasn't at all bad,' says Blood Pressure, nodding condescendingly at George. 'Perhaps a little uncertain off the tee, though.'

'I was going to mention that,' chimes in Fatty. 'You've got the classic hooker's grip, you know. It is a fault of all you young players. You can't see a knuckle when you drive. Took me years to cure myself. What you want to do, George, is to take a five iron before breakfast every morning and hold it in one hand and swing it forty times round your head. You'll find that gradually . . .'

And there it is time to leave them. The fantasies have taken over, truth has fled out of the door, and the course is diminishing in size with each drink. As for George, he won't play for them again, but will join a good club in Surrey where he will in time reach a single-figure handicap and play with real golfers.

But occasionally, in ten or twenty years' time, he will say in the bar, 'I don't know if I ever told you of a remarkable experience I had playing for the United British Corsets Ltd. Golf Society years ago . . . extraordinary crowd they were . . .'

So George will tell his tale. And nobody will believe a word.

Excerpt from 'The Art of Coarse Golf'
Published by Curtis-Brown Ltd.

Writers must get more mileage out of football than almost anything else – the game, and how its been lost, won, ruined, forgotten and disgraced; the players, the size of their tempers, the price of their transfers, where they went to school, what detergent powder washes their socks – above all what they are like to live with:

Mrs CRERAND'S DIARY

During one of his many tiffs with his club George Best was ordered to leave his house and live with team mate Paddy Crerand. Here, in her own words, is how Mrs. Crerand coped with her new guest:

Monday Our new lodger arrived today. What a commotion. We've given him upstairs and the lounge downstairs and Paddy and I are living in the kitchen. Still it's only temporary until he gets married and makes a nest of his own. He's such a lovely looking boy and very quiet. Ooops, there's the phone again. I'll have to answer it because our lodger has gone to town to have his hair done and Paddy's gone with him to make sure he doesn't get knocked down crossing Deansgate. Be back in a minute . . .

Well I never, it was some girl from Finland or one of those places, who said she'd come over specially to give our lodger a personal massage. I told her we could do without that sort of thing in Chorlton-cum-Hardy. Ah well, I've no more time for tittle-tattle. I've got to make the dinner. Steak and chips and mushy peas. As Paddy's always telling me, you've got to put back what you sweat away.

Tuesday That nice Mr O'Farrell paid a call today just to see if our lodger was settling in nicely. I asked him if if was all right to give him a key to the front door, but Mr O'Farrell said he thought not just yet. Perhaps in a year or two when he's nearing thirty, he said. Then he'll be able to come and go as he pleases. Of course, he might get married before that.

He's certainly very popular with the girls. The phone never stops ringing and it's always for our lodger. He doesn't bother though. What with training and having his hair done he doesn't get much time nowadays.

Ah well, enough of this tittle-tattle. Time to go upstairs and run his bath and then time for dinner. Tonight it's his favourite – sausage, egg and chips and rice pudding. As Paddy's always telling me, we've got to build him up.

Wednesday He's been with us three days now and not a bit of trouble. He's as good as gold. They're out at present. Paddy has taken him for a walk in the park. That girl from Finland was on the phone again today saying if she couldn't massage George could she give my Paddy a rub down. I told her to ring Maine Road and ask for Malcolm Allison. Saucy cat.

It's so peaceful with them out of the house. When they are at home they are so boisterous and noisy. Our lodger likes the telly and the radiogram switched on at the same time. Also he uses the fretwork set that kind Mr O'Farrell gave him the other day.

'Idle hands make mischief,' said Mr O'Farrell in that nice voice of his. How true. But our lodger has had his hands full ever since and already he's nearly finished making a plywood model of the Skol Hotel, Marbella. He's such a clever little fellow really.

Ah well, enough of this day dreaming. Time to put the chips on. As Mr O'Farrell said the other day: 'The First Division Championship is won or lost in the frying pan.'

Thursday Sir Matt called today with some flowers for me and a jigsaw for our lodger. He wasn't in because he had gone to town to have his hair done. Sir Matt wasn't cross or anything. He said he was used to George not being where he wanted him to be, if you know what I mean.

A traffic warden came to see me soon after Sir Matt had departed. Wanted to know why our car was parked in the street. When I explained that our garage was full with our lodger's cars she said it was perfectly all right in the circumstances and could she have two signed photographs for her sister's children in Cleethorpes.

For dinner tonight I've bought something special – a packet of frozen paella and a bottle of Spanish wine – because our lodger talks of nothing else but the good times he had when he went for a quiet holiday with sixty of his friends to the Costa del Sol.

He enjoyed the meal and said he particularly liked the chips I made to go with the paella.

Friday Panic stations! Our lodger got lost today. Paddy was very upset but it wasn't his fault. They went out for a walk and while Paddy was buying some frozen chips in the High Street, our lodger wandered off by himself. Well, we were all so worried until we got this message from the sergeant at Chorlton-cum-Hardy police station that they'd found him outside his old house, which has been converted into a supermarket.

When Mr O'Farrell heard our lodger was missing he was very angry, but later he calmed down and came over personally to deliver a blow-football set which he thought might while away many a happy hour. We didn't play tonight because our lodger wanted to take us out for a meal to say thank you for having him.

He took us to a Chinese restaurant where we had the best steak and chips we've had for ages. As that nice Mr O'Farrell said, a full stomach and a contented mind are what our lodger wants.

Excerpt from 'Sporting Fever' by Michael Parkinson
Published by The Hutchinson Publishing Group Ltd.

'. . . Blindtwit – that's an unusual name – how do you spell it?'

The famous elephant football team was once playing a home match against a team of mice. Everything was oing fine until shortly before half-time when one of he elephants stepped on one of the mice and squashed im flat.

As the other players gathered round, the referee ernly took out his notebook.

didn't mean to squash him, honest, ref,' said the ophant apologetically. 'I only meant to trip him.'

A group of local boys had arranged to play football one Sunday afternoon. They all turned up promptly at two-thirty as arranged, except for little Jimmy Green who arrived breathless at five minutes to three.

'Where on earth have you been?' asked the captain.

'Well,' said Jimmy, 'it was a toss-up whether I came to play football or went to Sunday School.'

'Why should that make you so late?'

'I had to toss up twenty-seven times.'

plication by the Sports Section of the Ashford Group for a grant to pay for their visit to Bad nstereifel, Ashford's twin town, has been rejected the town council.

council spokesman said: "The application failed o specify the sport in question. If they were proposing to send ten gay chess players it would be quite a different matter."

Milltown Rovers came out bottom of the league for the tenth season running. Coming away from the last match of the season, which Rovers had lost fifteen-nil, one fan said to another, 'Well, you've got to say this about the boys—they're good losers.'

'What do you mean good?' said his pal. 'They're perfect.'

A Coventry fan travelled over to Wolverhampton one Saturday to see his team play Wolves. He went into a pub for a few quick ones before the match but over-indulged so much that he forgot all about the game and caught the bus back home.

He fell asleep almost as soon as he got on the coach but woke with a start about half-way home. Glancing out of the window, he saw a signpost which read 'Coventry 29: Wolverhampton 21.'

'Hurray!' he shouted. 'I knew we could beat them!'

Since you mustn't breathe a word to fishermen on the job, and since it isn't safe to start a conversation with them afterwards because they'll only pin you to the wall and stuff you as full of tall stories as the trout in the glass case is full of cottonwool – (ever wondered why a fish looks at you so *doubtfully*) – maybe the less *said* about fishing the better. (Now you're going to catch it):

'I wish I could afford to take time off to go fishing.'
'But you're always going fishing.'
'I know, I just wish I could afford it.'

Fishing bore: Yes, talking about fishing reminds me of the time. . .
Bored listener: Good Lord, you're right. I had no idea it was so late.

'Did you know that a single herring can have over a million baby herrings?'
'Blimey, how many can the married ones have?'

Stanley said that he once cleaned a hundred fish in one day.
'Now that,' said his friend, 'takes guts!'

The despondent customer had been waiting an hour for his order. Finally, a waiter came up and said: 'Your fish will be here in a minute, sir.'
The customer looked up. 'Tell me, what bait are you using?'

Having heard the angler's story of his last monster catch, the polite listener asked:
'But if it was as long as you say, how did you get the fish home?'
'It wasn't easy,' admitted the angler, 'but luckily, I managed to get a corridor train.'

Two sardines were swimming along when a submarine passed by.
'What on earth's that?' said one.
'Don't worry,' said the other, 'It's just a can of people

1st angler: Of course experience tells. I've landed as many as twenty 12 lb trout in an hour. Can you say the same?
2nd angler: Yes, but not with such a straight face.

'I heard that guppies are just like rabbits, so I bought two. They're not like rabbits, though. I put some lettuce in the tank and they swam right past it.'
'Really?'
'Yeah, all 300 of them.'

The seaside angler had ordered the lobster at the nearby restaurant. When it arrived, however, it had obviously gone off some time ago.
'Waiter,' said the angler. 'Are you sure this lobster's fresh?'
'Oh yes sir,' affirmed the waiter. 'In fact it walked here from the beach this morning.'
The angler sniffed it suspiciously.
'Well,' he said, 'it must have trodden in something on the way.'

Two fishermen were standing on the dock, talking.
'See that man over there?' said the first. 'He was a famous shark fisherman. He had this great trick where he stuck his right arm down the shark's throat. They used to call him "Fearless".'
'What do they call him now?'
'Lefty.'

JOKES - In compiling these and some other jokes throughout this book, we are indebted to the excellent series of Joke Books published by Wolfe Publishing Ltd, entitled the Mini Ha Ha series.